GOOGLE CLOUD ASSOCIATE DATA ENGINEER CERTIFICATION

MASTER THE EXAM: 10 PRACTICE TESTS, 500 RIGOROUS QUESTIONS, SOLID FOUNDATIONS TO EXAM, GAIN WEALTH OF INSIGHTS, EXPERT EXPLANATIONS AND ONE ULTIMATE GOAL

ANAND M
AMEENA PUBLICATIONS

Copyright © 2023 ANAND M
All rights reserved.
ISBN: 9798869982766

DEDICATION

To the Visionaries in My Professional Odyssey

This book is dedicated to the mentors and leaders who guided me through triumph and adversity in my professional universe. Your guidance has illuminated the path to success and taught me to seize opportunities and surmount obstacles. Thank you for imparting the advice to those who taught me the value of strategic thinking and the significance of innovation to transform obstacles into stepping stones. Your visionary leadership has inspired my creativity and motivated me to forge new paths.

Thank you for sharing the best and worst of your experiences with me, kind and severe employers. As I present this book to the world, I am aware that you have been my inspiration. All of your roles as mentors, advisors, and even occasional adversaries have helped me become a better professional and storyteller.

This dedication is a tribute to your impact on my journey, a narrative woven with threads of gratitude, introspection, and profound gratitude for the lessons you've inscribed into my story.

With deep gratitude and enduring respect,
Anand M

FROM TECH TO LIFE SKILLS – MY EBOOKS COLLECTION

Dive into my rich collection of eBooks, curated meticulously across diverse and essential domains.

Pro Tips and Tricks Series: Empower yourself with life-enhancing skills and professional essentials with our well-crafted guides.

Hot IT Certifications and Tech Series: Stay ahead in the tech game. Whether you're eyeing certifications in AWS, PMP, or prompt engineering, harnessing the power of ChatGPT with tools like Excel, PowerPoint, Word, and more!, we've got you covered!

Essential Life Skills: Embark on a journey within. From yoga to holistic well-being, Master the art of culinary, baking, and more delve deep and rediscover yourself.

Stay Updated & Engaged
For an entire world of my knowledge, tips, and treasures, follow me on Amazon
https://www.amazon.com/author/anandm

Your Feedback Matters!
Your support, feedback, and ratings are the wind beneath my wings. It drives me to curate content that brings immense value to every aspect of life. Please take a moment to share your thoughts and rate the books. Together, let's keep the flame of knowledge burning bright!

Best Regards,

ANAND M

INTRODUCTION

Embarking on the journey to conquer the Google Cloud Associate Data Engineer Certification Exam? Your quest for the ideal study guide concludes here. Introducing "**Google Cloud Associate Data Engineer Certification: Master the Exam: 10 Practice Tests, 500 Rigorous Questions, Expert Explanations, and One Ultimate Goal**" – your comprehensive and definitive resource to ace this pivotal certification.

In the ever-evolving realm of data and cloud technologies, the Google Cloud Platform (GCP) stands out as a beacon of innovation and excellence. Attaining the Google Cloud Associate Data Engineer Certification is not merely about proving your technical skills; it embodies a profound comprehension of one of the most cutting-edge cloud platforms globally. This certification is essential, whether you're embarking on your cloud journey or enhancing your data engineering acumen.

This guide is meticulously crafted to ensure your preparation is thorough and all-encompassing. Each question is strategically designed to reflect the actual exam's nature, backed by detailed explanations to foster a deep understanding. This approach allows you to move beyond mere memorization, enabling you to grasp the intricacies of data engineering on GCP genuinely.

With the increasing demand for proficient data engineers, possessing a renowned certification like the Google Cloud Associate Data Engineer places you at the industry's forefront. Whether your goal is to specialize in cloud-based big data solutions, machine learning applications, or sophisticated data processing techniques, this book lays the foundation for your mastery in the Google Cloud landscape.

For those prepared to take on this gratifying challenge, here's what you can expect:

Duration: *2 hours of intensive examination.*
Enrollment Cost: *$125, subject to additional taxes depending on your location.*
Language Availability: *Mainly available in English.*
Exam Format: *A thorough test comprising multiple-choice and multiple-select questions, conducted in a professional testing setting.*
Prerequisites: *No formal prerequisites, though practical experience with GCP is beneficial.*
Recommended Experience: *At least 6 months of hands-on experience with Google Cloud services.*

Equipped with knowledge, strategic insights, and confidence, let this book be your beacon as you navigate towards achieving the Google Cloud Associate Data Engineer Certification.

ADVANTAGES OF CERTIFICATION

As you prepare to embark on the journey of achieving the Google Cloud Associate Data Engineer Certification, it's vital to appreciate the array of advantages this certification brings, charting a transformative trajectory for your career in the realms of cloud technology and data engineering.

Key Advantages of the Certification:

Market Demand and Recognition: In today's data-centric world, where cloud computing is at the forefront, the need for proficient Data Engineers is more critical than ever. This certification sets you apart in this competitive landscape, validating your skills in managing and processing data on the Google Cloud Platform. It's a mark of excellence that is recognized globally, enhancing your professional credibility.

Career Advancement: The Google Cloud Associate Data Engineer Certification is not merely a testament to your abilities; it's a cornerstone in your career development. Many professionals with this certification report unlocking new job opportunities and venturing into roles that were previously out of reach. This certification broadens your horizons, paving the way for advanced positions in data engineering and cloud technology.

Increased Earning Potential: A notable benefit of this certification is the potential for financial growth. Studies and professional feedback consistently demonstrate that certified individuals often command higher salaries and more rewarding job roles. This certification can significantly boost your financial prospects in the field of cloud data engineering.

Professional Distinction: In the ever-evolving and competitive world of cloud data engineering, standing out is paramount. Being a Google Cloud Certified Associate Data Engineer raises your professional profile, aiding in job attainment and positioning you for specialized, sought-after roles in the industry.

Practical Expertise: This certification goes beyond theoretical knowledge. It ensures that you acquire practical, hands-on experience with Google Cloud's data services and tools. This real-world proficiency is crucial for tackling complex data challenges and sets you apart from others who may lack such certified experience.

Career Catalyst: The Google Cloud Associate Data Engineer Certification is more than a validation of your skills; it acts as a catalyst, propelling your career forward in the rapidly advancing field of cloud data engineering.

In essence, the Google Cloud Associate Data Engineer Certification is a strategic and impactful investment in your future. It promises recognition, career progression, financial advancement, enhanced visibility, and practical skills in the burgeoning sector of cloud data engineering.

CONTENTS

SET 1 - QUESTIONS ONLY 8
SET 1 - ANSWERS ONLY 21
SET 2 - QUESTIONS ONLY 35
SET 2 - ANSWERS ONLY 49
SET 3 - QUESTIONS ONLY 62
SET 3 - ANSWERS ONLY 75
SET 4 - QUESTIONS ONLY 88
SET 4 - ANSWERS ONLY 101
SET 5 - QUESTIONS ONLY 114
SET 5 - ANSWERS ONLY 127
SET 6 - QUESTIONS ONLY 140
SET 6 - ANSWERS ONLY 154
SET 7 - QUESTIONS ONLY 168
SET 7 - ANSWERS ONLY 182
SET 8 - QUESTIONS ONLY 195
SET 8 - ANSWERS ONLY 209
SET 9 - QUESTIONS ONLY 222
SET 9 - ANSWERS ONLY 236
SET 10 - QUESTIONS ONLY 250
SET 10 - ANSWERS ONLY 264
About the Author 278

SET 1 - QUESTIONS ONLY

QUESTION 1

You are working as a cloud architect for a financial services firm. The firm uses a variety of GCP services, including Cloud Spanner for transactional data, Bigtable for audit logs, and Cloud Storage for historical data archiving. A new regulatory requirement mandates a consolidated view of transactions and audit logs for compliance reporting. How should you approach this task to minimize complexity and ensure data integrity?

A) Use Cloud Dataflow to periodically export data from Cloud Spanner and Bigtable to a new dataset in BigQuery, and use BigQuery for compliance reporting.
B) Create a Data Fusion instance to integrate data from Cloud Spanner, Bigtable, and Cloud Storage, and use this for reporting.
C) Implement a custom application on Compute Engine to query Cloud Spanner and Bigtable, aggregate the data, and store it in Cloud SQL for reporting.
D) Configure Cloud Pub/Sub to stream data changes from Cloud Spanner and Bigtable to a processing pipeline in Dataflow, which then writes the results to BigQuery.
E) Manually export data from Cloud Spanner and Bigtable to Cloud Storage, and use a combination of Cloud Dataprep and BigQuery for reporting.

QUESTION 2

Your company is implementing a multi-cloud strategy, integrating services from GCP and other cloud providers. You need to monitor resource usage across all platforms in a unified manner for cost optimization. What GCP service would you use?

A) Google Cloud Monitoring
B) BigQuery
C) Google Cloud Functions
D) Cloud Interconnect
E) Cloud Pub/Sub
F) Cloud Billing Report

QUESTION 3

You've been assigned to enhance the security of a GCP project in your organization. Your first task is to review and manage the access controls for Cloud Storage. You need to ensure that only specific team members can modify objects in a particular bucket. What approach should you take?

A) Modify the bucket's IAM policy to grant the 'Storage Object Admin' role to the specific team members.
B) Use Access Context Manager to create access levels for the bucket and assign them to the team members.
C) Implement VPC Service Controls to restrict access to the Cloud Storage bucket based on the team members' network location.

D) Set up Object Lifecycle Management on the bucket to control who can modify objects based on their age.
E) Create a custom IAM role with specific permissions for object modification and assign it to the team members.

QUESTION 4

You are a cloud engineer at a software company that utilizes GCP for hosting its web applications. The applications are deployed on GKE across multiple VPC-native clusters. You need to ensure network connectivity among these clusters without exposing the services to the public internet. What solution would you implement?

A) Set up External HTTP(S) Load Balancers for inter-cluster communication.
B) Implement Internal Load Balancing with Ingress for each cluster.
C) Use VPC Network Peering to connect the clusters' VPCs.
D) Create VPN tunnels between each cluster's VPC for secure communication.
E) Utilize Cloud Interconnect to establish private connectivity among clusters.

QUESTION 5

You are a cloud engineer managing multiple GCP projects for different teams in your organization. One of your responsibilities is to ensure that critical Compute Engine instances hosting key applications are not accidentally modified or deleted. What measures would you implement to safeguard these instances?

A) Apply IAM policies to restrict access to Compute Engine resources.
B) Enable deletion protection on the critical Compute Engine instances.
C) Use Snapshot schedules for regular backups of the instances.
D) Create a VPC Service Control perimeter around the Compute Engine resources.
E) Implement labels on the instances and enforce policies based on these labels.

QUESTION 6

As a data engineer, you need to grant access to a BigQuery dataset to another team for analysis purposes. You must ensure they can query and view the data but cannot modify or delete the dataset. What is the most appropriate role to assign?

A) roles/bigquery.dataViewer
B) roles/bigquery.dataEditor
C) roles/bigquery.user
D) Create a custom role excluding data modification and deletion permissions
E) roles/bigquery.dataOwner

QUESTION 7

Your company manages multiple GCP projects with a complex hierarchical structure. To enhance governance, you need to set up a system where the finance team can only view billing information across all projects. What is the most efficient way to grant this access?

A) Assign roles/billing.viewer role at the organization level.
B) Create a custom role with billing information access and assign it to the finance team.
C) Assign roles/viewer role at each project level for the finance team.
D) Use roles/iam.roleViewer at the organization level for the finance team.
E) Set up a Cloud Billing account and add the finance team as billing administrators.

QUESTION 8

You are managing multiple GCP projects in your startup and need to set up a centralized monitoring system for resource usage across these projects. What is the most efficient way to achieve this in GCP?

A) Create individual dashboards for each project in Cloud Monitoring and manually compare metrics.
B) Use Stackdriver to create a single dashboard that aggregates metrics from all projects.
C) Assign the roles/logging.viewer role to a central project and use its dashboard to monitor other projects.
D) Set up Cloud Pub/Sub to collect metrics from each project and display them in a custom application.
E) Configure a shared VPC across projects to centralize the monitoring data.

QUESTION 9

You are operating a website with high-resolution images on a GCP Compute Engine instance. To manage costs effectively, you need to be alerted when the monthly egress traffic cost reaches a specific threshold. How can you set up this cost monitoring and alerting mechanism in GCP?

A) Use Cloud Monitoring to set an alert based on egress traffic metrics.
B) Create a budget in Cloud Billing with a specific threshold for egress traffic costs and set up email notifications.
C) Export billing data to BigQuery and use a scheduled query to trigger an email alert when the threshold is reached.
D) Install a network monitoring agent on the Compute Engine instance to track egress traffic and send alerts.
E) Use Cloud Functions to analyze real-time network traffic data and trigger email alerts when the threshold is exceeded.

QUESTION 10

A team is tasked with deploying a Node.js application on Google Kubernetes Engine (GKE). They have a Dockerfile for the application. What steps should they follow to ensure a successful deployment, considering best practices for using GKE and Docker?

A) Use kubectl apply -f <dockerfilename> in your CLI.
B) Use gcloud app deploy <dockerfilename> in your CLI.
C) 1. Build a Docker image from the Dockerfile and upload it to Container Registry.
   2. Create a Deployment YAML file to point to the newly uploaded image.
   3. Use the kubectl command line utility to create the deployment with that file.
D) 1. Build a Docker image from the Dockerfile and upload it to Cloud Storage.
   2. Create a Deployment YAML file to point to the newly uploaded image.
   3. Use the kubectl command line utility to create the deployment with that file.

QUESTION 11

You are managing several GCP projects and need to set up centralized logging for all of them. What is the most efficient way to achieve this using Google Cloud's Operations Suite?

A) Set up individual logging for each project and manually aggregate the logs.
B) Use a Shared VPC to connect all projects and configure logging.
C) Create a single Operations Suite account and link all projects to it.
D) Deploy a third-party logging tool across all projects.

QUESTION 12

As the head of backend and database management, you need to connect to a newly upgraded SQL Server running on a Windows Compute Engine instance for testing and debugging. What steps should you follow to establish the connection using the fewest possible steps, considering GCP's best practices for security and efficiency?

A) Install an RDP client on your desktop and SSH into the VM on port 3389.
B) Install an RDP client on your desktop, set a Windows username and password in the GCP Console, and use these credentials to log in to the instance.
C) Set a Windows password in the GCP Console, verify that a firewall rule for port 22 exists, and click the RDP button in the GCP Console to log in using the credentials.
D) Set a Windows username and password in the GCP Console, verify that a firewall rule for port 3389 exists, and click the RDP button in the GCP Console, using the credentials to log in.

QUESTION 13

As a cloud architect in a financial services firm, you are transitioning a critical application from a test environment in Google Kubernetes Engine (GKE) to a production environment. This production environment requires a separate GCP project for compliance. What is the best approach for this migration?

A) Create a new GCP project using gcloud, set up a new GKE cluster in this project, and deploy the application.
B) In the existing GCP project, create a new GKE cluster and migrate the application to this cluster for production.
C) Duplicate the existing GKE cluster within the same project and label it as the production environment.
D) Use gcloud to copy the GKE configuration to a new project name specified in the migration command.

QUESTION 14

Your application, hosted on Compute Engine, requires access to read and write data to a specific BigQuery dataset. To align with Google's best practices, how should you configure the necessary permissions?

A) Assign the Compute Engine default service account the 'bigquery.dataEditor' role for the dataset.
B) Create a custom service account and grant it the 'bigquery.user' role for the entire project.
C) Create a custom service account with the 'bigquery.dataEditor' role specifically for the dataset.
D) Use the Compute Engine default service account and assign it the 'bigquery.admin' role.

QUESTION 15

As part of the Operations and Access Governance team, you are tasked with granting a group of developers the ability to deploy and manage applications in App Engine within a specific GCP project. Which IAM role should you assign to these developers?

A) Project Editor
B) App Engine Admin
C) App Engine Deployer
D) App Engine Service Admin

QUESTION 16

You need to share a confidential report temporarily with an external consultant who doesn't have a Google account. The report is stored in Cloud Storage and access should be revoked automatically after three hours. What is the most secure method to share this file following Google's best practices?

A) Generate a signed URL with a three-hour expiration for the file and share it with the consultant.
B) Set the file to public for three hours and then revert it to private.
C) Email the file directly to the consultant and delete it from Cloud Storage.
D) Create a temporary Cloud Storage bucket, move the file there, and delete the bucket after three hours.

QUESTION 17

Your e-commerce website is hosted on Google Cloud using a Managed Instance Group (MIG). To ensure high availability, you want at least one instance to be running at all times, even during periods of low traffic. Which configuration should you choose for the MIG?

A) Enable autoscaling and set the minimum number of instances to 1
B) Disable autoscaling and set the minimum number of instances to 0
C) Enable autoscaling and set the maximum number of instances to 1
D) Disable autoscaling and set the minimum number of instances to 1

QUESTION 18

Your organization needs to implement a secure and scalable method for authenticating users in a web application hosted on Google Cloud. Which GCP service should you consider to manage user identities, enable single sign-on (SSO), and integrate with identity providers?

A) Google Cloud SQL.
B) Google Cloud Storage.
C) Google Cloud Identity Platform.
D) Google Cloud Dataprep.

QUESTION 19

You are managing a Google Kubernetes Engine (GKE) cluster that runs critical workloads. To ensure high availability, you want to set up automatic node repair. Which GKE feature should you enable for this purpose?

A) HorizontalPodAutoscaling
B) NodeAffinity
C) NodeAutoRepair
D) NodePoolScaling

QUESTION 20

Your company's web service on App Engine is experiencing increased traffic from Europe. To improve performance for European users, you've been tasked to deploy the application in a region closer to them. How should you proceed, given GCP's limitations and best practices?

A) Migrate the existing App Engine application to a European region.
B) Create a new App Engine application in the same project, choosing a European region for deployment.
C) Set up a new GCP project and deploy the App Engine application in a European region.
D) Reconfigure the existing App Engine application to route European traffic to a closer region.

QUESTION 21

As a cloud administrator, you want to ensure your GKE clusters are always running on the most secure and stable versions of Kubernetes. How can you automate this process to maintain cluster security and reliability?

A) Enable Cluster Auto-Repair to automatically update Kubernetes versions.
B) Implement Cluster Auto-Upgrades to keep the Kubernetes version up to date.
C) Manually update the Kubernetes version regularly for each cluster.
D) Set up periodic scripts to automatically create new clusters with the latest Kubernetes version.

QUESTION 22

In a Kubernetes deployment, you notice that an API key is embedded as plain text in a pod's environment variable within the deployment YAML. What is the recommended approach to securely manage this API key?

A) Encrypt the API key and store it in the deployment YAML.
B) Store the API key in a Kubernetes Secret and reference it in the deployment YAML.
C) Place the API key in a ConfigMap and reference it in the deployment YAML.
D) Write the API key to a file and mount it to the pod using a Persistent Volume.

QUESTION 23

You are hosting a portfolio website on Google Cloud Storage, which includes image galleries in JPEG format. You want these images to be displayed directly in the browser when clicked, rather than being downloaded. How should you configure your Cloud Storage settings for these images?

A) Set the Content-Type metadata of each image object to 'image/jpeg'.
B) Enable 'Share publicly' on the image file objects in Cloud Storage.
C) Implement Cloud CDN to cache and display images.
D) Add a label to the storage bucket with a key of Content-Type and value of 'image/jpeg'.

QUESTION 24

Your application processes large datasets every day at 3 AM, with a job duration of approximately 3 hours. To optimize costs on GCP, what is the best approach for running these batch jobs?

A) Use a dedicated Google Kubernetes Engine (GKE) cluster with standard machine types.
B) Run the batch jobs on regular Compute Engine VMs with automatic shutdown scripts.
C) Utilize preemptible Compute Engine VMs for the batch processing.
D) Deploy the batch jobs on Cloud Functions for on-demand processing.
E) Implement a multi-node Dataproc cluster with high-memory machine types.
F) Schedule the batch jobs on App Engine with automatic scaling enabled.

QUESTION 25

For a financial application on Compute Engine, you need high availability and minimal downtime. How should you configure your Compute Engine instances to ensure they automatically restart after a crash and continue running during system maintenance?

A) Enable 'Automatic Restart' and set 'On-host maintenance' to 'Migrate VM instance'.
B) Disable 'Automatic Restart' and set 'On-host maintenance' to 'Terminate VM instance'.
C) Enable 'Automatic Restart' and set 'On-host maintenance' to 'Terminate VM instance'.
D) Disable 'Automatic Restart' and set 'On-host maintenance' to 'Migrate VM instance'.
E) Use preemptible VMs and set 'Automatic Restart' to on.
F) Configure an instance group with auto-healing and HTTP health checks.

QUESTION 26

For your financial services company, you need to log every access request to sensitive data in a Cloud Storage bucket. What GCP feature should you enable to meet this compliance requirement?

A) Turn on Cloud Audit Logs for all read operations in the Cloud Storage bucket.
B) Implement Identity-Aware Proxy (IAP) for controlled access and logging.
C) Use Cloud Functions to trigger a log entry for every read operation on the bucket.
D) Configure Data Loss Prevention (DLP) API to log access requests.
E) Enable Access Transparency for detailed access logging.
F) Set up Object Versioning and Access Logs in the Cloud Storage bucket.

QUESTION 27

You're using personal funds to pay for GCP services for a project at your startup and need to transition the billing to the company. How can you achieve this so that future charges are directly billed to the company?

A) Provide your financial team with IAM access to your personal billing account for direct monitoring.
B) Set up a BigQuery billing export with access for your financial department to analyze costs.
C) Contact Google Support to change the billing method from your credit card to the company's account.
D) Change the project's billing account to the company's GCP billing account.
E) Create a new project under the company's GCP account and migrate resources.
F) Use a company credit card to replace your personal card on the existing billing account.

QUESTION 28

Your company has developed a photo-sharing platform and expects fluctuating user traffic. How can you ensure that the Kubernetes cluster hosting this app on GCP automatically adjusts to traffic changes?

A) Implement Horizontal Pod Autoscaler for each service.
B) Use Vertical Pod Autoscaler for resource optimization.
C) Enable autoscaling on the GKE node pool.
D) Assign dedicated node pools for different components of the app.
E) Schedule manual scaling activities based on expected traffic trends.
F) Set up custom scaling metrics based on the number of photo uploads.

QUESTION 29

Your company is building a web application that needs to securely store sensitive customer data. Which Google Cloud service should you use for secure and scalable storage of this data?

A) Google Cloud Storage
B) Google Cloud Datastore
C) Google Cloud SQL
D) Google Cloud Bigtable
E) Google Cloud Firestore

QUESTION 30

In a hybrid cloud setup where GCP applications rely on an on-premises database, how can you manage connectivity without needing to reconfigure applications if the database IP changes?

A) Use Cloud Interconnect for stable IP management between on-premises and GCP.
B) Implement a custom script on GCP VMs to update the database IP address dynamically.
C) Set up a Cloud DNS private zone to manage the database hostname.
D) Store the database IP in a Secret Manager and periodically update it.
E) Configure a GCP Internal Load Balancer to redirect to the current database IP.
F) Use a Cloud VPN with static routing for consistent database connectivity.

QUESTION 31

How can you securely grant a partner company access to specific BigQuery datasets in your GCP project without exposing your entire project's resources?

A) Share your project's IAM credentials with the partner company.
B) Create a Service Account in your project and share it with the partner.
C) Have the partner create a Service Account in their project and grant it access to your BigQuery datasets.
D) Set up a shared VPC between your project and the partner's project.
E) Use BigQuery Data Transfer Service to replicate data to the partner's project.
F) Implement VPC Service Controls to manage cross-project resource sharing.

QUESTION 32

How can you implement a gradual rollout of a new update for a web app on Cloud Run for Anthos, allowing a small percentage of users to access the new version first?

A) Deploy the updated version as a new service and use a Load Balancer to distribute traffic.
B) Create a new revision of the existing service and configure traffic splitting between the new and old revisions.
C) Update the existing service and use Cloud Monitoring to control the percentage of users directed to the new version.
D) Deploy the updated version to a separate project and gradually redirect users using DNS routing.
E) Implement a feature flag system within the application to toggle between old and new versions for selected users.
F) Use a Cloud Function to distribute traffic between the old and new versions based on user criteria.

QUESTION 33

How can you ensure a Python function is executed every time a new object is uploaded to a Cloud Storage bucket?

A) Configure a Pub/Sub notification for the bucket to trigger a Compute Engine VM running the Python code.
B) Create a Cloud Function with the Python code and set the Cloud Storage bucket as a trigger.
C) Use Cloud Run to host the Python code and trigger it using Cloud Storage events.
D) Implement a CRON job on App Engine that checks the bucket for new uploads and runs the Python code.
E) Set up a Cloud Scheduler job that triggers a Cloud Function checking for new uploads in the bucket.
F) Use Google Kubernetes Engine to run a containerized application that responds to Cloud Storage events.

QUESTION 34

You are architecting a solution for a global e-commerce platform on GCP. The platform requires a highly available database that supports strong consistency and horizontal scaling. The application also needs to handle large-scale, complex queries. Considering cost-effectiveness and performance, which architecture would you recommend?

A) Deploying Cloud Spanner across multiple regions, using instance configurations to optimize cost and performance.
B) Using Cloud SQL with read replicas in multiple regions for scaling and a combination of BigQuery for complex query analysis.
C) Implementing a combination of Cloud Bigtable for horizontal scaling and Dataflow for processing complex queries.
D) Utilizing Cloud Firestore in Datastore mode for strong consistency and horizontal scaling, coupled with Cloud Dataproc for handling complex queries.
E) Setting up a multi-regional Kubernetes Engine cluster hosting a custom-built NoSQL database for scalability, and integrating with Cloud Pub/Sub for real-time data analysis.

QUESTION 35

Your company is implementing enhanced security measures on GCP and wants to monitor for any unauthorized access to Compute Engine instances. What is the most effective way to track and report such activities?

A) Enable VPC Flow Logs and analyze them using Cloud Logging.
B) Use Cloud Security Command Center to detect and report on unauthorized access attempts.
C) Set up Audit Logs for Compute Engine and analyze them with BigQuery.
D) Implement custom Stackdriver Monitoring alerts for Compute Engine instances.
E) Deploy Cloud IDS to monitor network traffic to and from Compute Engine instances.

QUESTION 36

You are working on a project that requires automated access to GCP services from a CI/CD pipeline. You have been given a JSON file containing the private key for a service account. How should you configure your CI/CD tool to authenticate to GCP using this service account?

A) Set the content of the JSON file as an environment variable in your CI/CD pipeline settings.
B) Use the gcloud auth activate-service-account command in your CI/CD script, referencing the JSON file.
C) Upload the JSON file to a secure location in Cloud Storage and reference it in your CI/CD scripts.
D) Convert the JSON file to a P12 key and use it with gcloud auth login in your CI/CD scripts.
E) Create a new service account in GCP IAM and use it in your CI/CD pipeline instead of the provided JSON key.

QUESTION 37

You are tasked with designing a highly available web application that needs to scale dynamically based on traffic. Which GCP service should you choose to achieve this goal while minimizing operational overhead?

A) Google Kubernetes Engine (GKE) with Auto Scaling and Load Balancing
B) Google Compute Engine instances with manual scaling
C) Google App Engine with App Engine Standard environment
D) Google Cloud Functions with serverless deployment
E) Google Cloud Run

QUESTION 38

You are tasked with designing a scalable and cost-effective solution for storing and analyzing large volumes of log data generated by your applications running on Google Cloud. The data needs to be archived for long-term retention. Which GCP services should you use for this purpose?

A) Use Google Cloud Bigtable for real-time log ingestion and Google Cloud Storage for long-term data archival.
B) Utilize Google Cloud Pub/Sub for log streaming and Google BigQuery for querying historical log data.
C) Set up Google Cloud Dataflow for log processing and Google Cloud Spanner for data storage.
D) Implement Google Cloud Logging for real-time log collection and Google Cloud Storage Nearline for long-term data retention.

E) Deploy Google Cloud Functions for log processing and store data in Google Cloud SQL.

QUESTION 39

Your company is running a fleet of virtual machines (VMs) on Google Cloud Compute Engine. You want to ensure that each VM can access specific Google Cloud APIs based on their roles. What should you do to achieve this access control?

A) Create a custom IAM role for each VM instance.
B) Use service accounts to grant permissions to each VM instance.
C) Assign a single project-level IAM role to all VM instances.
D) Use instance metadata to define API access for each VM.
E) Grant access to APIs directly from the VM's OS.

QUESTION 40

Your organization is migrating its on-premises database to Google Cloud SQL. You need to ensure that the migration process is as smooth as possible and that the database remains available during the transition. Which migration method should you choose to minimize downtime and ensure data consistency?

A) Use the "Create Backup" feature and restore it in Google Cloud SQL.
B) Perform a physical migration by copying the database files to Google Cloud SQL.
C) Use the Database Migration Service for online migration with minimal downtime.
D) Export the data to CSV files and import them into Google Cloud SQL.

QUESTION 41

You work as a senior cloud engineer at a premiere medical institute where your team is working on migrating the entire infrastructure of a legacy enterprise client to GCP Compute Engine. Some medical servers are accessible from the internet, others via the institute's internal intranet. All servers talk to each other over specific ports and protocols. You are studying the current network setup and you have found that the public servers rely on a demilitarized zone (DMZ) and the private servers use the Local Area Network (LAN). How can you design the networking setup on GCP with these requirements?

A) Use a single VPC with two subnets: one for the DMZ and one for LAN.
B) Use a single VPC with two subnets: one for the DMZ and one for LAN.
C) Create two separate VPCs: one for the DMZ and one for LAN.
D) Create two separate VPCs: one for the DMZ and one for LAN.

QUESTION 42

You are tasked with optimizing the costs of a Google Cloud project. The project contains a large dataset stored in Google Cloud Storage. Which approach should you consider to reduce storage costs while maintaining data accessibility?

A) Use Object Versioning to archive old data
B) Implement data compression on the dataset
C) Move the dataset to Google Cloud Coldline Storage
D) Configure data lifecycle policies to delete old data

QUESTION 43

Your company operates a daily mission-critical data analysis pipeline that relies on files stored in Cloud Storage. Users for this pipeline are located in Bangalore, India, and require frequent and dynamic access to the data. What is the most optimal and cost-effective storage configuration for these files on Cloud Storage?

A) Configure regional storage with nearline storage class for the region closest to the users. B) Configure regional storage with standard storage class for the region closest to the users. C) Configure dual-regional storage with nearline storage class for the dual region closest to the users. D) Configure dual-regional storage with standard storage class for the dual region closest to the users.

QUESTION 44

You are tasked with designing a highly available architecture on Google Cloud for a critical application. Which service would you choose to ensure automatic failover and redundancy across multiple regions?

A) Google Compute Engine (GCE)
B) Google Cloud Storage
C) Google Cloud Spanner
D) Google App Engine

QUESTION 45

Your organization is planning to deploy a web application that requires highly available and globally distributed storage. The application must provide low-latency access to users worldwide. Which Google Cloud storage service should you choose to meet these requirements effectively?

A) Google Cloud Storage Multi-Regional
B) Google Cloud Storage Regional
C) Google Cloud Storage Nearline
D) Google Cloud Filestore

QUESTION 46

Your organization has decided to implement a disaster recovery (DR) plan for its Google Cloud resources. You want to ensure data redundancy and failover capabilities across multiple regions. Which Google Cloud service should you use to achieve this DR strategy?

A) Google Cloud Storage
B) Google Cloud Pub/Sub
C) Google Cloud Spanner
D) Google Cloud Storage Multi-Regional

QUESTION 47

Your organization is designing a multi-tier web application on Google Cloud Platform (GCP). The application requires a distributed cache for storing frequently accessed data to reduce database load and improve performance. Which GCP service should you choose for implementing this distributed cache?

A) Implement a custom caching layer on Google Kubernetes Engine (GKE).
B) Use Google Cloud Bigtable as an in-memory cache.
C) Deploy Google Cloud Memorystore .
D) Set up a separate Google Cloud SQL database for caching.

QUESTION 48

Your organization is migrating a legacy on-premises application to Google Cloud. The application relies on an Oracle database. Which Google Cloud service can you use to host the Oracle database while minimizing operational overhead and ensuring compatibility?

A) Deploy the Oracle database on Google Compute Engine instances.
B) Use Google Cloud SQL for Oracle to manage the Oracle database.
C) Set up Oracle database on Google Kubernetes Engine (GKE) for containerized management.
D) Utilize Google Cloud Bigtable for hosting relational databases.

QUESTION 49

You are tasked with setting up a highly available database for a new global application. You've chosen Cloud Spanner for its scalability and consistency features. What should be your first action in GCP to start using Cloud Spanner for your application?

A) Enable the Cloud Spanner API in your GCP project.
B) Create a new Cloud Spanner instance and choose a multi-regional configuration.
C) Assign the Cloud Spanner Admin IAM role to your user account.
D) Set up a VPC network with subnetworks in the regions where your application will be available.

QUESTION 50

Your company is integrating its user accounts with Google Cloud Identity. Some employees have existing personal Google Accounts with their company email addresses. What is the best practice for resolving these conflicts?

A) Ask the employees to change the email address associated with their personal Google Accounts.
B) Initiate a Google Account transfer process for affected users to integrate their accounts into Cloud Identity.
C) Require employees to delete their personal Google Accounts.
D) Create new company email addresses for employees to use with Cloud Identity.
E) Merge the personal Google Accounts with the Cloud Identity accounts.

SET 1 - ANSWERS ONLY

QUESTION 1

Answer - D) Cloud Pub/Sub to Dataflow pipeline

A) Incorrect, as periodic export might not meet the real-time requirement of the new regulation.
B) Incorrect, Data Fusion is a powerful integration tool but might introduce unnecessary complexity for this use case.
C) Incorrect, implementing a custom application adds complexity and maintenance overhead.
D) Correct, streaming data changes using Cloud Pub/Sub to a Dataflow pipeline and writing results to BigQuery allows for real-time data integration and meets regulatory requirements.
E) Incorrect, manual processes are error-prone and do not provide the real-time integration needed for compliance.

QUESTION 2

Answer - A) Google Cloud Monitoring

A) Correct, Google Cloud Monitoring allows for monitoring resources and services across multiple clouds, providing a unified view for cost optimization.
B) Incorrect, BigQuery is a data warehouse service and not primarily used for monitoring resources across different clouds.
C) Incorrect, Cloud Functions is a serverless execution environment for building and connecting cloud services, not for monitoring resources.
D) Incorrect, Cloud Interconnect connects your network to Google's network, but it doesn't provide monitoring capabilities across clouds.
E) Incorrect, Cloud Pub/Sub is a messaging service for event-driven systems and doesn't provide resource monitoring capabilities.
F) Incorrect, Cloud Billing Report provides billing reports for GCP services only, not for resources on other clouds.

QUESTION 3

Answer - A) Modify the bucket's IAM policy

A) Correct, modifying the bucket's IAM policy to grant 'Storage Object Admin' to specific team members is the most direct way to control access.
B) Incorrect, Access Context Manager is more about defining and enforcing access based on user context, not specific bucket permissions.
C) Incorrect, VPC Service Controls are used for securing resources within a network perimeter, not for specific object modification permissions.
D) Incorrect, Object Lifecycle Management is for managing object's life cycle, not access control.
E) Incorrect, creating a custom IAM role is an option, but it's more complex and not necessary when predefined roles can suffice.

QUESTION 4

Answer - B) Internal Load Balancing with Ingress

A) Incorrect, External Load Balancers expose services to the public internet, which is not desired in this scenario.
B) Correct, Internal Load Balancing with Ingress allows for private, internal communication among clusters without exposing services to the public internet.
C) Incorrect, VPC Network Peering is used for connecting VPCs, not GKE clusters directly.
D) Incorrect, VPN tunnels are more suited for connecting different networks, and are an over-complication for inter-cluster communication within GCP.
E) Incorrect, Cloud Interconnect is typically used for connecting on-premises infrastructure to GCP, not for internal GCP communication.

QUESTION 5

Answer - B) Enable deletion protection

A) Incorrect, IAM policies control access but do not prevent accidental modifications or deletions by authorized users.
B) Correct, enabling deletion protection on Compute Engine instances prevents them from being accidentally deleted.
C) Incorrect, while snapshot backups are important for recovery, they do not prevent accidental modifications or deletions.
D) Incorrect, VPC Service Controls provide a security boundary for services, but do not specifically safeguard individual instances.
E) Incorrect, labels help in organizing and managing resources but do not provide protection against accidental modifications or deletions.

QUESTION 6

Answer - A) roles/bigquery.dataViewer

A) Correct, the roles/bigquery.dataViewer role allows users to view and query data without the ability to modify or delete the dataset.
B) Incorrect, roles/bigquery.dataEditor allows editing and potentially deleting data within the dataset.
C) Incorrect, roles/bigquery.user provides broader permissions that may include data manipulation.
D) Incorrect, while a custom role can be created, it's unnecessary when roles/bigquery.dataViewer suffices.
E) Incorrect, roles/bigquery.dataOwner provides full control over the dataset, including modification and deletion.

QUESTION 7

Answer - A) roles/billing.viewer at the organization level

A) Correct, assigning roles/billing.viewer at the organization level allows the finance team to view billing information across all projects.
B) Incorrect, creating a custom role is unnecessary when a predefined role like roles/billing.viewer exists.
C) Incorrect, roles/viewer at the project level would provide broader access than required for viewing

billing information.
D) Incorrect, roles/iam.roleViewer provides access to IAM policies, not billing information.
E) Incorrect, adding as billing administrators would give more access than needed for just viewing billing details.

QUESTION 8

Answer - B) Stackdriver for a unified dashboard

A) Incorrect, creating individual dashboards is not efficient for centralized monitoring.
B) Correct, Stackdriver (Cloud Monitoring) can be used to create a unified dashboard that aggregates metrics from multiple projects.
C) Incorrect, roles/logging.viewer allows viewing logs, not aggregating metrics across projects in a dashboard.
D) Incorrect, using Cloud Pub/Sub for this purpose is overly complex and not as direct as using Stackdriver.
E) Incorrect, a shared VPC centralizes network management, not monitoring of resource usage.

QUESTION 9

Answer - B) Budget in Cloud Billing

A) Incorrect, Cloud Monitoring tracks usage metrics but does not directly monitor costs.
B) Correct, creating a budget in Cloud Billing and setting up email notifications for a specific threshold is the most direct way to monitor egress traffic costs.
C) Incorrect, while exporting to BigQuery is possible, it's more complex than setting a budget in Cloud Billing.
D) Incorrect, network monitoring agents track usage but do not directly correlate to billing costs.
E) Incorrect, using Cloud Functions for real-time analysis is more complex and not necessary for cost monitoring.

QUESTION 10

Answer –C) 1. Build a Docker image from the Dockerfile and upload it to Container Registry.
   2. Create a Deployment YAML file to point to the newly uploaded image.
   3. Use the kubectl command line utility to create the deployment with that file.

A) Incorrect because kubectl apply -f expects a YAML file that describes the Kubernetes resources, not a Dockerfile.
B) Incorrect as gcloud app deploy is used for deploying applications to Google App Engine, not for deploying containerized applications to GKE.
C) Correct because this is the standard workflow for deploying containerized applications on GKE. It involves building a Docker image, pushing it to Container Registry, and then deploying it using a YAML configuration file with kubectl.
D) Incorrect because GKE requires images to be stored in Container Registry, not Cloud Storage. Cloud Storage is not used for storing Docker images for deployment on GKE.

QUESTION 11

Answer - C) Create a single Operations Suite account and link all projects to it.

A) Inefficient due to manual aggregation.
B) Shared VPC does not directly support logging aggregation.
C) Correct, as it provides a centralized logging solution across multiple projects.
D) Unnecessary with Operations Suite capabilities.

QUESTION 12

Answer - B) Install an RDP client on your desktop, set a Windows username and password in the GCP Console, and use these credentials to log in to the instance.

A) Incorrect as SSH is not used for Windows-based instances.
B) Correct, as it provides a straightforward and secure method to connect to a Windows VM on GCP using RDP.
C) Incorrect because port 22 is for SSH, not RDP, which uses port 3389.
D) Incorrect, as it does not mention the initial step of installing an RDP client, which is essential for connecting to a Windows VM.

QUESTION 13

Answer - A) Create a new GCP project using gcloud, set up a new GKE cluster in this project, and deploy the application.

A) This is the best practice for ensuring compliance and separation of environments. It allows for clear delineation between test and production environments in separate GCP projects.
B) This does not meet compliance requirements of having separate projects.
C) Duplicating within the same project fails to provide the necessary separation for compliance.
D) Gcloud does not support direct copying of GKE configurations to a new project in this manner.

QUESTION 14

Answer - C) Create a custom service account with the 'bigquery.dataEditor' role specifically for the dataset.

C) This approach adheres to the principle of least privilege by granting the necessary permissions to the specific resource (BigQuery dataset) and avoids giving broader access than required.
A) The default service account might have broader access than necessary.
B) The 'bigquery.user' role at the project level is too broad.
D) The 'bigquery.admin' role provides more permissions than needed for this task.

QUESTION 15

Answer - B) App Engine Admin

B) App Engine Admin role is appropriate as it provides permissions to manage all aspects of App Engine applications, including deployment and configuration, without overly broad project-level access.
A) Project Editor is too broad and violates the principle of least privilege.

C) App Engine Deployer allows deployment but not full management capabilities.
D) App Engine Service Admin role doesn't provide comprehensive application management permissions.

QUESTION 16

Answer - A) Generate a signed URL with a three-hour expiration for the file and share it with the consultant.

A) Creating a signed URL provides secure and time-limited access to the file without requiring a Google account, aligning with best practices for sharing sensitive data.
B) Setting the file to public poses a security risk and does not ensure automatic revocation.
C) Emailing the file is insecure and does not guarantee access revocation.
D) Creating a temporary bucket is less efficient and does not provide the same level of access control as a signed URL.

QUESTION 17

Answer - A) Enable autoscaling and set the minimum number of instances to 1

Option A: This is the correct choice as it enables autoscaling, ensuring the MIG can dynamically adjust the number of instances based on traffic. Setting the minimum number to 1 guarantees at least one instance is running at all times.
Option B: Disabling autoscaling contradicts the goal of ensuring high availability.
Option C: Setting the maximum number of instances to 1 may restrict scalability when needed.
Option D: Disabling autoscaling without specifying a minimum may result in zero instances during low traffic.

QUESTION 18

Answer - C) Google Cloud Identity Platform.

Option C is the correct choice as Google Cloud Identity Platform provides user identity management, SSO capabilities, and integration with identity providers for secure and scalable authentication in web applications.
Option A and Option B are unrelated to user authentication. Option D is for data preparation, not identity management.

QUESTION 19

Answer - C) NodeAutoRepair

Option C is the correct choice because enabling NodeAutoRepair in a GKE cluster allows for automatic node repair, ensuring the high availability of critical workloads by automatically repairing nodes that fail health checks. Options A, B, and D do not directly address the need for automatic node repair.

QUESTION 20

Answer - C) Set up a new GCP project and deploy the App Engine application in a European region.

C) This is the correct approach as each App Engine application is bound to the region it was initially

deployed in, and a GCP project can only have one App Engine app. Setting up a new project for a different region is the viable solution.
A) Migrating the existing application to a different region is not supported in App Engine.
B) It's not possible to create multiple App Engine applications in the same project.
D) App Engine does not support reconfiguring an existing application to route traffic based on region.

QUESTION 21

Answer - B) Implement Cluster Auto-Upgrades to keep the Kubernetes version up to date.

B) Cluster Auto-Upgrades automatically update nodes to match the cluster control plane's version, ensuring the latest Kubernetes patches and fixes are applied.
A) Cluster Auto-Repair fixes node health issues but doesn't update Kubernetes versions.
C) Manual updates are time-consuming and prone to delays.
D) Creating new clusters for each update is inefficient and disruptive.

QUESTION 22

Answer - B) Store the API key in a Kubernetes Secret and reference it in the deployment YAML.

B) Kubernetes Secrets are designed to store and manage sensitive information, such as API keys, securely. This approach is more secure than embedding plain text in the YAML file or using ConfigMaps, which are not intended for sensitive data.
A) Encryption alone doesn't manage the access and distribution of the key securely.
C) ConfigMaps are not designed for sensitive data.
D) Storing sensitive information on disk can pose a security risk.

QUESTION 23

Answer - A) Set the Content-Type metadata of each image object to 'image/jpeg'.

A) Setting the Content-Type metadata to 'image/jpeg' for each image file instructs the browser to display the image directly, rather than downloading it. This approach ensures the desired user experience when interacting with the image gallery.
B) Sharing publicly only makes the file accessible; it does not control how it's displayed.
C) Cloud CDN improves performance but doesn't affect how images are displayed.
D) Labels are for organization and don't impact file behavior.

QUESTION 24

Answer - C) Utilize preemptible Compute Engine VMs for the batch processing.

C) Preemptible VMs offer a cost-effective solution for batch jobs that can handle potential interruptions and don't require continuous runtime, making them ideal for time-constrained and resource-intensive tasks.
A) A dedicated GKE cluster may be more expensive due to continuous resource allocation.
B) Regular VMs don't offer the same cost savings as preemptible VMs.
D) Cloud Functions are more suited for lightweight, event-driven processes.
E) Dataproc provides managed Hadoop services, which may be overkill for simple batch jobs.

F) App Engine is best for web applications, not batch processing tasks.

QUESTION 25

Answer - A) Enable 'Automatic Restart' and set 'On-host maintenance' to 'Migrate VM instance'.

A) This is the correct configuration for high availability. 'Automatic Restart' ensures that the VMs reboot after crashes, and 'On-host maintenance' set to 'Migrate' keeps the instances running during maintenance by moving them to another host.
B) Disabling 'Automatic Restart' and setting 'On-host maintenance' to 'Terminate' would result in downtime, which is not acceptable for mission-critical applications.
C) While 'Automatic Restart' is correctly enabled, setting 'On-host maintenance' to 'Terminate' would cause downtime during maintenance.
D) Disabling 'Automatic Restart' would mean instances won't reboot automatically after crashes.
E) Preemptible VMs are not suitable for mission-critical applications due to their ephemeral nature.
F) Auto-healing in an instance group is useful, but it doesn't address the maintenance behavior.

QUESTION 26

Answer - A) Turn on Cloud Audit Logs for all read operations in the Cloud Storage bucket.

A) Cloud Audit Logs, specifically Data Access audit logs, are designed to log access requests to cloud resources, including Cloud Storage buckets. This will record every instance of data being read, which aligns with the compliance requirement.
B) IAP provides controlled access but doesn't specifically log data access operations in Cloud Storage.
C) Cloud Functions can be used for logging, but it's a more complex solution compared to using built-in audit logs.
D) The DLP API is used for data inspection and classification, not for logging access.
E) Access Transparency provides logs for Google's operations, not user access.
F) Object Versioning and Access Logs provide information about object changes and requests but don't specifically log all read operations.

QUESTION 27

Answer - D) Change the project's billing account to the company's GCP billing account.

D) Changing the project's billing account to your company's GCP billing account will ensure that all future charges for the project are directly billed to the company. This is the most direct and effective way to transition billing responsibilities.
A) IAM access allows monitoring but doesn't change who is billed.
B) BigQuery billing export is for analysis and doesn't affect billing responsibilities.
C) Contacting Google Support isn't necessary for this change; it can be done directly in the GCP Console.
E) Creating a new project is an option, but it's simpler to change the billing account of the existing project.
F) Replacing the credit card doesn't change the billing account to the company's account.

QUESTION 28

Answer - C) Enable autoscaling on the GKE node pool.

C) Enabling autoscaling on the GKE node pool allows the cluster to automatically adjust the number of nodes based on the workload, which is essential for a photo-sharing platform experiencing variable traffic.
A) Horizontal Pod Autoscaler scales pods but not the underlying nodes.
B) Vertical Pod Autoscaler adjusts pod resources, not the number of nodes.
D) Dedicated node pools don't automatically scale with varying traffic.
E) Manual scaling isn't efficient for unpredictable traffic.
F) Custom metrics are useful but more complex than necessary for basic scaling needs.

QUESTION 29

Answer - E) Google Cloud Firestore

Option E - Google Cloud Firestore is a NoSQL document database that provides secure and scalable storage for sensitive customer data. It is designed for flexible and reliable data storage.
Option A - Google Cloud Storage is for object storage, not database storage.
Option B - Google Cloud Datastore is a NoSQL database but may not be the best choice for sensitive customer data.
Option C - Google Cloud SQL is a relational database service.
Option D - Google Cloud Bigtable is a NoSQL database for large-scale analytical and operational workloads.

QUESTION 30

Answer - C) Set up a Cloud DNS private zone to manage the database hostname.

C) Using Cloud DNS private zone allows you to manage the database connection using a DNS hostname. When the IP address of the on-premises database changes, you only need to update the DNS record, and all GCP applications will automatically connect to the new IP without requiring any changes in their configuration.
A) Cloud Interconnect provides a dedicated connection but doesn't solve dynamic IP address management.
B) Custom scripts require maintenance and aren't as efficient as DNS management.
D) Secret Manager is for managing secrets, not dynamic IP addresses.
E) Internal Load Balancers are for balancing traffic within GCP, not for hybrid connections.
F) Cloud VPN with static routing doesn't accommodate dynamic IP address changes.

QUESTION 31

Answer - C) Have the partner create a Service Account in their project and grant it access to your BigQuery datasets.

C) This approach follows the principle of least privilege and maintains a clear boundary between the two projects. By having the partner create a Service Account in their project, you can grant specific access to only the necessary BigQuery datasets in your project. This ensures controlled access without exposing other resources in your project.
A) Sharing IAM credentials is not secure and exposes the entire project.
B) Sharing a Service Account from your project is less secure and can lead to broader access than necessary.

D) A shared VPC is not necessary for BigQuery dataset sharing and is more complex.
E) Data Transfer Service replicates data but may not be needed for simple access sharing.
F) VPC Service Controls are for broader access management and are more complex than necessary for this scenario.

QUESTION 32

Answer - B) Create a new revision of the existing service and configure traffic splitting between the new and old revisions.

B) Creating a new revision of the existing service and then using Cloud Run's built-in traffic splitting feature is the most efficient way to gradually roll out an update. This approach allows you to specify the percentage of traffic that should go to each revision, enabling controlled testing with live users.
A) Deploying as a new service makes traffic management more complex and is less efficient for gradual rollouts.
C) Cloud Monitoring is for insights and metrics, not for traffic management.
D) Using a separate project complicates management and does not offer the same level of control as traffic splitting.
E) Feature flags can control access but are more complex to implement for this purpose.
F) Cloud Functions are not typically used for traffic routing between service versions.

QUESTION 33

Answer - B) Create a Cloud Function with the Python code and set the Cloud Storage bucket as a trigger.

B) Cloud Functions are ideal for executing code in response to Cloud Storage events. By creating a Cloud Function with the Python code and setting the Cloud Storage bucket as a trigger, the function will automatically execute each time a new object is uploaded, providing a direct, efficient, and scalable solution.
A) Using Compute Engine with Pub/Sub is less efficient and more complex for this task.
C) Cloud Run is an option but Cloud Functions provide a more straightforward integration with Cloud Storage events.
D) A CRON job on App Engine would not provide real-time processing and is less efficient.
E) Cloud Scheduler is for time-based jobs, not event-driven triggers like new uploads.
F) Kubernetes Engine is overkill for this task and adds unnecessary complexity.

QUESTION 34

Answer – A) Cloud Spanner across multiple regions

A) Correct, Cloud Spanner offers global distribution, strong consistency, and horizontal scaling, suitable for large-scale applications.
B) Incorrect, Cloud SQL might not handle horizontal scaling efficiently, and BigQuery is an additional complexity for query handling.
C) Incorrect, Cloud Bigtable doesn't support SQL queries natively, and Dataflow is more about data transformation than complex query analysis.
D) Incorrect, Firestore in Datastore mode is more suitable for smaller-scale applications, and Dataproc, while powerful, adds complexity for query handling.
E) Incorrect, managing a custom database on Kubernetes is complex and might not offer the same level

of consistency and integration as native GCP services.

QUESTION 35

Answer – C) Audit Logs for Compute Engine, BigQuery

A) Incorrect, VPC Flow Logs focus on network traffic, not access to instances.
B) Incorrect, Cloud Security Command Center is more for overall security posture, not specific to Compute Engine access.
C) Correct, Audit Logs provide detailed information on access and activities, and BigQuery allows for effective analysis.
D) Incorrect, Stackdriver Monitoring is more for performance metrics, not specific access tracking.
E) Incorrect, Cloud IDS focuses on intrusion detection, not specific to instance access monitoring.

QUESTION 36

Answer – B) gcloud auth activate-service-account

A) Incorrect, setting it as an environment variable is not a secure practice.
B) Correct, this command will authenticate the CI/CD tool using the provided service account key.
C) Incorrect, storing keys in Cloud Storage is not recommended due to security concerns.
D) Incorrect, P12 keys are less secure and gcloud auth login is for user authentication, not service accounts.
E) Incorrect, it is unnecessary to create a new service account when one has already been provided.

QUESTION 37

Answer - E) Google Cloud Run (Correct)

Option A is incorrect because while GKE with Auto Scaling and Load Balancing is a scalable solution, it involves more operational overhead than Google Cloud Run, which is fully managed and serverless.
Option B is incorrect because manual scaling of Compute Engine instances is not as dynamic and automated as Google Cloud Run.
Option C is incorrect because App Engine Standard environment does not provide as much control and flexibility for dynamic scaling as Google Cloud Run.
Option D is incorrect because Google Cloud Functions are designed for event-driven, short-lived functions, and may not be suitable for a web application's continuous scaling needs.

QUESTION 38

Answer - D) Implement Google Cloud Logging for real-time log collection and Google Cloud Storage Nearline for long-term data retention. (Correct)

Option A is incorrect because while Bigtable is suitable for real-time data ingestion, it may not be the best choice for long-term archival of log data.
Option B is incorrect because Pub/Sub and BigQuery are suitable for real-time analytics but do not provide cost-effective long-term data retention.

Option C is incorrect because Dataflow and Spanner are not typically used for log data storage and retention.
Option E is incorrect because Cloud Functions and Cloud SQL may not be the most efficient solution for managing and retaining log data at scale.
Option D is correct because Google Cloud Logging (formerly Stackdriver Logging) is designed for real-time log collection, and Google Cloud Storage Nearline is a cost-effective option for long-term data retention, making it a practical and scalable solution for the scenario described.

QUESTION 39

Answer - B) Use service accounts to grant permissions to each VM instance. (Correct)

Option A is incorrect because creating a custom IAM role for each VM instance can become cumbersome to manage and may not provide the necessary flexibility.
Option C is incorrect because assigning a single project-level IAM role to all VM instances would grant the same permissions to all instances, which may not be suitable for granular access control.
Option D is incorrect because instance metadata is not used to define API access permissions.
Option E is incorrect because granting access to APIs directly from the VM's OS is not a recommended or controlled approach for managing Google Cloud API access.
Using service accounts allows you to assign specific roles and permissions to each VM instance, ensuring fine-grained access control.

QUESTION 40

Answer - C) Use the Database Migration Service for online migration with minimal downtime. (Correct)

Option A is incorrect because using the "Create Backup" feature and restoring it may result in downtime during the restoration process.
Option B is incorrect because performing a physical migration by copying database files is not an online migration method and may lead to significant downtime.
Option D is incorrect because exporting and importing data using CSV files may also result in downtime and is not the most efficient method for large databases.
Using the Database Migration Service allows for an online migration with minimal downtime, ensuring data consistency and availability during the transition.

QUESTION 41

Answer - A) Use a single VPC with two subnets: one for the DMZ and one for LAN.

Option B is a duplicate of Option A. Options C and D suggest creating two separate VPCs, which would not allow for the required communication between the DMZ and LAN servers. Option A is correct because it recommends using a single VPC with two subnets to separate the DMZ and LAN servers, allowing control of traffic between them using firewall rules and enabling public ingress traffic for the DMZ servers.

QUESTION 42

Answer - C) Move the dataset to Google Cloud Coldline Storage

Option C suggests moving the dataset to Google Cloud Coldline Storage, which is a lower-cost storage class suitable for archiving data while maintaining accessibility.
Option A (Object Versioning) doesn't directly reduce storage costs and is primarily for data integrity.
Option B (Data compression) can help but may not provide the same level of cost reduction as Coldline Storage.
Option D (Data lifecycle policies) can help with data deletion but doesn't address reducing storage costs for accessible data.

QUESTION 43

Answer - D) Configure dual-regional storage with standard storage class for the dual region closest to the users.

Option A is incorrect because regional storage with nearline storage class does not take into account the proximity of users in Bangalore and may result in increased latency and slower access times.
Option B is incorrect because regional storage with standard storage class also does not consider user proximity and may lead to latency issues.
Option C is incorrect because configuring dual-regional storage with nearline storage class may increase costs without necessarily improving performance for users in Bangalore.

QUESTION 44

Answer - C) Google Cloud Spanner

Option C is correct because Google Cloud Spanner is a globally distributed, strongly consistent, and highly available database service that provides automatic failover and redundancy across multiple regions. It is well-suited for critical applications that require high availability and scalability.
Option A (Google Compute Engine) provides virtual machines but does not offer automatic failover and multi-region redundancy out of the box.
Option B (Google Cloud Storage) is an object storage service and does not provide automatic failover for applications.
Option D (Google App Engine) is a platform-as-a-service (PaaS) offering but does not inherently provide multi-region redundancy.

QUESTION 45

Answer - A) Google Cloud Storage Multi-Regional

Option A is correct because Google Cloud Storage Multi-Regional is designed for high availability and global distribution, providing low-latency access to users worldwide.
Option B (Google Cloud Storage Regional) is suitable for regional storage but may not provide the same global availability.
Option C (Google Cloud Storage Nearline) is for archival storage and not designed for low-latency access.
Option D (Google Cloud Filestore) is a managed file storage service and does not address global distribution and low latency.

QUESTION 46

Answer - D) Google Cloud Storage Multi-Regional

Option D is correct because Google Cloud Storage Multi-Regional provides data redundancy and failover capabilities across multiple regions, making it suitable for implementing a disaster recovery plan.
Option A (Google Cloud Storage) is a storage service but does not inherently provide cross-region redundancy.
Option B (Google Cloud Pub/Sub) is a messaging service and not designed for disaster recovery.
Option C (Google Cloud Spanner) is a database service but may not be the best fit for disaster recovery needs.

QUESTION 47

Answer - C) Deploy Google Cloud Memorystore

Option C is correct because Google Cloud Memorystore is a fully managed in-memory data store service, specifically designed for implementing distributed caching in applications. It provides low-latency access to frequently accessed data, reducing the load on the database and improving performance. It's a suitable choice for implementing a distributed cache.
Option A is not the most efficient choice as it involves custom development and management on Google Kubernetes Engine (GKE) for caching, which may add complexity.
Option B is not the best choice because Google Cloud Bigtable is designed as a NoSQL database and is not typically used for in-memory caching.
Option D is not efficient because setting up a separate Google Cloud SQL database for caching adds unnecessary complexity and cost.

QUESTION 48

Answer - B) Use Google Cloud SQL for Oracle to manage the Oracle database

Option B is correct because Google Cloud SQL for Oracle is a fully managed database service that provides compatibility with Oracle databases while minimizing operational overhead. It allows you to host and manage Oracle databases in Google Cloud, ensuring a smooth migration of your legacy application.
Option A would require manual management of Oracle on Compute Engine instances, increasing operational overhead and complexity.
Option C is not the best choice for hosting Oracle databases, as it is more suitable for containerized workloads and may not provide the required compatibility.
Option D is not designed for relational databases like Oracle and is not a suitable choice for this use case.

QUESTION 49

Answer – A) Enable the Cloud Spanner API

A) Correct, enabling the Cloud Spanner API is the first step to use Cloud Spanner in a GCP project.
B) Incorrect, creating a new instance is a subsequent step after enabling the API.
C) Incorrect, assigning roles is part of access management and not the initial step.
D) Incorrect, setting up a VPC network is not a prerequisite for using Cloud Spanner.

QUESTION 50

Answer – B) Account transfer process

A) Incorrect, changing the email address of personal accounts is disruptive and doesn't integrate them with Cloud Identity.
B) Correct, initiating an account transfer allows users to retain their data and integrates their account with Cloud Identity.
C) Incorrect, deletion of personal accounts is unnecessary and can lead to data loss.
D) Incorrect, creating new email addresses is inefficient and confusing.
E) Incorrect, merging accounts is not a standard practice for resolving such conflicts.

SET 2 - QUESTIONS ONLY

QUESTION 1

As a cloud engineer in a multinational corporation, you are tasked with designing a disaster recovery plan for critical applications running on GCP. The applications are currently hosted in the us-central1 region. Your objective is to ensure minimal downtime and data loss in the event of a regional outage. What is the most appropriate disaster recovery strategy to implement?

A) Set up a hot standby environment in the europe-west1 region with real-time data replication from the primary site.
B) Use a cold standby approach by regularly backing up data to Cloud Storage in the asia-southeast1 region, with a manual failover process.
C) Implement a multi-regional GKE deployment that automatically fails over to the europe-west3 region in case of a primary region outage.
D) Configure a pilot-light environment in the us-west1 region with critical core elements always running and data replicated from us-central1.
E) Establish an active-active configuration with load balancing between the us-central1 and europe-north1 regions.

QUESTION 2

You are tasked with setting up a scalable and secure storage solution for your company's large datasets that must be accessible by various GCP services. Which GCP product should you choose?

A) Cloud Storage
B) Cloud SQL
C) Bigtable
D) Firestore
E) Cloud Spanner
F) Datastore

QUESTION 3

As part of the compliance requirements, your organization needs to regularly audit the use of service account keys in your GCP project. You are tasked with setting up a system to monitor the creation, deletion, and usage of these keys. Which combination of GCP services and features would best allow you to achieve this?

A) Use Cloud Audit Logs to monitor service account key events and set up Cloud Monitoring alerts based on these logs.
B) Implement custom logging in Cloud Functions that triggers on service account key events and sends notifications.
C) Configure Data Loss Prevention (DLP) API to scan and report on service account key usage across GCP services.
D) Set up a Pub/Sub notification system for events related to service account keys and process these

events with Dataflow.
E) Create custom metrics in Cloud Monitoring for service account key operations and set alerts for unusual activities.

QUESTION 4

As a cloud engineer, you are tasked with designing a disaster recovery plan for critical applications running on GKE. The applications are currently hosted in the asia-southeast1 region. Your goal is to ensure minimal downtime and data loss in the event of a regional outage. What strategy would you recommend for disaster recovery?

A) Create a secondary GKE cluster in the asia-southeast1 region and use regional persistent disks for storage.
B) Deploy a hot standby GKE cluster in the europe-west1 region with real-time data replication.
C) Implement a multi-regional GKE deployment that automatically fails over to the us-central1 region in case of a primary region outage.
D) Set up a cold standby GKE cluster in the asia-northeast1 region and regularly sync data from the primary cluster.
E) Configure a pilot-light environment in the australia-southeast1 region with critical components always running.

QUESTION 5

In your organization, multiple teams are deploying applications on GCP using Kubernetes Engine. You need to ensure that each team can only access their respective GKE clusters and not affect others. What is the best approach to achieve this?

A) Implement Network Policies within each GKE cluster for traffic control.
B) Use separate namespaces within a single GKE cluster for each team.
C) Create individual GKE clusters for each team and apply IAM roles and permissions.
D) Utilize VPC Network Peering to isolate traffic between different GKE clusters.
E) Configure Pod Security Policies in GKE to restrict access to resources.

QUESTION 6

Your team is managing sensitive user data in BigQuery. You need to ensure that only authorized team members can access this data. Additionally, the access logs of who viewed or queried the data must be retained for compliance. How should you configure access and auditing?

A) Enable BigQuery audit logs and grant roles/bigquery.dataOwner to authorized users.
B) Use VPC Service Controls and access levels to restrict data access and enable Cloud Audit Logs.
C) Grant roles/bigquery.dataViewer to authorized users and enable Data Access audit logs in BigQuery.
D) Create a custom role with view permissions and set up Stackdriver for monitoring access.
E) Implement Identity-Aware Proxy (IAP) to control access to BigQuery and enable access logs.

QUESTION 7

As part of your role in managing GCP projects, you need to ensure that the security team can audit IAM policies across the entire GCP organization without making any modifications. Which role should you assign to the security team?

A) roles/iam.securityReviewer
B) roles/iam.policyViewer
C) roles/iam.roleViewer
D) roles/resourcemanager.organizationViewer
E) roles/securitycenter.viewer

QUESTION 8

As a member of a small team responsible for maintaining uptime, you need to monitor network traffic along with CPU, memory, and disk usage across multiple GCP projects. Which GCP service should you primarily use for comprehensive monitoring?

A) Cloud Monitoring
B) Cloud IAM
C) Cloud Trace
D) Cloud Interconnect
E) Cloud SQL

QUESTION 9

As part of your cloud cost management strategy, you want to track and get notified when the overall monthly GCP costs of your project exceed a certain amount. What is the best way to implement this in GCP?

A) Set up a budget alert in Cloud Billing for the specified amount with email notifications.
B) Use Cloud Monitoring to create an alert policy based on estimated charges.
C) Write a custom script to pull billing data periodically and send notifications when the limit is exceeded.
D) Manually monitor the billing account and send email alerts.
E) Implement a third-party cost management tool integrated with GCP billing data.

QUESTION 10

For a data analytics project, you need to choose an appropriate data storage solution on GCP. The project requires high throughput for both read and write operations, and the data is semi-structured. Which GCP service is most suitable?

A) Bigtable
B) Firestore
C) Cloud Storage
D) BigQuery
E) Cloud SQL
F) Datastore

QUESTION 11

To monitor and analyze the performance of multiple applications across different GCP projects, which feature of Google Cloud's Operations Suite should you use?

A) Cloud Monitoring with custom metrics.
B) Cloud Trace for inter-project tracing.
C) VPC Flow Logs for network monitoring.
D) Cloud Debugger for application performance.

QUESTION 12

Your team is tasked with migrating a legacy application to GCP. The application is currently hosted on a physical server and uses a local MySQL database. The goal is to ensure high availability and scalability in the cloud. What migration and deployment strategy should you choose?

A) Migrate the application to a Compute Engine VM using a lift-and-shift approach, and migrate the MySQL database to Cloud SQL with replication for high availability.
B) Containerize the application, deploy it on Kubernetes Engine, and use Cloud Spanner for the database to ensure scalability and high availability.
C) Re-architect the application for a serverless model using Cloud Functions, and migrate the MySQL database to Firestore for simplified operations and scalability.
D) Use App Engine to host the application and integrate it with Cloud SQL using automatic failover for high availability.

QUESTION 13

Your team is developing a web application on GCP and is currently using Cloud Run as a serverless platform for the development environment. The application is now ready to be moved to a dedicated production environment. What is the most suitable approach to achieve this while adhering to best practices for environment segregation?

A) Create a new GCP project and deploy the application to Cloud Run in the new project.
B) Within the same GCP project, deploy the application to a new service in Cloud Run designated for production.
C) Generate a new version of the application in Cloud Run within the existing project and route production traffic to it.
D) Replicate the existing Cloud Run configuration in the same project and rename it as the production environment.

QUESTION 14

You are configuring a new application on Compute Engine that needs to interact with a Cloud SQL database. Following Google's recommended practices, how should you set up the service account for this application?

A) Use the Compute Engine default service account with 'cloudsql.client' role.
B) Create a new service account and assign it the 'cloudsql.editor' role for the specific Cloud SQL instance.
C) Create a new service account with 'cloudsql.client' role for the specific Cloud SQL instance.

D) Assign the project owner role to the Compute Engine default service account for comprehensive access.

QUESTION 15

Your organization's security policy mandates strict control over networking resources. A team requires permissions to manage Virtual Private Cloud (VPC) networks, subnets, and related resources in a GCP project. Which IAM role should you grant to this team?

A) Network Admin
B) Project Viewer
C) Compute Network Admin
D) Compute Admin

QUESTION 16

Your team has been collaborating on a sensitive project with a vendor who requires temporary access to a dataset stored in Cloud Storage. The vendor uses a non-Google email service. How should you grant and manage this access in a secure and timely manner?

A) Share a signed URL to the dataset with a specific expiration time matching the duration of the required access.
B) Change the dataset's permission to public for the duration of the project and then revert back.
C) Manually send the dataset files to the vendor and instruct them to delete after use.
D) Create a dedicated Cloud Storage bucket for the vendor and schedule its deletion after the project completion.

QUESTION 17

Your company is launching a new mobile app that requires a scalable and highly available backend. You want to ensure that the backend can withstand regional outages and distribute traffic efficiently. Which Google Cloud service should you consider?

A) Google Cloud Compute Engine
B) Google Cloud Load Balancer
C) Google Cloud CDN
D) Google Cloud Firestore

QUESTION 18

Your team is responsible for maintaining high availability of a critical application on Google Cloud. Which GCP service or feature should you leverage to ensure automatic scaling, load balancing, and redundancy across multiple regions?

A) Google Cloud VPN.
B) Google Cloud Pub/Sub.
C) Google Cloud Kubernetes Engine.
D) Google Cloud Managed Instance Group with Auto-Scaling.

QUESTION 19

You need to ensure that data stored in Google Cloud Storage buckets is encrypted at rest using customer-managed keys (CMEK). Which configuration should you choose to meet this requirement?

A) Enable default bucket encryption in the Google Cloud Console.
B) Use Google-managed keys (GMEK) for encryption and configure IAM policies.
C) Enable Cloud Identity and Access Management (IAM) for bucket access control.
D) Enable Customer-Managed Encryption Keys (CMEK) and specify the desired encryption key for each bucket in the Google Cloud Console.

QUESTION 20

As part of a global expansion strategy, your organization wants to serve its App Engine-based application from Asia to reduce latency for Asian customers. What steps should you follow to meet this requirement?

A) Replicate the existing App Engine application to a server located in Asia.
B) Configure the existing App Engine application to automatically serve traffic from Asia.
C) Create a new GCP project and deploy the application on App Engine in an Asian region.
D) Use a Network Load Balancer to route Asian traffic to the existing App Engine application.

QUESTION 21

Your company's GKE cluster hosts critical applications, and you need to minimize vulnerabilities. What is the best approach to ensure the Kubernetes nodes are always updated with the latest security patches?

A) Configure the GKE cluster to use the latest node image for ongoing updates.
B) Enable GKE Node Auto-Upgrades for continuous and automated Kubernetes updates.
C) Regularly recreate the GKE cluster with the latest Kubernetes version.
D) Use a custom tool to patch Kubernetes nodes independently of GKE management.

QUESTION 22

Your team is deploying a new service in Kubernetes that requires access to a sensitive database. The database credentials are currently included in the service's deployment YAML file. How should you handle these credentials to enhance security?

A) Encrypt the database credentials and keep them in the deployment YAML file.
B) Use a Kubernetes Persistent Volume to store the database credentials securely.
C) Store the database credentials in a Kubernetes Secret and reference them in the deployment YAML.
D) Keep the credentials in a ConfigMap for better manageability.

QUESTION 23

Your company's Cloud Storage bucket hosts various documents, including HTML files for a static website. You want these HTML files to be rendered in the browser upon access. What Cloud Storage setting should you configure for these HTML files?

A) Enable 'Share publicly' for each HTML file object.

B) Set Content-Type metadata of each HTML file to 'text/html'.
C) Use Cloud CDN for the HTML files.
D) Add a label to each HTML file with a key of Content-Type and value of 'text/html'.

QUESTION 24

You need to run a nightly data processing job that typically takes 4 hours to complete. The job requires significant compute resources but can tolerate interruptions. Which GCP service would be most cost-effective for this use case?

A) Deploy the job on a persistent Compute Engine VM with high CPU capacity.
B) Utilize a Google Kubernetes Engine (GKE) cluster with autoscaling.
C) Use Cloud Functions to execute the job in a serverless environment.
D) Run the job on preemptible Compute Engine VMs.
E) Set up a Dataproc cluster to handle the data processing.
F) Configure a Cloud Run service to execute the job.

QUESTION 25

You are setting up a Compute Engine environment for a critical trading application that requires continuous operation. How can you ensure that the VM instances automatically recover from failures and are not interrupted during host maintenance?

A) Set both 'Automatic Restart' and 'Preemptibility' to on.
B) Enable 'Automatic Restart' and configure 'On-host maintenance' to use live migration.
C) Use standard persistent disks and enable 'Autohealing' with TCP health checks.
D) Create the instances within a managed instance group with automatic scaling.
E) Configure the instances as preemptible and set 'On-host maintenance' to 'Migrate VM instance'.
F) Deploy the instances in a region with minimum two zones and enable 'Automatic Restart'.

QUESTION 26

Your client requires all read requests to their financial data in a GCP Cloud Storage bucket to be logged for auditing purposes. How can you achieve this?

A) Enable the Storage Object Viewer role for all users and audit their activities.
B) Activate VPC Flow Logs for the Cloud Storage bucket.
C) Implement bucket-level IAM policies to log every access request.
D) Enable Data Access audit logs in Cloud Audit Logs for the Cloud Storage service.
E) Use Stackdriver Monitoring to create custom access logs.
F) Configure Cloud Storage to use private access logs for each object.

QUESTION 27

As part of a startup, you need to move your GCP project billing from your personal account to your company's account. What is the most straightforward approach to accomplish this?

A) Update the payment method in your current billing account to the company's bank details.
B) Transfer ownership of the project to an IAM account controlled by the company.

C) Assign the role of Billing Administrator to a member of the company's finance team.
D) Link the project to the company's existing GCP billing account.
E) Request Google Cloud Support to migrate the billing account to the company.
F) Create a new billing account under the company's name and link the project to it.

QUESTION 28

For an online event streaming service you're developing on GCP, how can you ensure the Kubernetes cluster scales effectively with varying viewer numbers?

A) Set up a Horizontal Pod Autoscaler for each streaming component.
B) Configure Vertical Pod Autoscaler for efficient resource usage.
C) Activate node pool autoscaling in the GKE cluster settings.
D) Create individual node pools for each streaming service.
E) Regularly update node pool sizes based on viewer analytics.
F) Implement a custom metric for scaling based on streaming data.

QUESTION 29

You are tasked with designing a disaster recovery plan for your company's GCP resources. Which GCP service can help you create automated backups of your virtual machines?

A) Google Cloud Snapshot
B) Google Cloud Storage
C) Google Cloud Backup
D) Google Cloud Pub/Sub
E) Google Cloud Logging

QUESTION 30

For a hybrid cloud environment where GCP-hosted applications use an on-premises database, how can you ensure the applications maintain connectivity without manual reconfiguration if the database IP address changes?

A) Utilize Cloud SQL as an intermediary between GCP applications and the on-premises database.
B) Create a DNS entry in Cloud DNS private zone for the on-premises database.
C) Configure each GCP application to periodically check a centralized config file for the database IP.
D) Set up a VPN tunnel with dynamic routing between GCP and the on-premises network.
E) Implement an environment variable in GCP VMs that stores the database IP.
F) Use a GCP External Load Balancer to manage the connection to the on-premises database.

QUESTION 31

To collaborate with a partner company requiring access to certain BigQuery datasets in your warehouse, what is the best method to grant them the necessary access?

A) Grant the partner's existing user accounts direct access to your BigQuery datasets.
B) Create a shared database user for both companies to access the BigQuery datasets.
C) Ask the partner to create a Service Account and give it roles to access specific datasets in your

BigQuery.
D) Use BigQuery's managed data sharing features to share datasets with the partner.
E) Establish a cross-project data sharing agreement through GCP support.
F) Implement a custom API to provide the partner with access to the required datasets.

QUESTION 32

For a live web app update on Cloud Run for Anthos, how can you test the new version with a subset of users before a full rollout?

A) Set up a canary release by deploying the new version as a separate service and manually redirecting a portion of users.
B) Implement a blue-green deployment by switching traffic between two separate versions using a Load Balancer.
C) Create a new revision of the existing service and split traffic based on user attributes using Cloud Endpoints.
D) Use the new version to create a new revision within the same service and split traffic between revisions.
E) Duplicate the application to a new Cloud Run environment and gradually move users to the new version.
F) Route traffic through a Cloud CDN to control which users receive the new version based on geographic location.

QUESTION 33

What is the best method to run a Python function automatically each time an object is uploaded to a specific Cloud Storage bucket?

A) Deploy the Python function on a Compute Engine instance and use Cloud Storage FUSE to mount the bucket.
B) Create a Cloud Function triggered by Cloud Storage events to run the Python code.
C) Use a Cloud Dataflow job that polls the bucket for new objects and processes them with the Python code.
D) Configure a Cloud Scheduler job to periodically run the Python code and check for new objects in the bucket.
E) Implement an App Engine application that continuously monitors the bucket for new uploads.
F) Set up a Google Kubernetes Engine service that listens for Cloud Storage events and runs the Python function.

QUESTION 34

As a cloud architect, you are tasked with designing a disaster recovery plan for a critical application hosted on GCP. The application has a strict RTO (Recovery Time Objective) of 2 hours and RPO (Recovery Point Objective) of 15 minutes. The application is currently deployed in the us-central1 region. What would be the most appropriate disaster recovery strategy to meet these objectives?

A) Implementing a hot standby environment in the europe-west1 region with continuous data replication and automatic failover setup.
B) Using a cold standby setup in the asia-east1 region with daily backups and manual restoration

processes.

C) Setting up a warm standby in the us-east1 region, with data replication every 30 minutes and semi-automated failover processes.

D) Creating a multi-regional deployment with load balancing and real-time data replication across both us-central1 and europe-west3 regions.

E) Opting for backup and restore strategy with backups stored in multi-regional storage and a manual restoration process in the asia-northeast1 region.

QUESTION 35

As part of regulatory compliance, your financial services company needs to audit and report all administrative activities within its GCP environment, including changes to network configurations. Which approach would you use?

A) Enable Access Transparency and use its logs for audit.
B) Use Cloud Audit Logs with a focus on Admin Activity logs, and analyze using Data Studio.
C) Set up Cloud Asset Inventory to track and report changes in the network configurations.
D) Implement Cloud Security Scanner to regularly scan and report any changes in the environment.
E) Utilize Cloud Compliance Reports Manager for real-time tracking of administrative activities.

QUESTION 36

Your team is developing a Google Cloud Function that needs to access resources in a GCP project. You have been given a service account key in JSON format. How should you ensure the Cloud Function uses this service account for authorization?

A) Embed the JSON key directly in the Cloud Function's code.
B) Set the service account as the runtime service account for the Cloud Function in the GCP Console.
C) Use the gcloud functions deploy command and specify the path to the JSON key file.
D) Store the JSON key in Secret Manager and reference it in the Cloud Function.
E) Set the GOOGLE_APPLICATION_CREDENTIALS environment variable in the Cloud Function to the path of the JSON key.

QUESTION 37

You need to set up a secure and scalable data warehousing solution on GCP. The solution should allow you to analyze large datasets with minimal setup and maintenance. Which GCP service should you choose?

A) Google Bigtable
B) Google Cloud Dataprep
C) Google BigQuery
D) Google Cloud Dataflow
E) Google Cloud Pub/Sub

QUESTION 38

Your organization is expanding its presence to multiple regions, and you need to ensure data replication and availability across regions for your cloud-native applications. Which GCP service or feature can help you achieve this cross-region replication and high availability?

A) Configure Google Cloud VPN for cross-region data replication.
B) Implement Google Cloud Spanner for global transaction consistency and data replication.
C) Use Google Cloud Dataprep for ETL jobs and data synchronization across regions.
D) Deploy Google Cloud Run for serverless microservices with cross-region load balancing.
E) Set up Google Cloud Functions for event-driven data replication.

QUESTION 39

Your organization is building a data analytics platform on Google Cloud that involves processing large volumes of data. You want to ensure cost-effective data storage and processing. What Google Cloud service should you choose to store and analyze large datasets economically?

A) Use Google Cloud Bigtable for cost-effective storage and analysis of large datasets.
B) Implement Google Cloud Datastore for scalable and cost-effective data storage and processing.
C) Choose Google Cloud Storage and use Google BigQuery for cost-effective analysis.
D) Deploy Google Cloud SQL for efficient storage and analysis of large datasets.
E) Utilize Google Cloud Pub/Sub for economical data storage and processing.

QUESTION 40

Your team is responsible for optimizing cost management in a Google Cloud project that uses various GCP services. You want to identify opportunities for cost reduction and analyze resource usage. Which GCP service or feature can you use for cost optimization and resource usage analysis?

A) Implement Google Cloud Billing Reports for cost reduction and resource usage analysis.
B) Configure Google Cloud Monitoring for real-time cost tracking and analysis.
C) Utilize Google Cloud Cost Explorer for cost optimization and resource usage analysis.
D) Set up Google Cloud Security Command Center for cost management and resource usage analysis.

QUESTION 41

You are working on a project that involves processing a large amount of data using Google Cloud services. To optimize costs, you want to minimize data egress charges when transferring data out of Google Cloud Storage to the public internet. Which Google Cloud service should you use to achieve this optimization?

A) Google Cloud Pub/Sub
B) Google Cloud Dataflow
C) Google Cloud Transfer Appliance
D) Google Cloud CDN

QUESTION 42

Your team is developing a microservices-based application on Google Kubernetes Engine (GKE). You need a reliable way to manage and distribute configurations to the microservices. What should you use for this purpose?

A) Google Cloud Pub/Sub
B) Google Cloud Endpoints
C) Google Cloud Config Connector
D) Google Kubernetes ConfigMaps and Secrets

QUESTION 43

Your organization's data analysis pipeline relies on Cloud Storage for mission-critical data. Users are located in Bangalore, India, and need fast and frequent access to this data. Which storage configuration should you choose to optimize both performance and cost-effectiveness?

A) Configure multi-regional storage with nearline storage class. B) Configure multi-regional storage with standard storage class. C) Configure dual-regional storage with nearline storage class for the dual region closest to the users. D) Configure dual-regional storage with standard storage class for the dual region closest to the users.

QUESTION 44

Your organization is dealing with sensitive data, and you need to ensure encryption at rest for your Google Cloud Storage buckets. Which encryption option should you choose to achieve this while maintaining control over the encryption keys?

A) Google-managed keys
B) Customer-supplied keys
C) Firebase-managed keys
D) Google Identity Platform keys

QUESTION 45

Your team is responsible for optimizing the cost of Google Cloud resources in a multi-project environment. You want to allocate costs accurately to different departments within your organization. What Google Cloud feature or service should you use to achieve this cost allocation?

A) Google Cloud Audit Logs
B) Google Cloud Billing Reports and Cost Explorer
C) Google Cloud Identity and Access Management (IAM)
D) Google Cloud Project Labels

QUESTION 46

Your organization wants to set up a cost-effective and scalable data warehouse solution on Google Cloud. The data warehouse will be used for analyzing large datasets and generating business reports. Which Google Cloud data warehouse service should you choose for this purpose?

A) Google BigQuery
B) Google Cloud Datastore
C) Google Cloud Bigtable
D) Google Cloud Firestore

QUESTION 47

Your organization needs to securely store and manage secrets, such as API keys and database credentials, for applications running on Google Cloud. Which Google Cloud service should you use to store and manage secrets securely?

A) Utilize Google Cloud Identity and Access Management (IAM) for secret management.
B) Store secrets in Google Cloud Storage with restricted access.
C) Leverage Google Cloud Key Management Service (KMS) .
D) Create a custom database to store secrets.

QUESTION 48

Your organization is building a real-time analytics platform on Google Cloud. You need to ingest, process, and analyze large volumes of streaming data from various sources. Which GCP service can help you efficiently handle real-time data processing and analytics?

A) Use Google Cloud Dataprep for data preprocessing and batch analytics.
B) Implement Google Cloud Dataflow for stream processing and real-time analytics.
C) Deploy Google BigQuery for batch data processing and analysis.
D) Leverage Google Cloud Dataproc for long-running Hadoop and Spark jobs.

QUESTION 49

Your development team is creating a new application that requires a globally distributed, horizontally scalable database. They have chosen Cloud Spanner for its features. What is the initial step they should perform to start using Cloud Spanner?

A) Allocate a global IP address for the Cloud Spanner instance.
B) Enable the Cloud Spanner API in the GCP project.
C) Configure instance-level IAM permissions for the development team.
D) Design the database schema for the application's data structure.

QUESTION 50

In the process of migrating to Google Cloud Identity, you encounter user accounts that exist both as personal Google Accounts and within the company's domain. How should you handle these conflicting accounts to ensure a smooth transition?

A) Instruct users to transfer their data manually to new Cloud Identity accounts.
B) Use the Google Workspace Admin console to send account transfer requests to users with conflicting accounts.
C) Implement a policy to phase out personal Google Accounts in favor of Cloud Identity accounts.
D) Allow users to maintain separate personal and Cloud Identity accounts to avoid data migration issues.
E) Automatically convert all existing personal Google Accounts to Cloud Identity accounts without user intervention.

SET 2 - ANSWERS ONLY

QUESTION 1

Answer - C) Multi-regional GKE deployment

A) Incorrect, while hot standby ensures minimal downtime, cross-continental replication may introduce latency and complexity.
B) Incorrect, cold standby is cost-effective but does not meet the objective of minimal downtime and quick failover.
C) Correct, a multi-regional GKE deployment provides automatic failover and meets the requirements of minimal downtime and data loss.
D) Incorrect, a pilot-light approach in a nearby region reduces costs but may not ensure quick scaling during an outage.
E) Incorrect, active-active is highly resilient but can be complex to manage and might be overkill for certain applications.

QUESTION 2

Answer - A) Cloud Storage

A) Correct, Cloud Storage offers scalable and secure storage solutions for large datasets and is accessible by various GCP services.
B) Incorrect, Cloud SQL is a managed relational database service but not optimized for large datasets.
C) Incorrect, Bigtable is designed for large analytical and operational workloads but might not be the best fit for general-purpose storage.
D) Incorrect, Firestore is a NoSQL database for mobile, web, and server development but not suitable for large dataset storage.
E) Incorrect, Cloud Spanner is a scalable relational database service but might be overkill for just storage purposes.
F) Incorrect, Datastore is a NoSQL database for web and mobile applications and not ideal for large dataset storage.

QUESTION 3

Answer - A) Cloud Audit Logs and Cloud Monitoring alerts

A) Correct, Cloud Audit Logs can track service account key events, and Cloud Monitoring can be used to alert on these events.
B) Incorrect, custom logging in Cloud Functions is more complex and not directly designed for monitoring service account key events.
C) Incorrect, DLP API is for scanning sensitive data, not for monitoring service account key events.
D) Incorrect, while Pub/Sub can be used for event notification, it's more complex and Cloud Audit Logs provide a more direct solution.
E) Incorrect, creating custom metrics in Cloud Monitoring for this specific purpose is overly complex and not as straightforward as using Cloud Audit Logs.

QUESTION 4

Answer - B) Hot standby GKE cluster in europe-west1

A) Incorrect, having a secondary cluster in the same region does not protect against regional outages.
B) Correct, a hot standby GKE cluster in a different region like europe-west1 ensures minimal downtime and data loss with real-time replication.
C) Incorrect, a multi-regional deployment might be too broad for this use case and could introduce unnecessary complexity.
D) Incorrect, a cold standby approach in asia-northeast1 would result in slower recovery time during an outage.
E) Incorrect, a pilot-light environment in australia-southeast1 does not guarantee quick failover or minimal data loss.

QUESTION 5

Answer - C) Individual GKE clusters with IAM roles

A) Incorrect, Network Policies control traffic flow at the IP address or port level, but do not restrict cluster access.
B) Incorrect, namespaces provide a logical separation within a cluster but do not prevent access to other namespaces or clusters.
C) Correct, creating individual GKE clusters for each team and applying specific IAM roles and permissions ensures access is properly segregated.
D) Incorrect, VPC Network Peering is for connecting networks, not for access control within GKE.
E) Incorrect, Pod Security Policies define what a pod can do and do not provide access control to clusters.

QUESTION 6

Answer - C) roles/bigquery.dataViewer and Data Access audit logs

A) Incorrect, roles/bigquery.dataOwner provides excessive permissions for sensitive data.
B) Incorrect, VPC Service Controls are more about securing the environment rather than specific data access in BigQuery.
C) Correct, roles/bigquery.dataViewer restricts access to viewing and querying, and Data Access audit logs provide the necessary compliance tracking.
D) Incorrect, creating a custom role is unnecessary when roles/bigquery.dataViewer exists, and Stackdriver alone does not provide sufficient audit logging.
E) Incorrect, IAP is not typically used for BigQuery access control and does not provide the same level of detailed logging as BigQuery audit logs.

QUESTION 7

Answer - C) roles/iam.roleViewer

A) Incorrect, roles/iam.securityReviewer is not a predefined role in GCP.
B) Incorrect, roles/iam.policyViewer does not exist in GCP.
C) Correct, roles/iam.roleViewer allows viewing of IAM policies without the ability to modify them.
D) Incorrect, roles/resourcemanager.organizationViewer allows viewing organizational resources, not specifically IAM policies.

E) Incorrect, roles/securitycenter.viewer is specific to Google Cloud Security Command Center and does not focus on IAM policy auditing.

QUESTION 8

Answer - A) Cloud Monitoring

A) Correct, Cloud Monitoring provides comprehensive monitoring capabilities for CPU, memory, disk, and network traffic across multiple GCP projects.
B) Incorrect, Cloud IAM is used for access management, not resource monitoring.
C) Incorrect, Cloud Trace is used for performance analysis of applications, not for monitoring infrastructure.
D) Incorrect, Cloud Interconnect connects on-premises networks to GCP but does not provide monitoring functionality.
E) Incorrect, Cloud SQL is a database service and does not offer comprehensive monitoring for other resources.

QUESTION 9

Answer - A) Budget alert in Cloud Billing

A) Correct, setting up a budget alert in Cloud Billing with email notifications is a direct and efficient way to track and get notified about GCP costs.
B) Incorrect, Cloud Monitoring focuses on operational metrics rather than billing data.
C) Incorrect, writing a custom script is more complex and less reliable than using built-in Cloud Billing features.
D) Incorrect, manual monitoring is time-consuming and prone to errors.
E) Incorrect, a third-party tool is unnecessary when Cloud Billing provides the needed functionality.

QUESTION 10

Answer – A) Bigtable

A) Bigtable is designed for large volumes of semi-structured data and offers high throughput for read and write operations, making it ideal for analytics workloads.
B) Firestore is more suited for mobile and web application backends.
C) Cloud Storage is ideal for unstructured data storage, not for high-throughput data processing.
D) BigQuery is optimized for analytical queries on large datasets, not for high-throughput read/write operations.
E) Cloud SQL is a relational database service, better for structured data.
F) Datastore is good for semi-structured data but doesn't provide the same throughput as Bigtable.

QUESTION 11

Answer - A) Cloud Monitoring with custom metrics.

A) Correct, allows monitoring of applications across projects with custom metrics.
B) Useful for tracing but not for broad application performance monitoring.
C) More focused on network traffic than application performance.

D) Used for debugging, not performance monitoring.

QUESTION 12

Answer - B) Containerize the application, deploy it on Kubernetes Engine, and use Cloud Spanner for the database to ensure scalability and high availability.

A) A traditional approach but might not offer the best scalability.
B) Correct, provides a modern, scalable, and highly available architecture using GKE and Cloud Spanner.
C) Involves significant changes to the application architecture and may not be suitable for all legacy applications.
D) Suitable for high availability but may not provide the same level of scalability as Kubernetes Engine.

QUESTION 13

Answer - A) Create a new GCP project and deploy the application to Cloud Run in the new project.

A) Separating development and production environments into different GCP projects is a recommended practice for better management and security.
B) This keeps both environments in the same project, which is not ideal for segregation.
C) Using versions within the same project does not provide the necessary environmental separation.
D) Simply replicating configurations in the same project does not adhere to best practices for environment segregation.

QUESTION 14

Answer - C) Create a new service account with 'cloudsql.client' role for the specific Cloud SQL instance.

C) Provides the necessary permissions for interacting with Cloud SQL while adhering to the principle of least privilege, focusing on the specific instance.
A) Using the default service account is not a best practice for specific tasks.
B) The 'cloudsql.editor' role is more permissive than necessary.
D) The project owner role is excessively broad and not recommended for specific service tasks.

QUESTION 15

Answer - C) Compute Network Admin

C) Compute Network Admin role allows management of networking resources such as VPC networks and subnets, aligning with the specific requirements of the team.
A) Network Admin is not a specific predefined role in GCP.
B) Project Viewer only provides read-only access and is not sufficient.
D) Compute Admin is too broad, providing access to all Compute Engine resources.

QUESTION 16

Answer - A) Share a signed URL to the dataset with a specific expiration time matching the duration of the required access.

A) This method is secure and efficient, providing the vendor with temporary access without the need for

a Google account and ensuring automatic revocation of access.
B) Making the dataset public even temporarily is a security risk.
C) Sending files manually is insecure and relies on the vendor for compliance.
D) A dedicated bucket may not automatically control access duration and is less efficient.

QUESTION 17

Answer - B) Google Cloud Load Balancer

Option B: This is the correct choice as Google Cloud Load Balancer can distribute traffic across multiple regions, ensuring high availability and efficient traffic distribution.
Option A: Google Cloud Compute Engine provides VM instances but doesn't inherently ensure regional resilience.
Option C: Google Cloud CDN is for content delivery, not regional resilience.
Option D: Google Cloud Firestore is a NoSQL database and not designed for load balancing or regional resilience.

QUESTION 18

Answer - D) Google Cloud Managed Instance Group with Auto-Scaling.

Option D is the correct choice as a Managed Instance Group with Auto-Scaling provides automatic scaling, load balancing, and redundancy across multiple regions, ensuring high availability.
Option A is for secure network connections, Option B is a messaging service, and Option C is for container orchestration.

QUESTION 19

Answer - D) Enable Customer-Managed Encryption Keys (CMEK) and specify the desired encryption key for each bucket in the Google Cloud Console.

Option D is the correct choice because it aligns with the requirement to use customer-managed keys (CMEK) for encryption at rest in Google Cloud Storage buckets. You can specify the encryption key for each bucket in the Google Cloud Console. Options A, B, and C do not provide the same level of control over encryption keys as CMEK.

QUESTION 20

Answer - C) Create a new GCP project and deploy the application on App Engine in an Asian region.

C) This approach is necessary because App Engine applications are region-locked and cannot be migrated or replicated to another region within the same project. Creating a new project for the Asian region is the recommended practice.
A) App Engine does not support replication of applications across regions.
B) You cannot configure an existing App Engine application to automatically serve different regions.
D) Network Load Balancers cannot change the fundamental region-based hosting limitations of App Engine.

QUESTION 21

Answer - B) Enable GKE Node Auto-Upgrades for continuous and automated Kubernetes updates.

B) Node Auto-Upgrades automatically keep nodes up to date with the latest Kubernetes version, ensuring that security patches are applied promptly.
A) Using the latest node image doesn't guarantee automatic updates.
C) Recreating the cluster regularly is highly disruptive.
D) Custom tools can introduce complexity and may not be as reliable as GKE's built-in features.

QUESTION 22

Answer - C) Store the database credentials in a Kubernetes Secret and reference them in the deployment YAML.

C) Kubernetes Secrets are specifically meant for handling sensitive data like database credentials. Storing them in Secrets and referencing in the deployment is a secure approach that follows best practices.
A) Encryption is not sufficient for managing access to sensitive data.
B) Persistent Volumes are not designed for securing sensitive data.
D) ConfigMaps are not intended for sensitive information.

QUESTION 23

Answer - B) Set Content-Type metadata of each HTML file to 'text/html'.

B) Setting the Content-Type metadata to 'text/html' ensures that browsers properly render HTML files when accessed. This metadata tells the browser that the file is an HTML document, leading to appropriate rendering.
A) Sharing publicly makes files accessible but doesn't affect rendering.
C) Cloud CDN improves load times but doesn't impact how files are rendered.
D) Labels are for organizational purposes and don't dictate how browsers render files.

QUESTION 24

Answer - D) Run the job on preemptible Compute Engine VMs.

D) Preemptible VMs are cost-effective for jobs that can be interrupted and don't run continuously, offering significant cost savings for compute-intensive tasks.
A) Persistent VMs may incur higher costs due to continuous resource allocation.
B) GKE with autoscaling can be more expensive and complex for this scenario.
C) Cloud Functions are designed for short-lived, event-driven processes.
E) Dataproc is a managed service for big data processing but may be more expensive.
F) Cloud Run is optimal for stateless HTTP containers, not batch processing.

QUESTION 25

Answer - B) Enable 'Automatic Restart' and configure 'On-host maintenance' to use live migration.

B) Enabling 'Automatic Restart' ensures that the VMs will reboot automatically in case of failure. Configuring 'On-host maintenance' for live migration allows the VMs to continue operating without interruption during maintenance events.

A) Setting 'Preemptibility' to on is not suitable for critical applications, as it allows Google Cloud to terminate preemptible VMs.

C) 'Autohealing' is an attribute of instance groups, not individual VMs, and doesn't address maintenance scenarios.

D) Managed instance groups are helpful for scaling but don't directly address VM restarts or maintenance.

E) Preemptible instances are not appropriate for critical applications.

F) Deploying across zones is good for redundancy but doesn't specify behavior during maintenance or failures.

QUESTION 26

Answer - D) Enable Data Access audit logs in Cloud Audit Logs for the Cloud Storage service.

D) Data Access audit logs in Cloud Audit Logs are the appropriate tool for recording read operations on Cloud Storage, fulfilling the auditing requirement.

A) The Storage Object Viewer role allows viewing objects but doesn't provide logging.

B) VPC Flow Logs capture network flow data, not access to storage objects.

C) IAM policies manage access but don't inherently log access requests.

E) Stackdriver Monitoring is not specific enough for logging individual access requests.

F) Private access logs are more about object-level operations, not detailed read requests.

QUESTION 27

Answer - D) Link the project to the company's existing GCP billing account.

D) The most efficient way to handle this situation is to link the project directly to the company's existing GCP billing account. This ensures all future charges are billed to the company without needing to create new accounts or transfer ownership.

A) Updating payment methods doesn't transfer billing responsibilities to the company's account.

B) Transferring project ownership doesn't automatically change the billing account.

C) Assigning a Billing Administrator role is part of billing management but doesn't change the billing account.

E) It's unnecessary to involve Google Cloud Support for this task.

F) There's no need to create a new billing account if the company already has one.

QUESTION 28

Answer - C) Activate node pool autoscaling in the GKE cluster settings.

C) Activating node pool autoscaling in GKE allows the cluster to dynamically adjust its size in response to the viewer traffic, ensuring efficient resource allocation for the streaming service.

A) Horizontal Pod Autoscaler adjusts the number of pods, not nodes.

B) Vertical Pod Autoscaler optimizes pod resource limits.

D) Individual node pools require manual management for scaling.

E) Regular updates are less efficient for real-time scaling needs.

F) Custom metrics for scaling, while effective, might be more complex than node pool autoscaling.

QUESTION 29

Answer - A) Google Cloud Snapshot

Option A - Google Cloud Snapshot allows you to create automated backups of your virtual machine instances, making it a suitable choice for disaster recovery planning.
Option B - Google Cloud Storage is for object storage.
Option C - Google Cloud Backup is not a standard GCP service.
Option D - Google Cloud Pub/Sub is for event streaming, and
Option E - Google Cloud Logging deals with log management.

QUESTION 30

Answer - B) Create a DNS entry in Cloud DNS private zone for the on-premises database.

B) Creating a DNS entry for the on-premises database in a Cloud DNS private zone allows applications to connect using a hostname. Updating the DNS record to reflect the new IP address will enable seamless connectivity without needing to reconfigure each application when the database IP changes.
A) Cloud SQL doesn't directly address the issue of connecting to an on-premises database.
C) Periodic checks of a config file introduce delays and complexities.
D) VPN with dynamic routing provides stable connectivity but doesn't address dynamic IP management.
E) Environment variables require updates if the IP changes, leading to potential downtime.
F) External Load Balancers are not typically used for on-premises database connectivity.

QUESTION 31

Answer - C) Ask the partner to create a Service Account and give it roles to access specific datasets in your BigQuery.

C) Having the partner create a Service Account in their own project and then granting it specific roles to access the required datasets in your BigQuery is a secure and efficient way to collaborate. This approach ensures that access is confined to what's necessary, without exposing other resources.
A) Directly granting access to user accounts can be less secure and harder to manage.
B) A shared database user is not recommended due to security concerns and lack of fine-grained control.
D) BigQuery managed data sharing is an option, but it might not offer the same level of control as Service Account access.
E) Cross-project agreements through support are more complex and may not be necessary.
F) A custom API requires additional development and maintenance.

QUESTION 32

Answer - D) Use the new version to create a new revision within the same service and split traffic between revisions.

D) Using the new version to create a new revision within the same Cloud Run service and then splitting traffic allows for a controlled, gradual rollout to a subset of users. This method is efficient for testing updates without affecting all users and enables easy rollback if needed.
A) Deploying as a separate service is less efficient for gradual rollouts and can lead to configuration complexity.

B) Blue-green deployment is a valid strategy, but it's less granular than traffic splitting for gradual rollouts.
C) Cloud Endpoints can help manage user access but are not necessary for simple traffic splitting.
E) Duplicating the environment increases management overhead and is not necessary for traffic splitting.
F) Cloud CDN is for content delivery optimization, not for version-based traffic routing.

QUESTION 33

Answer - B) Create a Cloud Function triggered by Cloud Storage events to run the Python code.

B) Cloud Functions provide a native and efficient way to execute code in response to Cloud Storage events. By creating a Cloud Function that is triggered by Cloud Storage events, you can ensure that the Python function runs automatically and immediately whenever a new object is uploaded to the bucket. This approach is efficient, scalable, and requires minimal setup.
A) Compute Engine with FUSE is not as efficient or scalable for event-driven tasks.
C) Dataflow is more suited for large-scale data processing, not for individual object events.
D) Cloud Scheduler is not suitable for event-driven triggers and would introduce delays.
E) Continuously monitoring with App Engine is less efficient compared to event-driven Cloud Functions.
F) Kubernetes Engine is a more complex solution than necessary for this use case.

QUESTION 34

Answer – A) Hot standby in europe-west1

A) Correct, hot standby with continuous data replication and automatic failover in a geographically distant region meets the strict RTO and RPO requirements.
B) Incorrect, cold standby with daily backups won't meet the RTO and RPO requirements.
C) Incorrect, warm standby with 30-minute replication is close but may not consistently meet the 15-minute RPO.
D) Incorrect, while multi-regional deployment provides high availability, it may not align with the specified RTO and RPO for disaster recovery.
E) Incorrect, backup and restore with manual processes would not meet the required RTO.

QUESTION 35

Answer – B) Cloud Audit Logs, Data Studio

A) Incorrect, Access Transparency logs are for Google's operations, not user activities.
B) Correct, Cloud Audit Logs, specifically Admin Activity logs, are ideal for tracking administrative actions and can be effectively analyzed with Data Studio.
C) Incorrect, Cloud Asset Inventory is for asset management, not activity auditing.
D) Incorrect, Cloud Security Scanner is for vulnerability scanning, not for auditing administrative actions.
E) Incorrect, Cloud Compliance Reports Manager is more for compliance reporting, not detailed activity tracking.

QUESTION 36

Answer – B) Runtime service account in GCP Console

A) Incorrect, embedding keys in code is insecure.
B) Correct, setting the service account in the GCP Console ensures secure and proper authorization.
C) Incorrect, the gcloud functions deploy command does not have an option to specify a service account key file.
D) Incorrect, Secret Manager is for storing secrets, not for direct service account authentication.
E) Incorrect, environment variables in Cloud Functions do not work the same way as in local environments.

QUESTION 37

Answer - C) Google BigQuery (Correct)

Option A is incorrect because Google Bigtable is a NoSQL database and not ideal for data warehousing and analytical workloads.
Option B is incorrect because Cloud Dataprep is a data preparation tool and not a data warehousing solution.
Option D is incorrect because Cloud Dataflow is a data processing service, not a data warehousing service.
Option E is incorrect because Cloud Pub/Sub is a messaging service and not a data warehousing solution.

QUESTION 38

Answer - B) Implement Google Cloud Spanner for global transaction consistency and data replication. (Correct)

Option A is incorrect because Google Cloud VPN is primarily for network connectivity and secure communication and does not provide data replication and global consistency features.
Option C is incorrect because Google Cloud Dataprep is a data preparation tool, not a data replication or synchronization solution across regions.
Option D is incorrect because Google Cloud Run is a serverless container platform and cross-region load balancing is not its primary function.
Option E is incorrect because Google Cloud Functions are designed for event-driven serverless functions and may not be suitable for cross-region data replication.
Option B is correct because Google Cloud Spanner is a fully managed, globally distributed relational database service that provides global transaction consistency and automatic, synchronous data replication across regions, ensuring high availability and data consistency for cloud-native applications in multiple regions.

QUESTION 39

Answer - C) Choose Google Cloud Storage and use Google BigQuery for cost-effective analysis. (Correct)

Option A is incorrect because Google Cloud Bigtable is designed for NoSQL data storage and may not be the most cost-effective choice for analytical workloads on large datasets.
Option B is incorrect because Google Cloud Datastore is suitable for certain use cases but may not be

the most cost-effective solution for large-scale data analytics.
 Option D is incorrect because Google Cloud SQL is a traditional relational database service and may not be cost-effective for large-scale data storage and analysis.
 Option E is incorrect because Google Cloud Pub/Sub is a messaging service, not a data storage or analytics solution.
 Using Google Cloud Storage for data storage and Google BigQuery for analysis is a cost-effective approach for large datasets.

QUESTION 40

Answer - C) Utilize Google Cloud Cost Explorer for cost optimization and resource usage analysis. (Correct)

Option A is incorrect because Google Cloud Billing Reports are primarily for billing and invoice management, not for in-depth cost optimization and resource usage analysis.
 Option B is incorrect because Google Cloud Monitoring provides real-time monitoring and alerting capabilities but does not specialize in cost optimization analysis.
 Option D is incorrect because Google Cloud Security Command Center focuses on security-related aspects and does not directly address cost management and resource usage analysis.
 Option C is correct because Google Cloud Cost Explorer is a tool that allows you to analyze your Google Cloud spending, identify cost-saving opportunities, and gain insights into resource usage, making it a suitable choice for cost optimization and resource analysis in a GCP project.

QUESTION 41

Answer - D) Google Cloud CDN

Option A, Google Cloud Pub/Sub, is a messaging service and not related to data egress charges. Option B, Google Cloud Dataflow, is used for data processing and not specifically for minimizing data egress charges. Option C, Google Cloud Transfer Appliance, is a physical appliance used for data transfer, but it is not a service for optimizing egress charges. Option D, Google Cloud CDN (Content Delivery Network), can help optimize costs by caching and delivering content from Google Cloud Storage closer to the user, reducing data egress charges when transferring data to the public internet.

QUESTION 42

Answer - D) Google Kubernetes ConfigMaps and Secrets

Option D suggests using Google Kubernetes ConfigMaps and Secrets, which are designed for managing configuration data in microservices running on GKE.
 Option A (Google Cloud Pub/Sub) is a messaging service, not for configuration management.
 Option B (Google Cloud Endpoints) is for creating APIs, not for configuration distribution.
 Option C (Google Cloud Config Connector) focuses on managing Google Cloud resources but not microservice configurations.

QUESTION 43

Answer - D) Configure dual-regional storage with standard storage class for the dual region closest to the users.

Option A is incorrect because using multi-regional storage with nearline storage class may not provide the necessary performance for users in Bangalore and could increase costs.
Option B is incorrect because using multi-regional storage with standard storage class may not consider the proximity of users and could lead to latency issues.
Option C is incorrect because configuring dual-regional storage with nearline storage class may not optimize costs while still providing performance for users in Bangalore.

QUESTION 44

Answer - B) Customer-supplied keys

Option B is correct because using customer-supplied keys allows you to maintain control over the encryption keys used to encrypt data at rest in Google Cloud Storage. This is important for organizations that need to manage their encryption keys for compliance and security reasons.
Option A (Google-managed keys) means Google manages the keys, not the customer.
Option C (Firebase-managed keys) is related to Firebase, not Google Cloud Storage encryption.
Option D (Google Identity Platform keys) is not used for encrypting data at rest in Google Cloud Storage.

QUESTION 45

Answer - D) Google Cloud Project Labels

Option D is correct because Google Cloud Project Labels allow you to apply custom labels to projects, enabling accurate cost allocation to different departments or teams within your organization.
Option A (Google Cloud Audit Logs) is for auditing and monitoring but does not directly address cost allocation.
Option B (Google Cloud Billing Reports and Cost Explorer) helps analyze costs but does not allocate costs by itself.
Option C (Google Cloud IAM) manages access control and is not primarily for cost allocation.

QUESTION 46

Answer - A) Google BigQuery

Option A is correct because Google BigQuery is a cost-effective and scalable data warehouse service designed for analyzing large datasets and generating business reports.
Option B (Google Cloud Datastore) is a NoSQL database and not suitable for data warehousing.
Option C (Google Cloud Bigtable) is designed for NoSQL workloads and may not be the best fit for traditional data warehousing.
Option D (Google Cloud Firestore) is a NoSQL document database and is not primarily intended for data warehousing purposes.

QUESTION 47

Answer - C) Leverage Google Cloud Key Management Service (KMS)

Option C is correct because Google Cloud Key Management Service (KMS) is designed specifically for securely managing cryptographic keys and secrets. It provides strong encryption and access control for

secrets like API keys and credentials, making it the most suitable choice for secret management.
Option A is incorrect because Google Cloud IAM is for access control, not secret management.
Option B is not the recommended choice for secret management, as Google Cloud Storage is typically used for storing files and objects, not secrets.
Option D is not efficient because creating a custom database for storing secrets would require additional development and maintenance, which is unnecessary when Google Cloud offers dedicated services for this purpose.

QUESTION 48

Answer - B) Implement Google Cloud Dataflow for stream processing and real-time analytics

Option B is correct because Google Cloud Dataflow is a fully managed stream and batch data processing service that allows you to efficiently handle real-time data processing and analytics. It is well-suited for ingesting, processing, and analyzing large volumes of streaming data from various sources in real-time.
Option A focuses more on data preparation and batch analytics, not real-time processing.
Option C emphasizes batch data processing and analysis with BigQuery, which is not designed for real-time stream processing.
Option D is more suitable for long-running batch jobs using Hadoop and Spark but does not address real-time analytics needs.

QUESTION 49

Answer – B) Enable the Cloud Spanner API

A) Incorrect, allocating a global IP address is not necessary for Cloud Spanner.
B) Correct, enabling the Cloud Spanner API is the first step to use it in a project.
C) Incorrect, configuring IAM permissions is a subsequent step.
D) Incorrect, designing a database schema is a step after setting up the Cloud Spanner instance.

QUESTION 50

Answer – B) Admin console, transfer requests

A) Incorrect, manual data transfer is time-consuming and prone to errors.
B) Correct, using the Admin console to manage account transfers is the recommended approach for handling conflicting accounts.
C) Incorrect, phasing out accounts does not address the immediate conflict.
D) Incorrect, maintaining separate accounts doesn't resolve the conflict.
E) Incorrect, automatic conversion without user consent can lead to issues and dissatisfaction.

SET 3 - QUESTIONS ONLY

QUESTION 1

Your company has a large-scale application hosted on GCP, utilizing a mix of services including Compute Engine, Cloud SQL, and Cloud Storage. You need to implement a solution that automatically scales the Compute Engine instances based on CPU utilization and also scales the Cloud SQL instances based on the number of connections. Which combination of GCP services and features should you use to achieve this?

A) Deploy a managed instance group for Compute Engine with autoscaling based on CPU utilization and implement Cloud SQL with automatic storage increase.
B) Utilize Compute Engine with custom metrics for autoscaling and configure Cloud SQL with high availability and read replicas.
C) Implement a managed instance group for Compute Engine with autoscaling based on custom metrics and enable Cloud SQL's automatic scaling feature.
D) Use Compute Engine in an unmanaged instance group with a custom script for scaling and set up Cloud SQL with a failover replica for load distribution.
E) Configure a managed instance group for Compute Engine with autoscaling based on CPU utilization and Cloud SQL with connection-based autoscaling.

QUESTION 2

Your team is deploying an application on GCP that requires both relational and NoSQL databases. Which combination of services would best suit these requirements?

A) Cloud SQL and Firestore
B) Bigtable and Cloud Spanner
C) Cloud Storage and Datastore
D) Cloud Bigtable and Firestore
E) Cloud SQL and Bigtable
F) Datastore and Cloud Spanner

QUESTION 3

Your company's GCP environment is growing rapidly, and you are responsible for managing the costs. You notice that several older Compute Engine instances are running continuously, leading to higher costs. You need to implement a cost-effective solution to automatically stop these instances during off-peak hours. What is the best approach to accomplish this?

A) Use Cloud Scheduler to trigger Cloud Functions, which checks and stops the older instances based on a schedule.
B) Implement an instance group with autoscaling and autohealing policies to manage the lifecycle of the instances.
C) Configure the instances to use preemptible VMs and set shutdown scripts to control their availability.
D) Employ a custom script running on a small Compute Engine instance that periodically checks and stops the older instances.

E) Set up Cloud Monitoring with alert policies to notify administrators to manually stop the instances during off-peak hours.

QUESTION 4

Your team is developing a large-scale application that will be hosted on GCP. The application will heavily rely on Pub/Sub for event-driven architecture. You need to ensure that Pub/Sub can handle sudden spikes in message volume without losing messages. Which configuration should you prioritize to manage this requirement?

A) Enable message deduplication in Pub/Sub to prevent processing of duplicate messages during spikes.
B) Implement Dead Letter Queues in Pub/Sub to handle undeliverable messages efficiently.
C) Increase the number of subscriptions in Pub/Sub to distribute the load during high message volumes.
D) Use Cloud Dataflow to process messages from Pub/Sub and autoscale based on the volume of messages.
E) Set up custom alert policies in Cloud Monitoring for high message volume and manually increase resources when alerted.

QUESTION 5

You are responsible for managing a large dataset on GCP, which is accessed frequently by various analytics applications. The data must be stored in a way that allows high throughput and low-latency read/write access. Which GCP storage solution should you choose?

A) Cloud SQL for relational database management.
B) BigQuery for large-scale data analytics.
C) Cloud Bigtable for high-throughput, low-latency access.
D) Cloud Storage for durable object storage.
E) Firestore for document-oriented database needs.

QUESTION 6

In your GCP project, you have a BigQuery dataset containing large amounts of financial data. You need to allow financial analysts to run queries and create new tables based on the existing data but prevent them from modifying or deleting the original dataset. What access control strategy should you implement?

A) Assign the roles/bigquery.dataEditor role to the financial analysts.
B) Grant the roles/bigquery.user role to the analysts and use table-level permissions to restrict access.
C) Create a custom role with permissions to query and create tables, but not modify the original dataset.
D) Use roles/bigquery.dataViewer for the analysts and allow them to export data for analysis in separate datasets.
E) Implement row-level access controls in BigQuery for the financial analysts.

QUESTION 7

In your GCP environment, there's a need for the project management team to view the hierarchy and metadata of all resources across the organization without making any changes. What is the most appropriate role to grant them?

A) roles/viewer at the organization level.
B) roles/resourcemanager.organizationViewer
C) roles/browser at the organization level.
D) roles/cloudasset.viewer
E) roles/resourcemanager.projectViewer

QUESTION 8

To ensure proactive management of your digital simulation projects, you want to set up alerting for specific metrics like high CPU utilization across your GCP projects. What should you do to configure these alerts effectively?

A) Use Cloud Monitoring to create alert policies based on CPU utilization metrics from each project.
B) Configure individual alerts in each GCP project and manually manage them.
C) Implement a custom alerting tool using Cloud Functions to monitor CPU utilization.
D) Rely on default alerting mechanisms within each GCP service used by the projects.
E) Set up Cloud Logging to send logs to Cloud Monitoring and create alerts based on log data.

QUESTION 9

To maintain cost control over your GCP resources, you need to ensure that you are notified when there is an unusual spike in the costs of Compute Engine resources. Which tool or service should you use to set up this type of alert?

A) Configure cost anomaly detection in Cloud Billing.
B) Create a budget alert with a low threshold in the Cloud Billing dashboard.
C) Use Cloud Monitoring to track Compute Engine resource usage and costs.
D) Set up a Cloud Function to analyze Compute Engine billing data for spikes.
E) Implement a custom application to monitor billing reports for unusual cost increases.

QUESTION 10

A company is looking to deploy a set of microservices on GCP. They require quick deployment, easy scaling, and no server management. Which service should they use?

A) Kubernetes Engine
B) Compute Engine
C) Cloud Run
D) App Engine flexible environment
E) Cloud Functions
F) Cloud Build

QUESTION 11

When integrating multiple GCP projects into a single Google Cloud's Operations Suite workspace, what is the primary consideration to ensure effective monitoring?

A) Ensuring all projects use the same network.
B) Configuring appropriate IAM roles for cross-project access.

C) Using the same machine types across projects.
D) Maintaining a uniform naming convention for all resources.

QUESTION 12

You are setting up a secure and scalable web application environment on GCP. The application requires a robust caching mechanism to improve performance. Which combination of GCP services and configurations would best meet these requirements?

A) Use Compute Engine with Autoscaling and Load Balancer, and integrate Cloud CDN for caching.
B) Deploy the application on App Engine standard environment, and use Memorystore for Redis as a caching solution.
C) Host the application on Kubernetes Engine, and implement a custom caching solution using Compute Engine VMs.
D) Build the application on Cloud Run, and utilize Firestore for data caching and quick retrieval.

QUESTION 13

As a cloud solutions architect in a media company, you are responsible for migrating a content management system (CMS) from a legacy hosting environment to GCP. The CMS is currently being tested in a Compute Engine instance. For the production phase, you need to ensure operational separation. What should your approach be?

A) Migrate the CMS to a new GCP project by setting up a Compute Engine instance and replicating the test environment setup.
B) Create a new instance in the existing project and migrate the CMS, labeling this instance as the production environment.
C) Use the existing Compute Engine instance for production, but create a snapshot for rollback purposes.
D) Set up a managed instance group in the current project for the CMS and designate it as the production environment.

QUESTION 14

In your GCP environment, a Compute Engine instance needs to process and upload data to a designated Cloud Storage bucket. What is the best way to configure access for this task while following Google's recommended practices?

A) Use the default Compute Engine service account with the 'storage.objectCreator' role assigned for the specific bucket.
B) Create a new service account and give it the 'storage.objectAdmin' role for the bucket.
C) Assign the 'storage.admin' role to the default Compute Engine service account.
D) Create a new service account with the 'storage.objectCreator' role specifically for the bucket.

QUESTION 15

A data analysis team in your organization needs to perform BigQuery operations, including running queries and managing datasets, but should not have access to modify project settings. What IAM role will you assign?

A) BigQuery Data Editor
B) BigQuery User
C) BigQuery Admin
D) Project Editor

QUESTION 16

As a GCP administrator, you are tasked with providing a time-limited access to a set of confidential documents in Cloud Storage to an external auditor. The auditor does not have a Google account and needs access for just one day. Which approach should you take to ensure security and compliance?

A) Generate a signed URL for the documents with a 24-hour expiration and provide the URL to the auditor.
B) Temporarily add the auditor's email to the IAM with 'Storage Object Viewer' role and revoke it after one day.
C) Upload the documents to a shared drive with restricted access and remove them after one day.
D) Create a new bucket, transfer the documents, share the bucket URL, and delete the bucket after one day.

QUESTION 17

You're managing a complex microservices architecture on Google Kubernetes Engine (GKE). Each microservice requires its own isolated storage. What GCP resource should you use to achieve this isolation?

A) Google Cloud Virtual Machines
B) Google Cloud Persistent Disks
C) Google Cloud Kubernetes Engine Pods
D) Google Cloud Kubernetes Engine Clusters

QUESTION 18

Your project requires real-time analysis of streaming data from various sources. Which GCP service should you use to ingest, process, and analyze streaming data at scale, ensuring low-latency data processing?

A) Google Cloud Dataprep.
B) Google Cloud Bigtable.
C) Google Cloud Dataflow.
D) Google Cloud Firestore.

QUESTION 19

Your organization is using Google Cloud Pub/Sub to ingest data from various sources. You need to ensure that the data is retained for 30 days to meet compliance requirements. What should you configure in Cloud Pub/Sub?

A) Enable the "Data Retention" option in the Google Cloud Console.
B) Set up a Cloud Scheduler job to periodically archive data to Google Cloud Storage.

C) Configure the "Message Storage Policy" to retain data for 30 days in the Google Cloud Console.
D) Create a custom retention policy using Pub/Sub API to retain data for 30 days.

QUESTION 20

Your mobile application backend on App Engine needs to be closer to South American users to reduce latency. What is the best way to relocate your App Engine deployment to meet this geographic requirement?

A) Change the App Engine application's region settings to a South American region.
B) Duplicate the App Engine application and deploy it in a South American region within the same project.
C) Establish a new GCP project and redeploy the App Engine application in a South American region.
D) Use Google Cloud CDN to cache the App Engine content closer to South American users.

QUESTION 21

To maintain high security standards, you need to ensure your GKE cluster is always running a Kubernetes version with the latest security fixes. What strategy should you adopt to manage the Kubernetes version of your GKE cluster?

A) Set up a cron job to periodically update the Kubernetes version of your GKE cluster.
B) Enable Auto-Upgrades for your GKE cluster to automatically update the Kubernetes version.
C) Frequently check for updates and manually upgrade the Kubernetes version of your GKE cluster.
D) Use a third-party tool to manage Kubernetes version upgrades in your GKE cluster.

QUESTION 22

You are tasked with securing an application in Kubernetes that requires SSH keys for accessing a Git repository. The SSH keys are currently hardcoded in the application's deployment YAML. What should you do to secure the SSH keys?

A) Encrypt the SSH keys and store them directly in the deployment YAML.
B) Store the SSH keys in a Kubernetes Secret and inject them into the pods at runtime.
C) Keep the SSH keys in a ConfigMap and load them into the application.
D) Use a Kubernetes Persistent Volume to store and mount the SSH keys into the pods.

QUESTION 23

For a digital art exhibition, your team has uploaded multiple video files to a Cloud Storage bucket. To enhance user experience, you want these videos to play directly in the browser. How can you achieve this?

A) Change the storage class of the video files to Multi-Regional.
B) Enable 'Share publicly' for each video file.
C) Set the Content-Type metadata of the video files to the appropriate MIME type (e.g., 'video/mp4').
D) Use Cloud CDN to stream video files directly.

QUESTION 24

In your GCP project, you have a task that requires analyzing 50 GB of data every day at 1 AM, with an average run time of 2 hours. Which GCP solution offers the most cost-effective way to handle this task?

A) Use a small-sized Google Kubernetes Engine (GKE) cluster that runs continuously.
B) Schedule the task on Compute Engine VMs with high-memory machine types.
C) Deploy the task on preemptible Compute Engine VMs optimized for compute.
D) Execute the task using Cloud Functions with a high memory limit.
E) Run the task on a Dataproc cluster with preemptible worker nodes.
F) Configure a Cloud Run service with memory-optimized containers.

QUESTION 25

In a high-stakes stock trading application, you need your Compute Engine VMs to be resilient to failures and maintenance events. What combination of settings should you apply to achieve this?

A) Enable 'Automatic Restart', set 'On-host maintenance' to 'Terminate VM instance', and use instance groups.
B) Use preemptible VMs, set 'On-host maintenance' to 'Migrate VM instance', and enable 'Automatic Restart'.
C) Enable 'Automatic Restart', set 'On-host maintenance' to 'Migrate VM instance', and configure HTTP health checks.
D) Set 'On-host maintenance' to 'Migrate VM instance' and use standard VM instances with automatic scaling.
E) Enable 'Automatic Restart', configure 'On-host maintenance' to use live migration, and deploy in multiple zones.
F) Configure instances as preemptible, use automatic scaling, and set 'Automatic Restart' to off.

QUESTION 26

To comply with a client's requirement, you need to log every time someone reads data from a specific Cloud Storage bucket containing sensitive financial information. What should you configure in GCP?

A) Set up Cloud Storage Access Logs for each data read operation.
B) Enable Data Access audit logs for the Cloud Storage service.
C) Use Cloud IAM to log every access request to the bucket.
D) Configure custom logging in the Cloud Storage bucket using Cloud Functions.
E) Implement a VPC Service Control perimeter around the bucket.
F) Activate Access Context Manager to log data access.

QUESTION 27

To simplify the reimbursement process for GCP services used in your startup project, you want to ensure future costs are directly billed to your company. What action should you take in GCP?

A) Modify the billing settings in your personal account to send invoices directly to the company.
B) Link your project to your company's GCP billing account to directly charge the company.
C) Set up a budget alert in your personal account to notify the company of upcoming charges.
D) Provide the finance department with access to your billing account for expense tracking.

E) Use the company's credit card details to replace your personal card in the current billing setup.
F) Contact GCP sales to discuss transitioning the billing responsibilities to the company.

QUESTION 28

In managing a GCP-based e-commerce platform with fluctuating daily customer visits, what Kubernetes configuration ensures the platform scales effectively with the changing load?

A) Implement a Horizontal Pod Autoscaler for each microservice.
B) Utilize a Vertical Pod Autoscaler for all deployments.
C) Enable GKE node pool autoscaling for dynamic resource allocation.
D) Assign dedicated GKE node pools for high-traffic services.
E) Manually adjust the node pool size based on sales trends.
F) Use custom scaling metrics based on the number of transactions.

QUESTION 29

Your team is developing a web application on Google Cloud. You need a fully managed and scalable database service that supports both SQL and NoSQL data models. Which GCP service should you choose?

A) Google Cloud SQL
B) Google Cloud Datastore
C) Google Cloud Bigtable
D) Google Cloud Firestore

QUESTION 30

To ensure uninterrupted connectivity between GCP applications and an on-premises database, which method should you use to handle potential changes in the database's IP address?

A) Deploy a Redis instance on GCP to cache the on-premises database IP address.
B) Establish a Cloud DNS private zone for the on-premises database's hostname.
C) Use a GCP Service Directory to keep track of the on-premises database IP address.
D) Configure a custom service on Compute Engine to update applications with the database IP.
E) Create a persistent disk on GCP that stores the database IP address for shared access.
F) Implement a Pub/Sub mechanism to notify applications of IP address changes.

QUESTION 31

In a scenario where a partner company needs access to specific BigQuery datasets in your project, what's the most secure way to facilitate this access?

A) Allow the partner's IP addresses to access your GCP network and BigQuery datasets.
B) Set up a dedicated user in your GCP project for the partner to use for accessing BigQuery.
C) Have the partner create a Service Account in their project and assign it necessary permissions in your BigQuery datasets.
D) Share a service account key from your project with the partner for BigQuery access.
E) Duplicate the necessary datasets into the partner's BigQuery project.
F) Use a GCP Interconnect to establish a secure connection between the two projects.

QUESTION 32

What approach should you take to test a new application update on Cloud Run for Anthos with a limited number of users, before fully deploying it to everyone?

A) Use a Cloud Load Balancer to direct a fraction of the traffic to a new service hosting the updated version.
B) Deploy the update as a new service and gradually increase the number of users accessing it.
C) Create a new revision of the existing service with the update and split traffic to include the new revision.
D) Implement API Gateway to manage user access to different versions of the application.
E) Route user traffic through a VPN that determines access to the new version based on user profiles.
F) Set up a beta environment in Cloud Run and invite a select group of users to access the new version.

QUESTION 33

How can you automate the execution of a Python function on new file uploads to a Cloud Storage bucket?

A) Configure a Cloud Storage trigger in Cloud Functions to run the Python code upon new file uploads.
B) Use App Engine to deploy the Python function and set up a CRON job to check the bucket for new files.
C) Set up a Cloud Scheduler job to periodically invoke a Compute Engine instance running the Python function.
D) Create a custom script on a Compute Engine VM that uses the Cloud Storage API to detect new uploads.
E) Implement a Cloud Run service that is triggered by changes in the Cloud Storage bucket.
F) Deploy a Kubernetes cluster on GKE with a pod that monitors the bucket for new file uploads.

QUESTION 34

You are developing a data processing pipeline for a finance company on GCP. The pipeline must securely process sensitive transaction data, comply with industry regulations, and scale to handle varying loads. The processed data should be stored for analytics and reporting. Which combination of GCP services and configurations would you recommend for this scenario?

A) Utilizing Cloud Dataflow for data processing, encrypting data using Cloud KMS, and storing the processed data in BigQuery with access controls for analytics.
B) Configuring a Kubernetes Engine cluster with custom encryption for data processing, storing data in Cloud SQL with private IP, and using Data Studio for reporting.
C) Implementing Cloud Pub/Sub for data ingestion, Dataflow for processing, Cloud Storage with VPC Service Controls for storage, and BigQuery for analytics.
D) Setting up Dataprep for data processing, using Cloud HSM for encryption, storing processed data in Firestore, and leveraging Looker for analytics and reporting.
E) Deploying a Compute Engine-based custom data processing solution, storing data in Cloud Bigtable with IAM policies, and integrating with Cloud Dataproc for analytics.

QUESTION 35

You are tasked with setting up a system to monitor and alert any unauthorized attempts to access sensitive data stored in BigQuery. What combination of GCP services and features should you use to achieve this?

A) Implement Cloud DLP to scan BigQuery datasets and set up Cloud Monitoring alerts.
B) Use BigQuery Audit Logs, analyze with Cloud Logging, and set up alerts with Cloud Monitoring.
C) Enable Data Catalog for BigQuery datasets and monitor access with Cloud IAM policies.
D) Set up custom Dataflow jobs to stream BigQuery access logs and analyze with Cloud Pub/Sub.
E) Deploy Cloud Endpoint Security to monitor BigQuery and integrate with Stackdriver for alerts.

QUESTION 36

As a developer, you are tasked with running a script on your local machine that interacts with GCP services using a service account. You have been provided with a service account key file. What is the best practice to authenticate your script with GCP using this key?

A) Store the key file in a secure location and use the gcloud auth activate-service-account command with the key file path.
B) Embed the key file content as a string within your script and use it to authenticate API requests.
C) Upload the key file to Cloud Storage and reference its URL in your script.
D) Convert the key file to an OAuth 2.0 token and use it for gcloud authentication.
E) Set the GOOGLE_APPLICATION_CREDENTIALS environment variable in your script to the path of the key file.

QUESTION 37

You are designing a microservices architecture for an e-commerce platform on GCP. You want to ensure each microservice is independently scalable and fault-tolerant. Which GCP service should you use for managing containerized microservices?

A) Google Compute Engine with manual scaling
B) Google Kubernetes Engine (GKE)
C) Google App Engine
D) Google Cloud Functions
E) Google Cloud Run

QUESTION 38

Your team is working on a project that requires real-time data processing of streaming data from various sources. Which GCP service is best suited for ingesting, processing, and analyzing streaming data with low latency?

A) Use Google Cloud Dataflow for stream data ingestion and Google Cloud Dataprep for real-time data processing.
B) Implement Google Bigtable for stream data storage and analysis.
C) Set up Google Cloud Pub/Sub for data streaming and Google Cloud SQL for real-time data analysis.
D) Utilize Google Cloud Dataflow for stream data processing and Google Cloud BigQuery for real-time

analytics.

E) Deploy Google Cloud Functions for stream data processing and store data in Google Cloud Storage.

QUESTION 39

Your team is responsible for ensuring data security in a Google Cloud project that uses multiple GCP services. To enhance security, you want to implement centralized access control and fine-grained permissions management. Which GCP service or feature should you use for this purpose?

A) Utilize Google Cloud Identity-Aware Proxy (IAP) for centralized access control.
B) Implement Google Cloud Armor for fine-grained permissions management.
C) Set up Google Cloud IAM (Identity and Access Management) for centralized access control and fine-grained permissions management.
D) Deploy Google Cloud Pub/Sub for access control and permissions management.
E) Configure Google Cloud VPN for centralized access control.

QUESTION 40

Your organization is building a web application that requires low-latency access to a large dataset. The dataset is stored in Google Cloud Storage, and you want to optimize access performance. What should you use to achieve low-latency access to the dataset?

A) Utilize Google Cloud Pub/Sub for real-time data access.
B) Implement Google Cloud Datastore for low-latency data retrieval.
C) Choose Google Cloud Bigtable and use the HBase API for low-latency access.
D) Deploy Google Cloud SQL for efficient dataset access.

QUESTION 41

Your organization has multiple development teams working on different Google Cloud projects. Each team manages its own set of resources within their projects. To ensure resource isolation and minimize the risk of accidental deletion, which IAM best practice should you follow?

A) Grant the Organization Administrator role to all developers for centralized control.
B) Use a single Google Cloud project for all development teams to ensure uniform resource management.
C) Assign IAM roles at the project level, giving each team access only to their respective projects.
D) Share a single service account across all projects for consistent access control.

QUESTION 42

Your company is planning to deploy a web application on Google App Engine. The application requires auto-scaling based on traffic and zero-downtime deployments. Which environment should you choose for hosting your App Engine application?

A) App Engine Standard Environment

B) App Engine Flexible Environment
C) App Engine Standard Environment with manual scaling
D) App Engine Flexible Environment with automatic scaling

QUESTION 43

Your organization's data analysis pipeline relies on Cloud Storage for critical data, and users are based in Bangalore, India. What storage configuration can provide both performance and cost-efficiency for users in Bangalore?

A) Configure regional storage with nearline storage class. B) Configure regional storage with standard storage class. C) Configure dual-regional storage with nearline storage class for the dual region closest to the users. D) Configure dual-regional storage with standard storage class for the dual region closest to the users.

QUESTION 44

You are responsible for optimizing the cost of your organization's Google Cloud usage. Which service can help you analyze your Google Cloud spending patterns and recommend cost-saving measures?

A) Google Compute Engine (GCE)
B) Google Cloud Spanner
C) Google Cloud Billing
D) Google Kubernetes Engine (GKE)

QUESTION 45

Your organization needs to ensure data encryption at rest for sensitive information stored in Google Cloud Storage. You also want to manage the encryption keys yourself for added security control. Which encryption option should you choose to meet these requirements?

A) Google-managed keys for Google Cloud Storage
B) Customer-supplied keys for Google Cloud Storage
C) Google Cloud Identity and Access Management (IAM)
D) Google Cloud Key Management Service (KMS)

QUESTION 46

Your organization needs to ensure high availability and scalability for its web applications running on Google Cloud. You want to set up a load balancing solution that distributes traffic across multiple regions. Which Google Cloud load balancing service should you use for this requirement?

A) Google Cloud Network Load Balancer
B) Google Cloud HTTP(S) Load Balancer
C) Google Cloud Internal TCP/UDP Load Balancer
D) Google Cloud Armor

QUESTION 47

Your organization is building a global e-commerce platform on Google Cloud, and you need a distributed storage system that can handle large volumes of unstructured data, such as product images and videos. Which Google Cloud service is suitable for storing and serving this type of data?

A) Implement Google Cloud Storage with multiple regional buckets.
B) Use Google Cloud Datastore as a NoSQL data store.
C) Deploy Google Cloud Firestore for unstructured data storage.
D) Utilize Google Cloud BigQuery for large binary data storage .

QUESTION 48

Your organization is using Google Kubernetes Engine (GKE) to deploy containerized applications. You want to automate the scaling of your application based on custom metrics and conditions. Which GKE feature allows you to achieve this level of automation?

A) Implement GKE's Horizontal Pod Autoscaling (HPA) for scaling based on CPU and memory metrics.
B) Use GKE's Cluster Autoscaler for automatically resizing the GKE cluster based on resource demands.
C) Configure GKE's Node Pools for granular control of node scaling.
D) Leverage GKE's Persistent Disk Autoscaler for dynamically adjusting disk capacity.

QUESTION 49

You are building a large-scale application that requires a database with strong consistency and horizontal scaling across continents. You decide to use Cloud Spanner. Before creating an instance, what is the most important initial action to perform in your GCP project?

A) Select a region and zone for your Cloud Spanner instance.
B) Enable the Cloud Spanner API for your project.
C) Estimate the cost of operations for Cloud Spanner and set a budget.
D) Create service accounts with necessary permissions for Cloud Spanner.

QUESTION 50

As an IT administrator in a multinational corporation, you are tasked with managing user accounts as your company adopts Cloud Identity. Several employees have pre-existing Google Accounts with their work email. What's the recommended approach to manage these accounts?

A) Direct users to create new Cloud Identity accounts and abandon their old Google Accounts.
B) Initiate a company-wide email change for creating new Cloud Identity accounts.
C) Guide users through the account transfer process from their personal Google Accounts to Cloud Identity.
D) Retain the personal Google Accounts and link them with Cloud Identity accounts.
E) Suspend the personal Google Accounts and force a switch to Cloud Identity.

SET 3 - ANSWERS ONLY

QUESTION 1

Answer - E) Managed instance group and Cloud SQL autoscaling

A) Incorrect, as it does not address the scaling of Cloud SQL instances based on the number of connections.
B) Incorrect, custom metrics for Compute Engine might not accurately reflect CPU utilization, and read replicas do not automatically scale Cloud SQL.
C) Incorrect, Cloud SQL does not have an automatic scaling feature based on the number of connections.
D) Incorrect, unmanaged instance groups lack the sophistication needed for autoscaling, and failover replicas are for high availability, not scaling.
E) Correct, a managed instance group with CPU-based autoscaling for Compute Engine and connection-based autoscaling for Cloud SQL meets the requirements.

QUESTION 2

Answer - E) Cloud SQL and Bigtable

A) Incorrect, Cloud SQL is suitable for relational data, but Firestore is a NoSQL database designed mainly for mobile, web, and server development.
B) Incorrect, both Bigtable and Cloud Spanner are more specialized and may not cover both relational and NoSQL needs effectively.
C) Incorrect, Cloud Storage is not a database service, and Datastore is NoSQL only.
D) Incorrect, Cloud Bigtable is for large analytical and operational workloads, and Firestore is a NoSQL database, not suitable for relational data.
E) Correct, Cloud SQL is a fully-managed relational database, and Bigtable is a NoSQL service suitable for large-scale data needs.
F) Incorrect, Datastore is NoSQL only, and Cloud Spanner, although scalable, might be overkill for certain applications.

QUESTION 3

Answer - A) Cloud Scheduler and Cloud Functions

A) Correct, Cloud Scheduler can trigger Cloud Functions to automate the stopping of instances, providing a cost-effective solution.
B) Incorrect, instance groups with autoscaling are for managing instance availability and load, not for cost management of specific instances.
C) Incorrect, preemptible VMs are stopped by GCP after 24 hours but don't provide control over specific off-peak times.
D) Incorrect, a custom script on a Compute Engine instance is a more manual approach and may not be as reliable or efficient.
E) Incorrect, relying on administrators to manually stop instances is not efficient or scalable for cost management.

QUESTION 4

Answer - D) Cloud Dataflow with autoscaling

A) Incorrect, while deduplication is important, it doesn't address the issue of handling sudden spikes in message volume.
B) Incorrect, Dead Letter Queues are for handling undeliverable messages, not for scaling with message volume.
C) Incorrect, increasing the number of subscriptions does not directly address the scalability of message processing.
D) Correct, using Cloud Dataflow with autoscaling based on message volume allows for efficient processing during spikes.
E) Incorrect, relying on manual intervention for scaling is not efficient for handling sudden spikes in real-time.

QUESTION 5

Answer - C) Cloud Bigtable

A) Incorrect, Cloud SQL is a relational database service, which might not offer the necessary throughput for large datasets.
B) Incorrect, BigQuery is ideal for analytics but is not optimized for low-latency read/write access.
C) Correct, Cloud Bigtable is designed for high throughput and low-latency read/write access, suitable for large datasets accessed frequently by analytics applications.
D) Incorrect, Cloud Storage is best for object storage but may not meet the high throughput and low-latency requirements.
E) Incorrect, Firestore is a NoSQL document database, better suited for app development than high-throughput data access.

QUESTION 6

Answer - C) Custom role with specific permissions

A) Incorrect, roles/bigquery.dataEditor would allow modification of the original dataset.
B) Incorrect, roles/bigquery.user provides broader access and may not sufficiently restrict modifications to the dataset.
C) Correct, a custom role can be tailored to allow querying and table creation without the ability to alter the original dataset.
D) Incorrect, while roles/bigquery.dataViewer restricts modification, it doesn't allow analysts to create new tables within BigQuery.
E) Incorrect, row-level access controls manage data access within tables, not permissions to create or modify tables.

QUESTION 7

Answer - C) roles/browser at the organization level

A) Incorrect, roles/viewer provides broad viewing permissions which may include the ability to view data within resources.
B) Incorrect, roles/resourcemanager.organizationViewer focuses on organizational resources but may

not provide full visibility of the hierarchical structure.
C) Correct, roles/browser at the organization level allows viewing the hierarchy and metadata of all resources without edit permissions.
D) Incorrect, roles/cloudasset.viewer is more focused on Cloud Asset Inventory.
E) Incorrect, roles/resourcemanager.projectViewer is limited to viewing projects, not the entire resource hierarchy.

QUESTION 8

Answer - A) Cloud Monitoring alert policies

A) Correct, Cloud Monitoring allows you to create alert policies based on specific metrics like CPU utilization across multiple projects.
B) Incorrect, configuring alerts individually in each project is less efficient than using Cloud Monitoring.
C) Incorrect, creating a custom tool is unnecessary when Cloud Monitoring provides the needed functionality.
D) Incorrect, default alerting mechanisms might not cover all specific needs and metrics.
E) Incorrect, while Cloud Logging is useful, it's more efficient to create alerts directly from metrics in Cloud Monitoring.

QUESTION 9

Answer - A) Cost anomaly detection in Cloud Billing

A) Correct, cost anomaly detection in Cloud Billing is designed to alert users to unusual spikes in costs.
B) Incorrect, a budget alert with a low threshold might not specifically detect unusual cost spikes.
C) Incorrect, Cloud Monitoring focuses on resource usage, not cost analysis.
D) Incorrect, using a Cloud Function for this task is more complex than necessary.
E) Incorrect, building a custom application is not as efficient as using built-in Cloud Billing features.

QUESTION 10

Answer – C) Cloud Run

A) Kubernetes Engine is powerful but requires some level of server management.
B) Compute Engine requires server management and manual scaling.
C) Cloud Run offers quick deployment, easy scaling, and a fully managed environment, ideal for microservices without the need for server management.
D) App Engine flexible environment requires some server management and is less focused on containerized microservices.
E) Cloud Functions is event-driven and more suited for single-purpose functions rather than a set of microservices.
F) Cloud Build is a CI/CD platform, not a hosting service.

QUESTION 11

Answer - B) Configuring appropriate IAM roles for cross-project access.

A) Network configuration is unrelated to Operations Suite integration.

B) Correct, as IAM roles are crucial for access and management across projects.
C) Machine types do not impact monitoring integration.
D) Helpful but not critical for monitoring.

QUESTION 12

Answer - B) Deploy the application on App Engine standard environment, and use Memorystore for Redis as a caching solution.

A) Provides scalability but may not offer the most efficient caching mechanism.
B) Correct, leverages App Engine for scalability and Memorystore for efficient and managed caching.
C) Offers scalability but requires manual setup and maintenance of the caching layer.
D) Cloud Run is efficient for serverless deployment, but Firestore is not primarily a caching solution.

QUESTION 13

Answer - A) Migrate the CMS to a new GCP project by setting up a Compute Engine instance and replicating the test environment setup.

A) Creating a new project for the production environment is a best practice to ensure operational separation and reduce risks.
B) This approach does not provide sufficient separation between test and production environments.
C) Using the same instance for production lacks the necessary separation and increases risk.
D) Although managed instance groups offer scalability, they do not address the need for a separate production environment.

QUESTION 14

Answer - D) Create a new service account with the 'storage.objectCreator' role specifically for the bucket.

D) This approach is in line with best practices, granting the necessary permissions to the specific resource (Cloud Storage bucket) and avoiding unnecessary broader access.
A) It's preferable to use a custom service account rather than the default for specific tasks.
B) The 'storage.objectAdmin' role is more permissive than required.
C) The 'storage.admin' role grants broader administrative privileges that are unnecessary for this task.

QUESTION 15

Answer - B) BigQuery User

B) BigQuery User role provides the necessary permissions to run queries and manage datasets in BigQuery, which is suitable for a data analysis team's requirements.
A) BigQuery Data Editor allows editing datasets but is not necessary for running queries.
C) BigQuery Admin provides broader administrative privileges than required.
D) Project Editor provides extensive permissions beyond BigQuery and is not aligned with the principle of least privilege.

QUESTION 16

Answer - A) Generate a signed URL for the documents with a 24-hour expiration and provide the URL to the auditor.

A) This is the most secure and compliant method for sharing sensitive documents with external parties without Google accounts, as it provides controlled, temporary access.
B) Adding an external email to IAM is less secure and requires manual follow-up.
C) Using a shared drive is less secure and efficient for this purpose.
D) Creating a new bucket for temporary access is less efficient and secure compared to a signed URL.

QUESTION 17

Answer - C) Google Cloud Kubernetes Engine Pods

Option C: This is the correct choice as Google Cloud Kubernetes Engine Pods are the smallest deployable units in GKE and can have their own storage, providing isolation for microservices.
Option A: Google Cloud Virtual Machines are not specific to microservices and may not provide the same level of isolation.
Option B: Google Cloud Persistent Disks provide storage but are attached to VMs or pods, not for isolation.
Option D: Google Cloud Kubernetes Engine Clusters manage the overall cluster, not individual microservice isolation.

QUESTION 18

Answer - C) Google Cloud Dataflow.

Option C is the correct choice as Google Cloud Dataflow is designed for ingesting, processing, and analyzing streaming data at scale, offering low-latency data processing capabilities.
Option A is for data preparation, Option B is a NoSQL database, and Option D is a document database.

QUESTION 19

Answer - C) Configure the "Message Storage Policy" to retain data for 30 days in the Google Cloud Console.

Option C is the correct choice because you can configure the "Message Storage Policy" in the Google Cloud Console to retain data in Cloud Pub/Sub for the specified duration, in this case, 30 days, to meet compliance requirements. Options A, B, and D do not directly address data retention in Cloud Pub/Sub.

QUESTION 20

Answer - C) Establish a new GCP project and redeploy the App Engine application in a South American region.

C) Since App Engine applications are region-locked and cannot be moved post-creation, the best solution is to create a new GCP project and deploy the application in the desired South American region.
A) It's not possible to change the region of an existing App Engine application.
B) You cannot have multiple App Engine applications in the same project.

D) While Google Cloud CDN can improve content delivery, it does not change the fundamental hosting region of the App Engine application.

QUESTION 21

Answer - B) Enable Auto-Upgrades for your GKE cluster to automatically update the Kubernetes version.

B) Enabling Auto-Upgrades is the most efficient and reliable way to ensure your GKE cluster is always running a secure and updated version of Kubernetes.
A) Cron jobs can automate updates but lack the integration and reliability of GKE's built-in features.
C) Manual upgrades are time-consuming and can lead to delays in applying critical patches.
D) Third-party tools are unnecessary and may not be fully compatible with GKE's update mechanisms.

QUESTION 22

Answer - B) Store the SSH keys in a Kubernetes Secret and inject them into the pods at runtime.

B) Kubernetes Secrets are the most appropriate resource for managing sensitive data like SSH keys. Storing them in Secrets and injecting them into pods at runtime ensures security and prevents exposure in the YAML file.
A) Merely encrypting the keys isn't a complete solution for secure management.
C) ConfigMaps are not secure for sensitive data like SSH keys.
D) Persistent Volumes are not the best choice for storing sensitive data like SSH keys.

QUESTION 23

Answer - C) Set the Content-Type metadata of the video files to the appropriate MIME type (e.g., 'video/mp4').

C) Correctly setting the Content-Type metadata to the appropriate MIME type for each video file (such as 'video/mp4') informs the browser to play the video directly. This ensures a seamless user experience for visitors to the digital art exhibition.
A) Storage class affects data storage but not how files are displayed in a browser.
B) Making files public doesn't dictate their playback behavior in browsers.
D) While Cloud CDN can improve performance, it doesn't control how files are displayed.

QUESTION 24

Answer - C) Deploy the task on preemptible Compute Engine VMs optimized for compute.

C) Preemptible VMs are ideal for batch jobs that can be interrupted and have a short, predictable run time, providing a cost-effective solution for compute-intensive tasks.
A) A continuous GKE cluster may lead to unnecessary costs outside the job's run time.
B) Regular VMs with high-memory machine types can be more expensive than necessary.
D) Cloud Functions are not suitable for long-running, data-intensive tasks.
E) Dataproc is useful for big data but might be over-provisioned for this specific task.
F) Cloud Run is more appropriate for stateless, event-driven applications.

QUESTION 25

Answer - E) Enable 'Automatic Restart', configure 'On-host maintenance' to use live migration, and deploy in multiple zones.

E) This configuration provides the highest level of availability. 'Automatic Restart' handles VM failures, live migration during 'On-host maintenance' avoids downtime, and deploying in multiple zones protects against zone-level failures.
  A) Setting 'On-host maintenance' to 'Terminate' contradicts the need for continuous operation.
  B) Preemptible VMs are not suitable for critical applications due to their temporary nature.
  C) HTTP health checks are good for monitoring but don't address maintenance handling.
  D) While live migration is correct, it doesn't mention 'Automatic Restart' for handling VM failures.
  F) Preemptible instances and disabling 'Automatic Restart' are not conducive to high availability.

QUESTION 26

Answer - B) Enable Data Access audit logs for the Cloud Storage service.

B) Data Access audit logs are designed to track access to data, including read operations, in Cloud Storage, making them suitable for this compliance need.
  A) Cloud Storage Access Logs are more about requests to the bucket, not specific read operations.
  C) Cloud IAM controls access but doesn't log individual data access operations.
  D) While possible, creating custom logging with Cloud Functions is a more complex approach.
  E) VPC Service Control provides security perimeters but does not inherently log all data access requests.
  F) Access Context Manager manages access but does not provide detailed logging of data reads.

QUESTION 27

Answer - B) Link your project to your company's GCP billing account to directly charge the company.

B) Linking the project to your company's GCP billing account is the most effective way to transition billing responsibilities, ensuring that all future charges are directly billed to the company.
  A) Modifying billing settings to send invoices doesn't change the billing responsibility.
  C) Budget alerts are for monitoring, not for billing transitions.
  D) Providing access for tracking is helpful but doesn't change who is billed.
  E) Updating payment methods doesn't transfer the billing account to the company.
  F) Involving GCP sales is not necessary for this administrative change.

QUESTION 28

Answer - C) Enable GKE node pool autoscaling for dynamic resource allocation.

C) Enabling GKE node pool autoscaling allows the cluster to automatically scale its resources in response to the e-commerce platform's variable customer visits, ensuring consistent performance during peak and off-peak hours.
  A) Horizontal Pod Autoscaler manages pod count but doesn't address node scaling.
  B) Vertical Pod Autoscaler adjusts resources within existing pods.
  D) Dedicated node pools don't inherently scale with traffic changes.
  E) Manual scaling isn't reactive enough for sudden traffic changes.
  F) Custom metrics are an advanced solution and might be more than what's needed for basic scaling.

QUESTION 29

Answer - D) Google Cloud Firestore

Option D - Google Cloud Firestore is a fully managed, scalable, serverless, and multi-model database service that supports both SQL and NoSQL data models. It's suitable for web applications requiring flexible data storage.
Option A - Google Cloud SQL is a managed relational database service.
Option B - Google Cloud Datastore is a NoSQL database.
Option C - Google Cloud Bigtable is a NoSQL database for large-scale analytical and operational workloads.

QUESTION 30

Answer - B) Establish a Cloud DNS private zone for the on-premises database's hostname.

B) Using Cloud DNS private zone to manage the hostname of the on-premises database provides a centralized way to control the IP address mapping. If the database IP changes, updating the DNS record in the private zone will ensure all connected applications automatically resolve to the new address without needing any reconfiguration.
A) Redis caching isn't a direct solution for managing dynamic IP addresses.
C) Service Directory is for service discovery within GCP, not for external database IP management.
D) Custom services require additional maintenance and are less efficient than DNS management.
E) Storing the IP on a persistent disk doesn't provide real-time updates or easy scalability.
F) Pub/Sub for IP notifications introduces unnecessary complexity and potential delays.

QUESTION 31

Answer - C) Have the partner create a Service Account in their project and assign it necessary permissions in your BigQuery datasets.

C) This method provides a secure and controlled way to grant access. By having the partner create their own Service Account, you can then assign specific permissions for accessing only the required BigQuery datasets. This minimizes risk and keeps the access scope limited to what is necessary.
A) Allowing IP address access is less secure and does not provide granular control.
B) Creating a dedicated user in your project can be less secure and more challenging to manage.
D) Sharing service account keys is not recommended due to security risks.
E) Duplicating datasets might be unnecessary and could incur additional costs.
F) GCP Interconnect is for network connectivity, not specific for dataset access management.

QUESTION 32

Answer - C) Create a new revision of the existing service with the update and split traffic to include the new revision.

C) Creating a new revision of the existing service for the update and then using Cloud Run's traffic splitting feature to include the new revision allows for a controlled and scalable rollout. This method enables you to specify the exact percentage of users who will access the new version, facilitating a gradual and safe deployment process.
A) Using a Load Balancer adds unnecessary complexity for a feature that Cloud Run natively supports.

B) Deploying as a new service complicates the management of different versions.
D) API Gateway is for managing API traffic, not for splitting application traffic between revisions.
E) Routing through a VPN is not practical for application version management and adds complexity.
F) Setting up a beta environment may not reflect real-world usage as effectively as traffic splitting.

QUESTION 33

Answer - A) Configure a Cloud Storage trigger in Cloud Functions to run the Python code upon new file uploads.

A) Utilizing Cloud Functions with a Cloud Storage trigger is the most efficient and direct way to automate the execution of a Python function upon new file uploads. This setup ensures that the function is triggered automatically and immediately every time a new file is uploaded, without the need for polling or manual intervention.
B) App Engine with a CRON job would not provide real-time execution and is less efficient for event-driven tasks.
C) Cloud Scheduler is for scheduling tasks at specific times, not for responding to storage events.
D) A custom script on Compute Engine requires continuous polling and is not as efficient.
E) Cloud Run can respond to events but requires additional setup compared to Cloud Functions.
F) A GKE cluster is more complex and resource-intensive than needed for this task.

QUESTION 34

Answer – C) Cloud Pub/Sub, Dataflow, Cloud Storage with VPC Service Controls, BigQuery

A) Incorrect, while Dataflow and BigQuery are suitable, this option lacks specific compliance measures like VPC Service Controls.
B) Incorrect, Kubernetes Engine might be overly complex for this use case, and Cloud SQL may not be the best fit for analytics.
C) Correct, this combination ensures scalability, security, and compliance, with each service playing a key role in the pipeline.
D) Incorrect, Dataprep and Firestore are not the best fit for high-scale transaction data processing and analytics in this context.
E) Incorrect, a custom Compute Engine solution adds complexity and might not meet compliance and scalability needs efficiently.

QUESTION 35

Answer – B) BigQuery Audit Logs, Cloud Logging, Cloud Monitoring

A) Incorrect, Cloud DLP is for data protection, not access monitoring.
B) Correct, BigQuery Audit Logs provide access details, Cloud Logging for analysis, and Cloud Monitoring for alerts.
C) Incorrect, Data Catalog is for data discovery and metadata, not for access monitoring.
D) Incorrect, overly complex and not direct for monitoring access.
E) Incorrect, Cloud Endpoint Security is not specific to BigQuery access monitoring.

QUESTION 36

Answer – A) gcloud auth activate-service-account

A) Correct, this is the most secure and recommended way to authenticate a script using a service account.
B) Incorrect, embedding the key in the script is not secure.
C) Incorrect, storing keys in Cloud Storage is not secure.
D) Incorrect, converting to an OAuth token is unnecessary and less secure.
E) Incorrect, GOOGLE_APPLICATION_CREDENTIALS is typically used for applications running on servers, not for local scripts.

QUESTION 37

Answer - B) Google Kubernetes Engine (GKE) (Correct)

Option A is incorrect because manual scaling of Compute Engine instances does not provide the level of automation and container orchestration that GKE offers.
Option C is incorrect because App Engine is a platform-as-a-service (PaaS) that abstracts container management, which may not meet the requirement for fine-grained control.
Option D is incorrect because Cloud Functions are designed for serverless functions, not containerized microservices.
Option E is incorrect because Cloud Run is a serverless container platform, but GKE offers more advanced features for managing containerized microservices.

QUESTION 38

Answer - D) Utilize Google Cloud Dataflow for stream data processing and Google Cloud BigQuery for real-time analytics. (Correct)

Option A is incorrect because while Dataflow can be used for stream data processing, Dataprep is not typically used for real-time data processing.
Option B is incorrect because Bigtable is suitable for certain types of data storage but may not provide real-time analytics capabilities.
Option C is incorrect because Pub/Sub is for data streaming but Cloud SQL is not typically used for real-time data analysis.
Option E is incorrect because Cloud Functions may not provide the same level of real-time analytics as BigQuery.
Option D is correct because Google Cloud Dataflow is designed for stream data processing, and Google Cloud BigQuery is a powerful tool for real-time analytics on streaming data, making it a suitable combination for the described scenario.

QUESTION 39

Answer - C) Set up Google Cloud IAM (Identity and Access Management) for centralized access control and fine-grained permissions management. (Correct)

Option A is incorrect because Google Cloud Identity-Aware Proxy (IAP) primarily focuses on identity verification and access control for web applications and does not provide fine-grained permissions management.
Option B is incorrect because Google Cloud Armor is a DDoS protection service and does not offer fine-grained permissions management.
Option D is incorrect because Google Cloud Pub/Sub is a messaging service and not designed for access control and permissions management at the project level.
Option E is incorrect because Google Cloud VPN is for network connectivity and does not provide centralized access control and fine-grained permissions management.
Option C is correct because Google Cloud IAM (Identity and Access Management) allows for centralized access control and fine-grained permissions management at the project level, enhancing data security across multiple GCP services.

QUESTION 40

Answer - C) Choose Google Cloud Bigtable and use the HBase API for low-latency access. (Correct)

Option A is incorrect because Google Cloud Pub/Sub is a messaging service, not a direct data access solution, and it does not provide low-latency access to datasets.
Option B is incorrect because Google Cloud Datastore may not provide the same level of low-latency access as Google Cloud Bigtable with the HBase API for large datasets.
Option D is incorrect because Google Cloud SQL is a relational database service and may not offer low-latency access for certain use cases.
Google Cloud Bigtable with the HBase API is designed for low-latency access to large datasets and is a suitable choice for optimizing access performance.

QUESTION 41

Answer - C) Assign IAM roles at the project level, giving each team access only to their respective projects.

Option A is incorrect because granting the Organization Administrator role to all developers does not provide resource isolation and can lead to excessive permissions. Option B is incorrect because using a single Google Cloud project for all development teams does not allow for proper isolation and resource management. Option D is incorrect because sharing a single service account across all projects can lead to security and access control issues. Option C is correct because assigning IAM roles at the project level allows each team to have access only to their respective projects, ensuring resource isolation and minimizing the risk of accidental deletion.

QUESTION 42

Answer - D) App Engine Flexible Environment with automatic scaling

Option D recommends using the App Engine Flexible Environment with automatic scaling, which offers auto-scaling based on traffic and supports zero-downtime deployments.
Option A (App Engine Standard Environment) provides automatic scaling but may have limitations for certain applications.
Option B (App Engine Flexible Environment) provides auto-scaling and more flexibility, suitable for this

scenario.
Option C (App Engine Standard Environment with manual scaling) is not ideal for auto-scaling based on traffic.

QUESTION 43

Answer - D) Configure dual-regional storage with standard storage class for the dual region closest to the users.

Option A is incorrect because regional storage with nearline storage class may not offer the necessary performance for users in Bangalore.
Option B is incorrect because regional storage with standard storage class may not optimize performance for users in Bangalore.
Option C is incorrect because configuring dual-regional storage with nearline storage class may not strike the right balance between cost and performance for users in Bangalore.

QUESTION 44

Answer - C) Google Cloud Billing

Option C is correct because Google Cloud Billing provides tools and reports to analyze Google Cloud spending patterns and offers cost-saving recommendations. It helps organizations optimize their cloud costs.
Option A (Google Compute Engine) provides virtual machines but does not offer cost analysis or optimization features.
Option B (Google Cloud Spanner) is a database service and not focused on cost analysis.
Option D (Google Kubernetes Engine) is a managed Kubernetes service and does not provide cost analysis tools.

QUESTION 45

Answer - B) Customer-supplied keys for Google Cloud Storage

Option B is correct because using customer-supplied keys for Google Cloud Storage allows you to manage the encryption keys yourself, ensuring data encryption at rest and providing enhanced security control.
Option A (Google-managed keys) means Google manages the keys, not the customer.
Option C (Google Cloud IAM) is for access control and does not directly address data encryption.
Option D (Google Cloud KMS) is a key management service but is not specific to Google Cloud Storage encryption.

QUESTION 46

Answer - B) Google Cloud HTTP(S) Load Balancer

Option B is correct because Google Cloud HTTP(S) Load Balancer is a global, fully-distributed load balancer that can distribute traffic across multiple regions, providing high availability and scalability for web applications.
Option A (Google Cloud Network Load Balancer) is regional and may not distribute traffic across multiple

regions.
Option C (Google Cloud Internal TCP/UDP Load Balancer) is for internal load balancing within a single VPC.
Option D (Google Cloud Armor) is a security service and not primarily a load balancing service.

QUESTION 47

Answer - D) Utilize Google Cloud BigQuery for large binary data storage

Option D is correct because Google Cloud BigQuery is not typically used for storing binary data like images and videos. It's a fully managed, serverless data warehouse designed for running analytical queries on large datasets, and it's not suitable for storing unstructured binary data.
Option A is not the best choice for storing binary data as Google Cloud Storage is primarily designed for object storage rather than serving unstructured binary files directly.
Option B and C are not appropriate for storing unstructured binary data as they are NoSQL databases, typically used for structured data and documents, not large binary files.

QUESTION 48

Answer - A) Implement GKE's Horizontal Pod Autoscaling (HPA) for scaling based on CPU and memory metrics

Option A is correct because GKE's Horizontal Pod Autoscaling (HPA) allows you to automate the scaling of your application pods based on custom metrics, including CPU and memory utilization. It provides fine-grained control over application scaling based on application-specific requirements.
Option B focuses on cluster-level scaling and is not as granular as HPA for application pod scaling.
Option C is related to node pool management and does not directly address application scaling.
Option D is specifically for adjusting disk capacity and does not handle application scaling.

QUESTION 49

Answer – B) Enable the Cloud Spanner API

A) Incorrect, selecting a region and zone is a subsequent step.
B) Correct, the first action is to enable the Cloud Spanner API.
C) Incorrect, estimating costs is important but not the initial technical step.
D) Incorrect, creating service accounts is done after enabling the API.

QUESTION 50

Answer – C) Account transfer process

A) Incorrect, abandoning old accounts can result in data loss and user dissatisfaction.
B) Incorrect, changing email addresses is disruptive and unnecessary.
C) Correct, guiding users through the account transfer process is the most efficient and user-friendly approach.
D) Incorrect, linking accounts is not a typical solution for this scenario.
E) Incorrect, suspending accounts is disruptive and may lead to data loss.

SET 4 - QUESTIONS ONLY

QUESTION 1

In an educational technology company, you are responsible for optimizing the cost of GCP services. The company's application is deployed on a Kubernetes cluster managed by GKE. The application experiences predictable traffic patterns, with peak usage during weekdays and minimal usage on weekends. What strategies would you employ to optimize costs without compromising performance during peak times?

A) Implement a horizontal pod autoscaler in GKE to automatically adjust the number of pods based on CPU and memory usage, and use preemptible VMs for the node pool.
B) Configure a GKE cluster with node auto-provisioning and use committed use discounts for Compute Engine resources.
C) Use a combination of horizontal and vertical pod autoscalers in GKE, and schedule scaling down of resources during weekends using Cloud Scheduler.
D) Set up a custom script to manually scale the GKE cluster based on time-of-day and day-of-week patterns, and utilize sustained use discounts.
E) Employ a GKE cluster with a mix of standard and high-memory machine types, adjusting the allocation of workloads based on predicted traffic.

QUESTION 2

For a critical application, your team needs to implement a disaster recovery plan on GCP. Which of the following would be a key component in this plan?

A) Cloud DNS
B) Cloud Load Balancing
C) Cloud SQL
D) Cloud Storage with multi-regional buckets
E) Virtual Private Cloud (VPC)
F) Cloud Spanner

QUESTION 3

In your GCP environment, you need to set up a secure and efficient way to manage SSH access to Compute Engine instances for multiple team members. You want to ensure that access is controlled and audited without managing individual SSH keys. What solution should you implement?

A) Configure the Compute Engine instances to use OS Login and manage access through IAM roles and permissions.
B) Set up individual SSH keys for each team member and store them in Secret Manager for secure access.
C) Use Identity-Aware Proxy (IAP) to control SSH access to Compute Engine instances based on team members' IAM roles.
D) Implement a third-party SSH key management tool to handle SSH access centrally and integrate it with GCP.
E) Create a VPN connection to the VPC and manage SSH access through network-level controls and firewall rules.

QUESTION 4

In your organization, you are responsible for managing the security of Compute Engine instances. These instances host sensitive applications and need to be protected against unauthorized access. What combination of GCP features and best practices would you employ to enhance the security of these instances?

A) Use OS Login for managing instance access and apply Shielded VMs for enhanced security against rootkits and bootkits.
B) Implement VPC Service Controls to isolate the instances and use Cloud IAM for fine-grained access control.
C) Set up Identity-Aware Proxy for controlling instance access based on user identity and context, and enable Access Transparency logs.
D) Configure private Google Access for instances to prevent access from the public internet, and use Cloud Armor for additional protection.
E) Utilize custom firewalls in the VPC and regularly update instance security patches manually for each VM.

QUESTION 5

As a cloud engineer in a financial services company, you are tasked with ensuring the security and compliance of Compute Engine instances. These instances contain sensitive financial data. What security best practices would you implement for these instances?

A) Enable Shielded VMs to protect against rootkits and bootkits.
B) Use VPC Service Controls to isolate the Compute Engine instances.
C) Configure Identity-Aware Proxy to manage access to the instances.
D) Apply customer-managed encryption keys (CMEK) to encrypt instance disks.
E) Implement regular vulnerability scanning and patch management.

QUESTION 6

As part of your role in data governance, you are required to oversee who has write access to certain critical datasets in BigQuery within your organization. You need to regularly audit and report on these access permissions. What approach would you use to effectively manage and monitor these permissions?

A) Utilize IAM policy audits with Cloud Identity and Access Management.
B) Regularly export BigQuery IAM policies to CSV and manually review them.
C) Implement custom scripts to query and report on BigQuery IAM roles.
D) Use Cloud Audit Logs to monitor and record all changes to IAM policies.
E) Set up Data Loss Prevention (DLP) scans on BigQuery to detect unauthorized access.

QUESTION 7

Your organization requires that the compliance team has the ability to view and audit resource configurations and settings across GCP projects, but they should not be able to modify any settings. Which role would you assign to the compliance team to facilitate this?

A) roles/compute.viewer

B) roles/cloudasset.viewer
C) roles/complianceAuditor
D) roles/iam.roleViewer
E) roles/securitycenter.auditViewer

QUESTION 8

You need to ensure that the storage utilization across all your GCP projects is monitored and reported monthly to optimize costs. What approach should you take to automate this reporting?

A) Set up a Cloud Scheduler job to generate monthly storage utilization reports from Cloud Monitoring.
B) Manually extract storage utilization data from each project at the end of the month.
C) Use the Cloud Billing API to programmatically retrieve storage utilization and generate reports.
D) Configure Cloud Monitoring dashboards to display storage utilization and manually review them monthly.
E) Implement a custom data extraction and reporting tool using BigQuery and Data Studio.

QUESTION 9

You are managing multiple GCP services in your project, and you want to set up a system that alerts you when the total GCP spending for a particular service exceeds a predefined limit. What is the most effective way to achieve this?

A) Create individual budgets for each service in the Cloud Billing dashboard.
B) Use labels to categorize resources by service and set up budget alerts based on these labels.
C) Monitor each service's usage with Cloud Monitoring and set up billing alerts for each service.
D) Export billing data for each service to BigQuery and analyze it for cost overruns.
E) Manually review the monthly billing statement for each service and send alerts.

QUESTION 10

You need to implement a disaster recovery strategy for a critical application on GCP. The strategy should ensure minimal data loss and a recovery time objective (RTO) of less than an hour. Which approach should you recommend?

A) Multi-regional storage with scheduled snapshots
B) Cross-region replication with Cloud SQL
C) GKE multi-cluster with regional clusters
D) Datastore with automated export to a different region
E) Persistent Disk with Regional SSDs
F) Cloud Spanner with multi-region configuration

QUESTION 11

How can you set up alerting for resource usage spikes across multiple applications in different GCP projects using Google Cloud's Operations Suite?

A) Configure individual alerts in each project.
B) Use Cloud Functions to trigger alerts based on resource usage.

C) Set up centralized alerting policies in the Operations Suite workspace.
D) Implement third-party monitoring tools for alerting.

QUESTION 12

You are overseeing the deployment of a new data-intensive application in GCP. The application will generate and process large volumes of data daily and requires a storage solution that optimizes for performance and cost. How should you configure your storage architecture to meet these requirements?

A) Utilize Cloud Bigtable for data storage, leveraging its high throughput and scalability for large-scale data processing.
B) Store the data in Cloud Storage Coldline to optimize for cost, and use Dataflow for processing.
C) Implement a multi-tiered storage strategy: use Cloud Storage Standard for the first 30 days, then transfer to Nearline, and finally to Coldline after 90 days.
D) Deploy a Cloud SQL instance with high memory and storage capacity, ensuring it is geographically located near your primary users to reduce latency.

QUESTION 13

In your role as a cloud engineer for an e-commerce company, you are leading the migration of a shopping cart application from a development stage in App Engine Flexible Environment to production. To comply with company policy, the production environment must reside in a distinct GCP project. What is the recommended method to proceed with this migration?

A) Establish a new GCP project and redeploy the shopping cart application to App Engine Flexible in this project.
B) In the current GCP project, create a new version of the App Engine application and allocate it for production use.
C) Convert the existing App Engine application to a managed instance group within the same project for production.
D) Copy the App Engine application settings to a new project using the gcloud app copy command.

QUESTION 14

Your team has developed a new service on Compute Engine that requires access to read data from a specific Pub/Sub topic. To ensure security and compliance, how should you configure the service account for this service?

A) Attach the 'pubsub.subscriber' role to the default Compute Engine service account for the specific topic.
B) Create a new service account and assign it the 'pubsub.viewer' role for the entire project.
C) Create a new service account and grant it the 'pubsub.subscriber' role for the specific topic.
D) Use the default Compute Engine service account and grant it 'pubsub.editor' role for broad access.

QUESTION 15

A new project requires a group of users to have permissions to create, view, and manage Compute Engine instances, but they should not have access to other GCP services. What is the most appropriate IAM role to grant?

A) Compute Engine Admin
B) Compute Instance Admin (v1)
C) Project Owner
D) Compute Viewer

QUESTION 16

You are responsible for optimizing costs in Google Cloud, and you want to analyze the billing data and track resource costs. Which GCP service should you use for this purpose?

A) Google Cloud Monitoring
B) Google Cloud Logging
C) Google Cloud Cost Management
D) Google Cloud Identity and Access Management

QUESTION 17

Your organization is planning to migrate a mission-critical on-premises database to Google Cloud. You aim to minimize downtime during the migration process. Which GCP service is designed to facilitate database migration with minimal downtime?

A) Google Cloud Storage
B) Google Cloud Compute Engine
C) Google Cloud Dataflow
D) Google Cloud Database Migration Service

QUESTION 18

Your team needs to establish a secure and dedicated connection between your on-premises data center and Google Cloud to ensure low-latency access and high bandwidth. Which GCP networking product should you choose for this requirement?

A) Google Cloud VPN.
B) Google Cloud Interconnect.
C) Google Cloud DNS.
D) Google Cloud CDN.

QUESTION 19

You are tasked with optimizing costs for your Google Cloud project. You notice that your Compute Engine instances run 24/7, but they are only required during business hours. What should you implement to reduce costs while ensuring the availability of the instances during business hours?

A) Use preemptible instances for business hours and regular instances for off-hours.
B) Configure custom machine types to lower the instance costs.
C) Implement instance scheduling using Cloud Scheduler to start and stop instances at specific times.
D) Use committed use contracts to reduce instance costs.

QUESTION 20

Your organization's interactive media application, hosted on App Engine, has gained significant user base in Australia. To optimize performance, you are asked to redeploy the application to a region closer to these users. How should you proceed while adhering to GCP constraints?

A) Relocate the existing App Engine application to an Australian region.
B) Create a new App Engine application within the same project for deployment in Australia.
C) Initiate a new GCP project and deploy the App Engine application in an Australian region.
D) Configure the existing App Engine application to prioritize Australian traffic.

QUESTION 21

In your organization, GKE clusters are used for various applications. To enhance security, you are tasked with keeping the Kubernetes versions up to date. What is the most effective method to achieve this across all clusters?

A) Regularly monitor Kubernetes release notes and manually update each GKE cluster.
B) Utilize a Continuous Integration tool to deploy updates to Kubernetes versions in GKE clusters.
C) Enable the GKE Master Auto-Upgrade and Node Auto-Upgrade features for all clusters.
D) Develop a custom script to check for updates and apply them to GKE clusters.

QUESTION 22

In reviewing your Kubernetes environment, you find a deployment where an encryption key is stored as a plain text environment variable in a pod specification. What is the recommended way to store this encryption key securely in Kubernetes?

A) Store the encryption key within the Docker image of the container.
B) Encrypt the key and include it in the deployment YAML file.
C) Use a Kubernetes Secret to store the encryption key and reference it in the pod specification.
D) Save the key in a file on a Persistent Volume and mount it into the container.

QUESTION 23

You have created an online resume as an HTML file hosted in a Cloud Storage bucket. You want to ensure that when employers click the link, the resume is displayed as a webpage, not downloaded. What should you do to achieve this?

A) Share the HTML file publicly and provide the link to employers.
B) Set the Content-Type metadata for the HTML file to 'application/octet-stream'.
C) Ensure the HTML file's Content-Type metadata is set to 'text/html'.
D) Convert the HTML file to a PDF and set its Content-Type to 'application/pdf'.

QUESTION 24

Your team is tasked with processing a large dataset every night, which takes around 5 hours. The job can be interrupted without issues. To minimize GCP costs, what is the recommended approach?

A) Set up a dedicated GKE cluster with standard machine types to run the job.

B) Schedule the job on a persistent Compute Engine VM with an automatic shutdown script.
C) Run the job on preemptible Compute Engine VMs with custom machine types.
D) Implement the job as a series of Cloud Functions triggered sequentially.
E) Create a Dataproc cluster with autoscaling enabled for nightly jobs.
F) Use Cloud Run to execute the job in a containerized environment.

QUESTION 25

For a Compute Engine setup in a financial services application, ensuring uninterrupted service during maintenance and quick recovery from crashes is crucial. Which of the following configurations would best meet these requirements?

A) Enable 'Automatic Restart' and set 'Preemptibility' to off.
B) Set 'On-host maintenance' to 'Migrate VM instance' and use preemptible VMs.
C) Deploy the VMs in an instance group with auto-scaling and auto-healing.
D) Enable 'Automatic Restart' and configure 'On-host maintenance' to 'Migrate VM instance'.
E) Use standard VM instances with SSD persistent disks and TCP health checks.
F) Configure the VMs with custom machine types and enable 'Automatic Restart'.

QUESTION 26

As part of a compliance mandate, your financial services company requires that all read operations on a Cloud Storage bucket with client data are logged. What is the best way to ensure this in GCP?

A) Configure the bucket with uniform bucket-level access and log all access requests.
B) Enable Object Lifecycle Management to log reads and manage data retention.
C) Utilize the Cloud Storage Data Access audit logs feature in Cloud Audit Logs.
D) Apply labels to all objects in the bucket and monitor access through Stackdriver.
E) Set up a Cloud Pub/Sub notification for every access to the bucket's data.
F) Implement a custom logging solution using a combination of Cloud Functions and BigQuery.

QUESTION 27

Your startup has been using your personal GCP account for a project, and now you need to transition the billing to be directly handled by the company. What is the most efficient way to do this?

A) Instruct your company's finance team to reimburse you based on your personal GCP account statements.
B) Change the credit card information in your GCP account to the company's corporate card.
C) Transfer the project to a new GCP account created under the company's name.
D) Reconfigure the project's billing to be associated with the company's GCP billing account.
E) Create a detailed report of expenses and submit it to the company for reimbursement.
F) Set up a billing subaccount under your GCP account with the company's payment details.

QUESTION 28

You are tasked with optimizing a Google Kubernetes Engine (GKE) cluster's resource utilization. Which GKE feature can automatically adjust the CPU and memory requests and limits for pods based on their usage?

A) Horizontal Pod Autoscaler (HPA)
B) Vertical Pod Autoscaler (VPA)
C) Cluster Autoscaler
D) Pod Disruption Budgets
E) GKE Node Pool Scaling

QUESTION 29

Your company needs to ensure data retention compliance for customer records. Which GCP service can help you automatically delete data that exceeds a specified retention period?

A) Google Cloud Storage
B) Google Cloud Datastore
C) Google Cloud Pub/Sub
D) Google Cloud Data Loss Prevention (DLP)
E) Google Cloud Bigtable

QUESTION 30

In a hybrid cloud setup, how can you manage the connection from GCP applications to an on-premises database to adapt to changes in the database's IP address without needing app-level configuration updates?

A) Configure a GCP Endpoint Service to route traffic to the current on-premises database IP.
B) Set up a Cloud DNS private zone with a DNS entry for the on-premises database.
C) Implement a Cloud Function that updates GCP applications with the new database IP.
D) Use environment variables in GCP VMs to store and retrieve the on-premises database IP.
E) Create a shared VPC to automatically synchronize the on-premises database IP.
F) Use a Cloud Memorystore instance to maintain the current database IP for applications.

QUESTION 31

Your company needs to provide a partner firm with access to specific BigQuery datasets for a collaborative project. How can you securely set up this access?

A) Create a new project in GCP for joint access and migrate the necessary datasets.
B) Implement API-based access controls for the partner to query your BigQuery datasets.
C) Have the partner create a Service Account in their project, then grant it necessary access to your datasets.
D) Use BigQuery's dataset sharing features to share the required datasets with the partner.
E) Establish a bilateral IAM policy to govern access to datasets across both projects.
F) Set up a VPN tunnel between the two GCP projects for secure dataset access.

QUESTION 32

How can you safely test a new update of your Cloud Run for Anthos-based application with a portion of your user base before a complete rollout?

A) Introduce a feature toggle in the application code to switch between old and new versions for certain

users.
B) Deploy the new version in a staging environment and redirect a segment of live traffic there.
C) Use version tags in Cloud Run to direct specific users to the new or old version of the application.
D) Create a new revision of the current service for the update and use traffic splitting to control user access.
E) Configure a Cloud Endpoint to selectively route users to the new version based on predefined criteria.
F) Set up a dedicated testing project in GCP for the new version and monitor user interactions.

QUESTION 33

To automatically run a Python function in response to new uploads in a Cloud Storage bucket, which GCP service should you use?

A) Create a Cloud Function with a trigger set on the Cloud Storage bucket to execute the Python code.
B) Deploy the Python function on Google Kubernetes Engine and use Pub/Sub for storage event notifications.
C) Set up an App Engine application with a background service to monitor and process new bucket uploads.
D) Use Cloud Dataflow to stream data from the bucket and process it with the Python function.
E) Implement a Compute Engine instance that regularly checks the bucket for new uploads and runs the Python code.
F) Configure a Cloud Scheduler job to trigger the Python function at regular intervals to process new files.

QUESTION 34

Your organization is implementing a new cloud-based IoT solution that involves collecting data from thousands of sensors. The data needs to be ingested in real-time, processed, and made available for immediate analysis and long-term storage. Which GCP services and architecture would best fit these requirements?

A) Deploying Cloud IoT Core for device management, using Cloud Pub/Sub for data ingestion, Dataflow for real-time processing, and BigQuery for analysis and archival.
B) Using Compute Engine instances to manage IoT devices, implementing custom scripts for data ingestion into Cloud SQL, and using Cloud Dataproc for processing and analysis.
C) Setting up Kubernetes Engine for IoT device management, Cloud Storage for data ingestion and storage, and BigQuery with Data Studio for analysis and reporting.
D) Implementing App Engine for device management, Firestore for real-time data ingestion and storage, and Cloud Dataprep for data processing and analysis.
E) Configuring Cloud Run for managing IoT devices, Firebase Realtime Database for data ingestion, and using Looker for analysis and Cloud Storage for long-term archival.

QUESTION 35

Your organization requires a detailed analysis of user access patterns to Cloud SQL databases for optimizing security protocols. How should you gather and analyze this data?

A) Use Cloud SQL Audit Logs, export them to BigQuery, and utilize ML models for pattern analysis.
B) Enable Cloud SQL Insights and use its dashboard for analyzing access patterns.

C) Implement Cloud IDS to monitor and log access to Cloud SQL instances.
D) Deploy a third-party monitoring tool to track access to Cloud SQL databases.
E) Set up VPC Flow Logs and analyze them using Cloud Logging for access patterns.

QUESTION 36

Your application running on Compute Engine needs to access other GCP services within the same project. You are provided with a service account key file. How should you use this key file to authenticate your application to other GCP services?

A) Attach the service account to the Compute Engine VM and set the key file as metadata.
B) Use the gcloud compute instances set-service-account command and specify the key file.
C) Store the key file in a secure local directory and reference it in your application's code.
D) Set the GOOGLE_APPLICATION_CREDENTIALS environment variable in the VM to the path of the key file.
E) Upload the key file to a private GCP repository and pull it into the VM when needed.

QUESTION 37

Your organization has a global presence, and you need to set up a secure, global content delivery network (CDN) for your website. Which GCP service should you choose to achieve low-latency content delivery worldwide?

A) Google Cloud Storage
B) Google Cloud CDN
C) Google App Engine
D) Google Cloud Endpoints
E) Google Cloud Load Balancing

QUESTION 38

Your company has a global presence, and you need to set up a secure, global content delivery network (CDN) for your website. Which GCP service should you choose to achieve low-latency content delivery worldwide?

A) Configure Google Cloud Load Balancing for regional content delivery.
B) Use Google Cloud CDN (Content Delivery Network) with Google Cloud Storage for static content hosting.
C) Implement Google Cloud Identity-Aware Proxy (IAP) for website security.
D) Deploy Google Cloud Functions for serverless website serving.
E) Set up Google Cloud Pub/Sub for content distribution.

QUESTION 39

Your organization is migrating its on-premises data center to Google Cloud, and you need to set up a hybrid cloud architecture to facilitate the migration. You want to maintain a private connection between your on-premises network and Google Cloud. Which Google Cloud networking solution should you choose to establish this private connection?

A) Deploy Google Cloud VPN for secure hybrid connectivity.
B) Implement Google Cloud Direct Peering for direct on-premises-to-cloud communication.
C) Set up Google Cloud Interconnect for dedicated, private network connections.
D) Configure Google Cloud VPC Peering for network isolation.
E) Utilize Google Cloud CDN for hybrid cloud communication.

QUESTION 40

Your team is responsible for ensuring data security in a Google Cloud project that uses multiple GCP services. To enhance security, you want to implement centralized access control and fine-grained permissions management. Which GCP service or feature should you use for this purpose?

A) Utilize Google Cloud Identity-Aware Proxy (IAP) for centralized access control.
B) Implement Google Cloud Armor for fine-grained permissions management.
C) Set up Google Cloud IAM (Identity and Access Management) for centralized access control and fine-grained permissions management.
D) Deploy Google Cloud Pub/Sub for access control and permissions management.

QUESTION 41

Your company is using Google Cloud Storage to store and manage large datasets. You want to implement a cost-effective solution to analyze and process this data using Google Cloud services. Which GCP service should you choose for cost-effective data processing with features like serverless data analysis and automatic scaling?

A) Google Cloud Dataprep
B) Google Cloud Dataproc
C) Google Cloud Dataflow
D) Google Cloud Datastore

QUESTION 42

Your team is responsible for managing a Google Cloud project with multiple Google Compute Engine instances. You need to ensure high availability and fault tolerance for your virtual machines. Which configuration should you implement to achieve this?

A) Use preemptible VM instances
B) Deploy VM instances in a single zone
C) Implement regional managed instance groups
D) Configure daily snapshots for VM disks

QUESTION 43

Your company's data analysis pipeline heavily relies on Cloud Storage for daily operations. Users in Bangalore, India, require fast and dynamic access to this data. What storage configuration should you select to ensure both performance and cost-efficiency?

A) Configure multi-regional storage with nearline storage class. B) Configure multi-regional storage with standard storage class. C) Configure dual-regional storage with nearline storage class for the dual region closest to the users. D) Configure dual-regional storage with standard storage class for the dual region closest to the users.

QUESTION 44

Your team is working on a global application with users in multiple regions. You need a service that can efficiently distribute content and deliver it with low latency. Which Google Cloud service should you use for content delivery?

A) Google Cloud CDN
B) Google Cloud Interconnect
C) Google Cloud Load Balancing
D) Google Cloud Storage

QUESTION 45

Your organization is deploying a web application that requires automatic scaling based on traffic load. You want to choose a Google Cloud service that provides managed compute resources and automated scaling. Which service should you select to meet these requirements?

A) Google Compute Engine
B) Google Kubernetes Engine (GKE)
C) Google Cloud Run
D) Google Cloud Dataprep

QUESTION 46

Your organization wants to set up a continuous integration and continuous deployment (CI/CD) pipeline on Google Cloud for its microservices-based applications. You need a managed service that automates the building, testing, and deployment of containerized applications. Which Google Cloud service should you choose for this CI/CD pipeline?

A) Google Cloud Composer
B) Google Cloud Dataflow
C) Google Cloud Build
D) Google Kubernetes Engine (GKE)

QUESTION 47

Your organization is planning to deploy a machine learning model on Google Cloud and needs a service that can automate the process of training, hyperparameter tuning, and deployment. Which Google Cloud service should you use for this purpose?

A) Utilize Google Cloud Dataflow for machine learning model automation.
B) Use Google Cloud AutoML for end-to-end machine learning model creation.
C) Deploy Google Cloud Dataprep for automated machine learning pipelines.

D) Leverage Google Cloud AI Platform .

QUESTION 48

Your organization is running a critical application on Google Cloud Compute Engine virtual machines (VMs). You need to ensure high availability and redundancy for the application in case of VM failures. Which GCP feature can help you achieve this goal?

A) Configure GCP's Regional Managed Instance Groups (MIGs) for distributing VMs across multiple zones within a region .
B) Use GCP's Virtual Private Cloud (VPC) for network isolation and security.
C) Implement GCP's Shared VPC for resource sharing across multiple projects.
D) Leverage GCP's Identity-Aware Proxy (IAP) for secure remote access to VMs.

QUESTION 49

As a cloud engineer, you're planning to deploy a new application that will leverage Cloud Spanner for its database requirements. What should you ensure is done first in your GCP environment before proceeding with the Cloud Spanner instance setup?

A) Configure the network settings to allow traffic to and from Cloud Spanner.
B) Enable the Cloud Spanner API in your GCP project.
C) Create a detailed database schema and data model for your application.
D) Set up Cloud Spanner instances in each region where your application will be deployed.

QUESTION 50

Your organization is transitioning to Cloud Identity, and some users have existing Google Accounts under the company's domain. What action should you take to integrate these accounts into Cloud Identity without losing user data?

A) Require users to back up their data from personal Google Accounts and then delete them.
B) Encourage users to maintain both personal and Cloud Identity accounts separately.
C) Facilitate the process of account transfer for users from their existing Google Accounts to Cloud Identity.
D) Convert all existing Google Accounts to Cloud Identity accounts automatically.
E) Create secondary email aliases for existing Google Accounts to differentiate them from Cloud Identity accounts.

SET 4 - ANSWERS ONLY

QUESTION 1

Answer - A) Horizontal pod autoscaler and preemptible VMs

A) Correct, horizontal pod autoscaling adjusts resources based on usage, and preemptible VMs reduce costs during low-usage periods.
B) Incorrect, while node auto-provisioning and committed use discounts are cost-effective, they do not dynamically adjust to traffic patterns.
C) Incorrect, vertical pod autoscalers are not as effective for predictable traffic patterns, and scheduled scaling might not react quickly to unexpected changes.
D) Incorrect, manual scaling is less efficient and prone to errors compared to automated solutions.
E) Incorrect, while using different machine types can be effective, it doesn't dynamically adjust to traffic patterns and might lead to over-provisioning.

QUESTION 2

Answer - D) Cloud Storage with multi-regional buckets

A) Incorrect, Cloud DNS manages domain names but isn't a disaster recovery solution.
B) Incorrect, Cloud Load Balancing distributes user traffic across multiple instances, which aids in high availability but isn't a disaster recovery solution per se.
C) Incorrect, Cloud SQL is a database service and not specifically a disaster recovery solution.
D) Correct, Cloud Storage with multi-regional buckets ensures data redundancy and availability across regions, essential for disaster recovery.
E) Incorrect, VPC allows you to manage your network but doesn't directly contribute to disaster recovery.
F) Incorrect, Cloud Spanner is a database service and not specifically designed for disaster recovery.

QUESTION 3

Answer - A) OS Login and IAM roles

A) Correct, OS Login integrates with IAM roles to manage SSH access efficiently and securely without handling individual SSH keys.
B) Incorrect, managing individual SSH keys, even with Secret Manager, adds complexity and doesn't offer centralized control.
C) Incorrect, IAP is primarily used for web applications, not for managing SSH access to Compute Engine instances.
D) Incorrect, a third-party tool adds complexity and may not be necessary when GCP offers integrated solutions like OS Login.
E) Incorrect, a VPN adds network complexity and doesn't provide an efficient way to manage SSH access at the user level.

QUESTION 4

Answer - A) OS Login and Shielded VMs

A) Correct, OS Login provides secure instance access management, and Shielded VMs offer additional security against sophisticated attacks.
B) Incorrect, VPC Service Controls are more about securing data within services and not directly related to instance access security.
C) Incorrect, Identity-Aware Proxy is generally used for web applications, not for Compute Engine instances.
D) Incorrect, while private Google Access restricts public internet access, it doesn't provide comprehensive security for instance access.
E) Incorrect, manual patch updates are less efficient, and custom firewalls alone do not provide comprehensive security measures for instances.

QUESTION 5

Answer - D) Customer-managed encryption keys (CMEK)

A) Incorrect, Shielded VMs add a layer of security, but encrypting data is crucial for sensitive financial information.
B) Incorrect, VPC Service Controls provide network-level isolation but do not directly encrypt data on instances.
C) Incorrect, Identity-Aware Proxy controls access to applications, not encryption or compliance of data on VMs.
D) Correct, using customer-managed encryption keys (CMEK) ensures that the financial data on instance disks is encrypted and meets compliance requirements.
E) Incorrect, while vulnerability scanning and patch management are important, they do not directly address data encryption and compliance.

QUESTION 6

Answer - A) IAM policy audits with Cloud IAM

A) Correct, performing IAM policy audits using Cloud IAM provides a structured and reliable way to oversee and report on access permissions.
B) Incorrect, exporting policies to CSV for manual review is time-consuming and prone to human error.
C) Incorrect, writing custom scripts is unnecessary when Cloud IAM provides the needed functionality.
D) Incorrect, while Cloud Audit Logs record changes, they are not as efficient for regular auditing of current access permissions.
E) Incorrect, DLP is more about data content scanning and does not specifically audit access permissions.

QUESTION 7

Answer - B) roles/cloudasset.viewer

A) Incorrect, roles/compute.viewer is limited to Compute Engine resources.
B) Correct, roles/cloudasset.viewer allows the compliance team to view resource configurations and settings across GCP projects without modification capabilities.
C) Incorrect, roles/complianceAuditor is not a standard role in GCP.

D) Incorrect, roles/iam.roleViewer is focused on viewing IAM policies.
E) Incorrect, roles/securitycenter.auditViewer is specific to the Security Command Center and does not provide broad visibility across all GCP resources.

QUESTION 8

Answer - A) Cloud Scheduler with Cloud Monitoring

A) Correct, using Cloud Scheduler to automate the generation of storage utilization reports from Cloud Monitoring is efficient for monthly reporting.
B) Incorrect, manual extraction is time-consuming and prone to errors.
C) Incorrect, while the Cloud Billing API provides cost data, Cloud Monitoring is more direct for storage utilization metrics.
D) Incorrect, manual review is less efficient than automated reporting.
E) Incorrect, creating a custom tool using BigQuery and Data Studio is more complex than using existing Cloud Monitoring and Cloud Scheduler capabilities.

QUESTION 9

Answer - A) Individual budgets for each service

A) Correct, creating individual budgets for each service in the Cloud Billing dashboard allows for specific monitoring and alerting of spending limits.
B) Incorrect, while labels help categorize resources, they do not directly facilitate budget alerts for individual services.
C) Incorrect, Cloud Monitoring focuses on operational metrics, not detailed billing data for individual services.
D) Incorrect, exporting to BigQuery for analysis is more complex than using Cloud Billing's budget feature.
E) Incorrect, manual review is time-consuming and prone to errors.

QUESTION 10

Answer – F) Cloud Spanner with multi-region configuration

A) Multi-regional storage provides data redundancy but may not ensure quick recovery for complex applications.
B) Cross-region replication with Cloud SQL offers data redundancy but may not meet the RTO of less than an hour for all scenarios.
C) GKE multi-cluster provides resilience but may not ensure the required RTO for critical applications.
D) Datastore automated exports provide a backup but may not support rapid recovery.
E) Regional SSDs offer redundancy but do not cover all aspects of a comprehensive disaster recovery strategy.
F) Cloud Spanner with a multi-region configuration provides high availability, strong consistency across regions, and rapid recovery, meeting the requirements for minimal data loss and a quick RTO.

QUESTION 11

Answer - C) Set up centralized alerting policies in the Operations Suite workspace.

A) Inefficient and does not provide a centralized view.
B) Overly complex for this requirement.
C) Correct, provides a centralized and efficient way to manage alerts across projects.
D) Unnecessary given Operations Suite's capabilities.

QUESTION 12

Answer - C) Implement a multi-tiered storage strategy: use Cloud Storage Standard for the first 30 days, then transfer to Nearline, and finally to Coldline after 90 days.

A) Suitable for large-scale data processing but may not be the most cost-effective for data storage.
B) Coldline is cost-effective for long-term storage but not optimal for frequent access and processing.
C) Correct. This multi-tiered approach balances performance needs with cost optimization, suitable for varying access patterns over time.
D) Cloud SQL may not be the best fit for high-volume data processing and storage, especially for data-intensive applications.

QUESTION 13

Answer - A) Establish a new GCP project and redeploy the shopping cart application to App Engine Flexible in this project.

A) This approach aligns with best practices for operational separation between development and production environments, ensuring compliance and risk management.
B) This does not fulfill the requirement of having the production environment in a separate GCP project.
C) Managed instance groups do not provide the same level of separation as a different project.
D) The gcloud app copy command does not exist, and this approach does not meet the requirement for a separate project.

QUESTION 14

Answer - C) Create a new service account and grant it the 'pubsub.subscriber' role for the specific topic.

C) Correctly aligns with the principle of least privilege by granting access to read from the specific Pub/Sub topic without unnecessary broader project-level permissions.
A) Using the default service account for specific access needs is not a best practice.
B) The 'pubsub.viewer' role at the project level is broader than necessary.
D) The 'pubsub.editor' role provides more access than required and using the default service account is not recommended for specific tasks.

QUESTION 15

Answer - B) Compute Instance Admin (v1)

B) Compute Instance Admin (v1) is the suitable role as it provides permissions to manage Compute Engine instances without granting access to other GCP services.
A) Compute Engine Admin might provide broader access than required.
C) Project Owner gives full control over all resources in the project, which is excessive.
D) Compute Viewer only allows viewing and does not permit instance management.

QUESTION 16

Answer - C) Google Cloud Cost Management

Option C: This is the correct choice as Google Cloud Cost Management provides tools and features for analyzing billing data and tracking resource costs, helping you optimize expenses.
 Option A: Google Cloud Monitoring is used for monitoring system performance, not billing analysis.
 Option B: Google Cloud Logging is for collecting and analyzing logs, not billing data.
 Option D: Google Cloud IAM is for managing access to resources, not for cost analysis.

QUESTION 17

Answer - D) Google Cloud Database Migration Service

Option D: This is the correct choice as Google Cloud Database Migration Service is specifically designed for migrating databases with minimal downtime. It helps ensure a smooth transition from on-premises to the cloud.
 Option A: Google Cloud Storage is for object storage, not database migration.
 Option B: Google Cloud Compute Engine provides VM instances but doesn't offer specialized database migration services.
 Option C: Google Cloud Dataflow is a data processing service, not designed for database migration.

QUESTION 18

Answer - B) Google Cloud Interconnect.

Option B is the correct choice as Google Cloud Interconnect provides dedicated and high-bandwidth connections between on-premises data centers and Google Cloud, ensuring low-latency access.
 Option A is for encrypted site-to-site connections, Option C is for domain name resolution, and Option D is for content delivery acceleration.

QUESTION 19

Answer - C) Implement instance scheduling using Cloud Scheduler to start and stop instances at specific times.

Option C is the correct choice because implementing instance scheduling with Cloud Scheduler allows you to start and stop instances at specific times, ensuring availability during business hours while reducing costs during off-hours. Options A, B, and D do not provide the same level of cost optimization and scheduling control.

QUESTION 20

Answer - C) Initiate a new GCP project and deploy the App Engine application in an Australian region.

C) The most viable solution is to start a new GCP project and deploy the App Engine application in a region closer to the Australian user base, as App Engine applications are locked to their initial deployment region.
 A) It's not possible to relocate an existing App Engine application to a different region.
 B) A single GCP project cannot have multiple App Engine applications.

D) App Engine does not offer the capability to configure traffic prioritization by region.

QUESTION 21

Answer - C) Enable the GKE Master Auto-Upgrade and Node Auto-Upgrade features for all clusters.

C) Enabling both Master and Node Auto-Upgrades ensures that the entire GKE cluster, including its control plane and nodes, is consistently updated with the latest Kubernetes version, enhancing overall security and stability.
 A) Manual monitoring and updating are inefficient and prone to human error.
 B) CI tools might not be specifically tailored for GKE Kubernetes upgrades.
 D) Custom scripts require maintenance and may not be as reliable as built-in GKE features.

QUESTION 22

Answer - C) Use a Kubernetes Secret to store the encryption key and reference it in the pod specification.

C) Using Kubernetes Secrets is the best practice for storing sensitive data like encryption keys, as it allows the key to be securely managed and injected into pods as needed, without exposing it in the deployment configurations.
 A) Storing sensitive data in Docker images is not secure.
 B) Simply encrypting the key does not address the issue of securely managing and distributing it.
 D) Persistent Volumes are not ideal for handling sensitive keys and add complexity.

QUESTION 23

Answer - C) Ensure the HTML file's Content-Type metadata is set to 'text/html'.

C) Setting the Content-Type metadata of the HTML file to 'text/html' is essential for browsers to recognize and display it as a webpage. This approach will render the resume directly in the browser window.
 A) Public sharing alone does not determine how a file is displayed.
 B) 'application/octet-stream' is used for binary data and would prompt a download.
 D) Converting to PDF changes the nature of the file and may not meet the requirement of displaying it as a webpage.

QUESTION 24

Answer - C) Run the job on preemptible Compute Engine VMs with custom machine types.

C) Using preemptible VMs for interruptible, nightly jobs is a cost-effective strategy, especially when custom machine types are utilized to match the job's resource requirements.
 A) A dedicated GKE cluster might be more costly due to continuous resource allocation.
 B) Persistent VMs are less cost-effective compared to preemptible VMs.
 D) Cloud Functions are better for short, event-driven processes, not long-running jobs.
 E) Dataproc could be more expensive and is more suited for big data applications.
 F) Cloud Run is ideal for stateless HTTP workloads, not long-running batch jobs.

QUESTION 25

Answer - D) Enable 'Automatic Restart' and configure 'On-host maintenance' to 'Migrate VM instance'.

D) This setup ensures that VMs automatically restart in case of crashes ('Automatic Restart') and remain operational during maintenance events ('Migrate VM instance' for 'On-host maintenance').
A) While enabling 'Automatic Restart' is correct, it doesn't address maintenance handling.
B) Preemptible VMs are not suitable for mission-critical applications.
C) Instance groups are good for managing VMs but don't specify individual VM settings for maintenance and restarts.
E) SSDs and TCP checks improve performance but don't address restarts or maintenance.
F) Custom machine types provide flexibility but don't directly address the core requirements.

QUESTION 26

Answer - C) Utilize the Cloud Storage Data Access audit logs feature in Cloud Audit Logs.

C) Data Access audit logs in Cloud Audit Logs are specifically intended for logging data access events, including read operations, which aligns perfectly with the compliance requirements.
A) Uniform bucket-level access controls access but doesn't log specific read operations.
B) Object Lifecycle Management is for managing the lifecycle of objects, not for logging access.
D) Labels and Stackdriver can monitor usage, but they don't provide detailed access logs.
E) Pub/Sub notifications can alert on events but aren't a substitute for detailed access logs.
F) A custom solution is unnecessarily complex when Cloud Audit Logs provides the needed functionality.

QUESTION 27

Answer - D) Reconfigure the project's billing to be associated with the company's GCP billing account.

D) Associating the project with the company's GCP billing account is the most direct way to ensure all future charges are billed to the company, streamlining the billing process and eliminating the need for personal reimbursements.
A) This continues the reimbursement process, which the company aims to streamline.
B) Changing payment methods doesn't transition the billing account to the company.
C) Transferring to a new account is more complex than changing the billing association.
E) Reporting expenses for reimbursement is what the company wants to avoid.
F) Creating a subaccount doesn't change the primary billing responsibility.

QUESTION 28

Answer - B) Vertical Pod Autoscaler (VPA)

Option B - Vertical Pod Autoscaler (VPA) automatically adjusts the CPU and memory requests and limits for pods based on their actual resource usage, optimizing resource allocation.
Option A - Horizontal Pod Autoscaler (HPA) scales the number of pod replicas, not resource allocation.
Option C - Cluster Autoscaler manages node scaling, not pod resource limits.
Option D - Pod Disruption Budgets set constraints on pod disruptions, and
Option E - GKE Node Pool Scaling is related to the cluster's node pool size.

QUESTION 29

Answer - D) Google Cloud Data Loss Prevention (DLP)

Option D - Google Cloud Data Loss Prevention (DLP) allows you to automatically delete data that exceeds a specified retention period to ensure data retention compliance. It provides powerful data inspection and redaction capabilities.
Option A - Google Cloud Storage is for object storage.
Option B - Google Cloud Datastore is a NoSQL database.
Option C - Google Cloud Pub/Sub is for event streaming.
Option E - Google Cloud Bigtable is a NoSQL database for large-scale analytical and operational workloads.

QUESTION 30

Answer - B) Set up a Cloud DNS private zone with a DNS entry for the on-premises database.

B) Setting up a Cloud DNS private zone for the on-premises database allows applications to use a DNS name for connectivity. This approach centralizes IP management, and any change in the database IP only requires an update to the DNS record, not to each individual application.
A) GCP Endpoint Service is not designed for managing dynamic IP addresses of on-premises databases.
C) Cloud Functions can update IPs, but this adds complexity and potential delays in updates.
D) Environment variables are static and would require updates if the IP changes.
E) Shared VPCs facilitate network sharing but don't manage dynamic IPs.
F) Cloud Memorystore is for data caching, not for IP address management.

QUESTION 31

Answer - C) Have the partner create a Service Account in their project, then grant it necessary access to your datasets.

C) This is the most secure and manageable approach. The partner's Service Account creation in their project ensures they maintain control over their access, while you retain control over your datasets by granting specific permissions. This method respects the boundaries of each company's resources while enabling collaboration.
A) Creating a new project and migrating datasets is more complex and might not be necessary.
B) API-based access is an option but requires additional development and maintenance.
D) Dataset sharing is a feature in BigQuery but may not offer the same level of control and security as Service Account access.
E) Bilateral IAM policies are complex and might lead to broader access than needed.
F) A VPN tunnel is more about network connectivity, not specific to dataset access.

QUESTION 32

Answer - D) Create a new revision of the current service for the update and use traffic splitting to control user access.

D) Creating a new revision of the current service and then utilizing traffic splitting is an effective way to test the new update with a subset of users. This approach allows for precise control over the distribution of traffic between the old and new versions, making it possible to conduct a phased rollout and gather feedback before a full deployment.

A) Feature toggles can be used but are less straightforward than Cloud Run's built-in traffic splitting.

B) Using a staging environment does not accurately represent live user interactions.

C) Version tags are useful but do not offer the same level of control as traffic splitting.

E) Cloud Endpoints are more about API management, not for traffic distribution between application versions.

F) A dedicated testing project does not provide live user interaction data like traffic splitting does.

QUESTION 33

Answer - A) Create a Cloud Function with a trigger set on the Cloud Storage bucket to execute the Python code.

A) Cloud Functions are specifically designed for such event-driven tasks. By creating a Cloud Function with a trigger on the Cloud Storage bucket, the Python function will be executed automatically each time a new file is uploaded. This approach is highly efficient, scalable, and requires minimal maintenance.

B) Kubernetes Engine with Pub/Sub is a more complex solution than necessary for this scenario.

C) App Engine would require constant polling, making it less efficient for real-time processing.

D) Dataflow is more suitable for continuous data streams, not discrete file uploads.

E) A Compute Engine instance with regular checks is less efficient and real-time.

F) Cloud Scheduler is not suitable for immediate, event-driven execution.

QUESTION 34

Answer – A) Cloud IoT Core, Cloud Pub/Sub, Dataflow, BigQuery

A) Correct, this setup provides a comprehensive solution for real-time IoT data management, processing, analysis, and storage.

B) Incorrect, Compute Engine and custom scripts may not efficiently handle the scale and real-time requirements.

C) Incorrect, Kubernetes Engine and Cloud Storage don't provide the best real-time ingestion and analysis capabilities for IoT data.

D) Incorrect, App Engine and Firestore are not the ideal choices for large-scale IoT data management and processing.

E) Incorrect, Cloud Run and Firebase Realtime Database are not the best fit for the scale and complexity of IoT data management and analysis.

QUESTION 35

Answer – A) Cloud SQL Audit Logs, BigQuery, ML models

A) Correct, Audit Logs provide access data, BigQuery enables analysis, and ML models can identify patterns.

B) Incorrect, Cloud SQL Insights is more for performance monitoring, not specific user access patterns.

C) Incorrect, Cloud IDS is for intrusion detection, not specific to database access monitoring.

D) Incorrect, third-party tools might not integrate as seamlessly with Cloud SQL.

E) Incorrect, VPC Flow Logs are for network traffic, not specific to database access.

QUESTION 36

Answer – D) GOOGLE_APPLICATION_CREDENTIALS

A) Incorrect, attaching the key as metadata is not a secure practice.
B) Incorrect, the set-service-account command does not specify a key file.
C) Incorrect, storing the key file on the VM is less secure than using instance metadata.
D) Correct, this is the standard way to authenticate applications on Compute Engine with a service account.
E) Incorrect, uploading keys to repositories is not recommended due to security risks.

QUESTION 37

Answer - B) Google Cloud CDN (Correct)

Option A is incorrect because Google Cloud Storage is an object storage service and not a CDN.
Option C is incorrect because App Engine is a platform-as-a-service (PaaS) and does not directly provide CDN capabilities.
Option D is incorrect because Cloud Endpoints is an API management platform, not a CDN.
Option E is incorrect because Cloud Load Balancing provides load balancing but not CDN functionality.

QUESTION 38

Answer - B) Use Google Cloud CDN (Content Delivery Network) with Google Cloud Storage for static content hosting. (Correct)

Option A is incorrect because Google Cloud Load Balancing is primarily for load distribution, and while it provides regional content delivery, it may not offer the same edge caching and CDN capabilities as Google Cloud CDN.
Option C is incorrect because Google Cloud Identity-Aware Proxy (IAP) is focused on access control and security and does not provide CDN capabilities for content delivery.
Option D is incorrect because Google Cloud Functions are designed for serverless functions and may not be the most efficient way to serve static website content with low latency.
Option E is incorrect because Google Cloud Pub/Sub is a messaging service and not designed for content distribution or CDN functionality.
Option B is correct because Google Cloud CDN, when used in conjunction with Google Cloud Storage for hosting static content, provides a secure and global content delivery network with low-latency content delivery worldwide, meeting the requirements for a global website presence.

QUESTION 39

Answer - C) Set up Google Cloud Interconnect for dedicated, private network connections. (Correct)

Option A is incorrect because while Google Cloud VPN provides secure connectivity, it may not offer the same level of dedicated, private network connections as Google Cloud Interconnect.
Option B is incorrect because Google Cloud Direct Peering focuses on direct internet-based communication and may not provide the private connection needed for hybrid cloud architecture.

Option D is incorrect because Google Cloud VPC Peering is used for network isolation within GCP, not for connecting on-premises networks.
Option E is incorrect because Google Cloud CDN is for content delivery and not for establishing private connections between on-premises and cloud networks.
Option C is correct because Google Cloud Interconnect is designed for dedicated, private network connections, making it suitable for maintaining a private connection between on-premises networks and Google Cloud in a hybrid cloud architecture.

QUESTION 40

Answer - C) Set up Google Cloud IAM (Identity and Access Management) for centralized access control and fine-grained permissions management. (Correct)

Option A is incorrect because Google Cloud Identity-Aware Proxy (IAP) primarily focuses on identity verification and access control for web applications and does not provide fine-grained permissions management.
Option B is incorrect because Google Cloud Armor is a DDoS protection service and does not offer fine-grained permissions management.
Option D is incorrect because Google Cloud Pub/Sub is a messaging service and not designed for access control and permissions management at the project level.
Option C is correct because Google Cloud IAM (Identity and Access Management) allows for centralized access control and fine-grained permissions management at the project level, enhancing data security across multiple GCP services.

QUESTION 41

Answer - C) Google Cloud Dataflow

Option A, Google Cloud Dataprep, is a data preparation tool and not a serverless data processing service. Option B, Google Cloud Dataproc, is used for running Apache Spark and Hadoop clusters and does not provide serverless data analysis. Option D, Google Cloud Datastore, is a NoSQL database and not a data processing service. Option C, Google Cloud Dataflow, is a serverless data processing service that offers automatic scaling and is suitable for cost-effective data processing with ease of use.

QUESTION 42

Answer - C) Implement regional managed instance groups

Option C recommends implementing regional managed instance groups, which distribute VM instances across multiple zones to achieve high availability and fault tolerance.
Option A (Preemptible VM instances) offer cost savings but are not suitable for high availability.
Option B (Deploy VM instances in a single zone) lacks redundancy and fault tolerance.
Option D (Daily snapshots for VM disks) is for backup, not for achieving high availability.

QUESTION 43

Answer - D) Configure dual-regional storage with standard storage class for the dual region closest to the users.

Option A is incorrect because multi-regional storage with nearline storage class may not provide the necessary performance for users in Bangalore and could increase costs.
Option B is incorrect because multi-regional storage with standard storage class may not consider the proximity of users and could lead to latency issues.
Option C is incorrect because configuring dual-regional storage with nearline storage class may not strike the right balance between cost and performance for users in Bangalore.

QUESTION 44

Answer - A) Google Cloud CDN

Option A is correct because Google Cloud CDN (Content Delivery Network) efficiently distributes content and delivers it with low latency to users worldwide. It caches content at edge locations, reducing the distance data needs to travel.
Option B (Google Cloud Interconnect) is for connecting on-premises networks to Google's network and is not focused on content delivery.
Option C (Google Cloud Load Balancing) balances traffic across instances and regions but does not specifically handle content delivery.
Option D (Google Cloud Storage) is an object storage service and not designed for content delivery like a CDN.

QUESTION 45

Answer - C) Google Cloud Run

Option C is correct because Google Cloud Run is a managed serverless platform that offers automatic scaling based on traffic load, making it suitable for web applications that require scalability without managing infrastructure.
Option A (Google Compute Engine) provides virtual machines but requires manual scaling and management.
Option B (Google Kubernetes Engine) offers container orchestration but may involve more manual configuration for auto-scaling.
Option D (Google Cloud Dataprep) is a data preparation tool and not designed for web application scaling.

QUESTION 46

Answer - C) Google Cloud Build

Option C is correct because Google Cloud Build is a managed CI/CD service that automates the building, testing, and deployment of containerized applications, making it suitable for CI/CD pipelines.
Option A (Google Cloud Composer) is for workflow orchestration and not primarily for CI/CD.
Option B (Google Cloud Dataflow) is for data processing and not a CI/CD service.
Option D (Google Kubernetes Engine - GKE) is a managed Kubernetes service and may be used in conjunction with CI/CD but is not a standalone CI/CD service.

QUESTION 47

Answer - D) Leverage Google Cloud AI Platform

Option D is correct because Google Cloud AI Platform is specifically designed for end-to-end machine learning, including automated training, hyperparameter tuning, and deployment of machine learning models.
Option A is not the best choice as Google Cloud Dataflow is primarily used for data processing and does not focus on machine learning model automation.
Option B is incorrect because Google Cloud AutoML is for custom machine learning model creation but does not automate the entire machine learning process.
Option C is not suitable for automating the entire machine learning process, as Google Cloud Dataprep is more focused on data preparation and cleansing.

QUESTION 48

Answer - A) Configure GCP's Regional Managed Instance Groups (MIGs) for distributing VMs across multiple zones within a region

Option A is correct because Google Cloud's Regional Managed Instance Groups (MIGs) allow you to distribute VM instances across multiple zones within a region, providing high availability and redundancy. In case of VM failures in one zone, the application can continue to run in other zones within the same region.
Option B, C, and D are not directly related to achieving high availability and redundancy for VMs and applications in case of failures.

QUESTION 49

Answer – B) Enable the Cloud Spanner API

A) Incorrect, network configuration is not the first step for Cloud Spanner.
B) Correct, enabling the API is the prerequisite step for using Cloud Spanner.
C) Incorrect, creating a database schema is subsequent to instance creation.
D) Incorrect, setting up instances in each region comes after enabling the API.

QUESTION 50

Answer – C) Facilitate account transfer

A) Incorrect, backing up and deleting accounts is cumbersome and risky.
B) Incorrect, maintaining separate accounts doesn't solve the conflict issue.
C) Correct, facilitating account transfers is the recommended method to integrate accounts while preserving data.
D) Incorrect, automatic conversion might not be feasible or user-consent compliant.
E) Incorrect, creating aliases does not address the underlying account conflict.

SET 5 - QUESTIONS ONLY

QUESTION 1

A logistics company is planning to enhance its vehicle tracking system hosted on GCP. The system collects real-time data from GPS devices on trucks and needs to process this data to provide insights into vehicle performance, fuel efficiency, and route optimization. What GCP services and architecture should you recommend for processing and analyzing this real-time data?

A) Use Cloud Pub/Sub for data ingestion from GPS devices, process the data in real-time with Dataflow, and store the processed data in BigQuery for analysis.
B) Collect GPS data directly into Bigtable, utilize Dataflow for periodic batch processing, and export the results to Cloud Storage for long-term analysis.
C) Implement a custom IoT solution on Compute Engine to receive GPS data, use Cloud Functions for processing, and store results in Firestore for real-time analysis.
D) Deploy a Cloud IoT Core solution for device management and data collection, process data using Cloud Dataproc, and analyze with Cloud AI Platform.
E) Stream GPS data into Cloud SQL using a custom API, apply machine learning models in AI Platform for analysis, and visualize results in Data Studio.

QUESTION 2

Your organization requires real-time analytics of its operational data on GCP. Which service combination would you recommend for this requirement?

A) Dataflow and BigQuery
B) Pub/Sub and Datastore
C) Bigtable and Cloud Functions
D) Dataflow and Cloud SQL
E) BigQuery and Cloud Storage
F) Dataproc and Firestore

QUESTION 3

You are tasked with designing a network architecture for a set of applications that will be deployed on GCP. The applications require isolation from each other but need to communicate securely with a shared database. Which of the following approaches would best meet these requirements?

A) Create separate VPCs for each application and use VPC peering to connect them to a shared VPC hosting the database.
B) Deploy all applications in a single VPC, use network tags to isolate traffic, and employ Cloud Armor for additional security.
C) Implement Shared VPC to host the database and connect individual service projects for each application.
D) Utilize separate subnets within a single VPC for each application and set up firewall rules for secure communication with the database.

E) Set up a VPN tunnel between each application's VPC and the database's VPC for secure and isolated communication.

QUESTION 4

You are configuring a highly available application on GCP that requires a relational database. The database should be accessible from multiple regions for read and write operations with minimal latency. Which database solution and configuration would be most appropriate for this requirement?

A) Deploy Cloud SQL with read replicas in different regions and a failover replica in the primary region.
B) Utilize Cloud Spanner with a multi-regional configuration for global data distribution and low-latency read-write access.
C) Implement a self-managed MySQL database on Compute Engine VMs in multiple regions with data replication.
D) Set up Cloud Bigtable with multi-regional instances for low-latency access across regions.
E) Use Firestore in Datastore mode with a multi-regional setup for distributed data storage and access.

QUESTION 5

Your company is planning to deploy a new application in GCP that will have variable traffic patterns and requires auto-scaling capabilities. The application also needs to connect to a Cloud SQL database. What is the most cost-effective and efficient deployment strategy for this application?

A) Deploy the application on App Engine standard environment with automatic scaling enabled and connect to Cloud SQL.
B) Use Compute Engine with custom machine types and manual scaling based on traffic patterns.
C) Implement the application in a GKE cluster with horizontal pod autoscaling and a Cloud SQL connector.
D) Configure the application on Cloud Functions, triggered based on usage, and connect to Cloud SQL.
E) Set up a managed instance group in Compute Engine with autoscaling and a Cloud SQL connection.

QUESTION 6

You are setting up a new BigQuery dataset for a project that involves multiple teams. You need to ensure that each team can only access and query the data relevant to their work, without exposing other teams' data. What is the best way to configure this data access segregation in BigQuery?

A) Use BigQuery row-level security to restrict data access based on team roles.
B) Create separate datasets for each team and assign appropriate IAM roles.
C) Implement VPC Service Controls to isolate data access between teams.
D) Apply labels to data and configure IAM policies based on these labels.
E) Encrypt data with different encryption keys for each team and manage access via IAM.

QUESTION 7

You need to set up access control so that the development team can view GCP resource usage and costs across all projects in the organization, but they should not have the ability to view the content within the resources. What role should you assign to the development team to achieve this?

A) roles/viewer at the organization level.
B) roles/monitoring.viewer at the organization level.
C) roles/billing.viewer at the project level.
D) roles/resourcemanager.folderViewer
E) roles/cloudasset.viewer

QUESTION 8

As part of maintaining high availability for your digital simulation projects, you need to track the uptime and health of various Compute Engine instances across multiple GCP projects. Which feature or service in GCP should you primarily utilize for this purpose?

A) Use Cloud Monitoring to set up dashboards and uptime checks for Compute Engine instances.
B) Implement custom health-check scripts on each Compute Engine instance and report to a centralized server.
C) Rely on the automatic email alerts from Compute Engine for any instance downtimes.
D) Use Compute Engine's metadata server to log uptime status and review it periodically.
E) Configure Cloud Trace on each instance to monitor and analyze their performance and uptime.

QUESTION 9

In your GCP environment, you want to ensure that you receive notifications when the usage of Cloud Storage exceeds a set amount to prevent unexpected charges. Which feature should you use to monitor and alert on Cloud Storage usage?

A) Set up a Cloud Monitoring alert based on Cloud Storage metrics.
B) Create a budget in Cloud Billing specifically for Cloud Storage usage.
C) Implement a Cloud Function to analyze Cloud Storage logs for usage patterns.
D) Use the Object Lifecycle Management feature in Cloud Storage to monitor usage.
E) Configure a Cloud Pub/Sub notification for Cloud Storage usage thresholds.

QUESTION 10

A finance company uses GCP to process sensitive customer data. They need to ensure that access to this data is tightly controlled and monitored. Which combination of GCP features should be used to enhance security and access control?

A) Identity-Aware Proxy and Cloud IAM
B) VPC Service Controls and Cloud Endpoints
C) Cloud Armor and Cloud Data Loss Prevention (DLP)
D) Cloud Audit Logs and Cloud Security Scanner
E) Kubernetes Network Policies and Cloud IAM
F) Cloud IAM and Cloud Key Management Service (KMS)

QUESTION 11

What is the best practice for managing access to monitoring data of multiple GCP projects in Google Cloud's Operations Suite?

A) Create separate user accounts for each project.
B) Use service accounts with limited permissions for each project.
C) Implement organization-level IAM policies for monitoring access.
D) Restrict access to monitoring data to project owners only.

QUESTION 12

Your company is deploying several IoT devices globally, which will continuously stream data to your GCP environment. To manage and analyze this data effectively, you need to choose an appropriate GCP service that can handle real-time data ingestion and analysis. Which service should you use and why?

A) Use Cloud IoT Core to manage device connections and Pub/Sub for real-time data ingestion, combined with Dataflow for stream processing and analysis.
B) Implement Cloud Spanner for its global scalability and strong consistency, using it to ingest and analyze the IoT data in real time.
C) Deploy a network of Compute Engine VMs across multiple regions to ingest data, and use BigQuery for real-time analysis.
D) Utilize Cloud Storage for immediate data ingestion, and periodically process the data using Cloud Dataproc for analysis.

QUESTION 13

Your organization is developing an AI-powered analytics tool on GCP, currently hosted in a Machine Learning (ML) environment using AI Platform. The tool has been validated in this development environment and is now ready for a production rollout, which must be isolated in a new GCP project as per organizational standards. How should you approach this deployment?

A) Provision a new GCP project and set up the AI Platform environment to mirror the development setup, then deploy the ML model.
B) Within the existing project, create a new AI Platform environment labeled as 'production' and deploy the model there.
C) Clone the existing AI Platform project settings to a new project using an AI Platform-specific cloning tool.
D) Transition the ML model to a Compute Engine based solution in the same project, designating it as the production environment.

QUESTION 14

You are setting up a Compute Engine instance that needs to interact with Cloud Spanner for querying and writing data. What is the most secure way to configure the service account for this Compute Engine instance, according to Google Cloud best practices?

A) Use the default Compute Engine service account with 'spanner.databaseUser' role for the relevant Spanner database.
B) Create a new service account with 'spanner.databaseAdmin' role for the specific Spanner database.
C) Assign the 'spanner.databaseUser' role to a new service account for the specific Spanner database.
D) Provide the Compute Engine default service account with project owner access for comprehensive permissions.

QUESTION 15

Your team is responsible for managing Cloud SQL instances in a project. You need to assign a role to a new team member that allows them to create, configure, and delete Cloud SQL instances without granting broader project-wide permissions. Which IAM role should you choose?

A) Cloud SQL Admin
B) Cloud SQL Editor
C) Project Editor
D) Database Admin

QUESTION 16

Your organization wants to ensure that data stored in Google Cloud Storage is encrypted both at rest and in transit. Which GCP services or features should you configure to achieve this dual encryption?

A) Google Cloud Storage encryption
B) Google Cloud Key Management Service (KMS)
C) Google Cloud Identity-Aware Proxy (IAP)
D) Google Cloud Armor

QUESTION 17

Your data analytics team needs to analyze a massive dataset to gain insights. You require a service that can handle complex queries and deliver results quickly. Which GCP service is best suited for this analytical workload?

A) Google Cloud Bigtable
B) Google Cloud Datastore
C) Google Cloud BigQuery
D) Google Cloud Pub/Sub

QUESTION 18

You are responsible for managing access control and permissions for your Google Cloud resources. You need a centralized solution for defining, managing, and enforcing access policies across services. Which GCP feature should you use for this purpose?

A) Google Cloud IAM (Identity and Access Management).
B) Google Cloud Identity.
C) Google Cloud Security Command Center.
D) Google Cloud Key Management Service.

QUESTION 19

Your organization is planning to implement a disaster recovery (DR) strategy for its Google Cloud resources. You want to ensure that data and services can be quickly restored in case of a disaster. What GCP service should you consider for this purpose?

A) Google Cloud Storage for data archival.

B) Google Cloud Dataflow for data transformation.
C) Google Cloud Dataprep for data preparation.
D) Google Cloud Deployment Manager for infrastructure as code (IaC).

QUESTION 20

To improve service for East Asian users, your team decides to host a version of your App Engine application in a region closer to them. Considering GCP's limitations, what is the best approach to achieve this regional deployment?

A) Transfer the existing App Engine application to an East Asian region.
B) In the current GCP project, create a new instance of the App Engine application in an East Asian region.
C) Construct a new GCP project and replicate the App Engine application in an East Asian region.
D) Implement a Global Load Balancer to distribute traffic from East Asia to the existing App Engine application.

QUESTION 21

Your GKE clusters host applications that require strict compliance with security standards. To ensure compliance, Kubernetes versions must be regularly updated with the latest security patches. How should you manage these updates within GKE?

A) Configure each GKE cluster to automatically pull and install updates for Kubernetes.
B) Enable automatic security patching for GKE nodes while manually updating the control plane.
C) Implement GKE's Node Auto-Upgrades feature to ensure Kubernetes versions are always current.
D) Assign a team to track Kubernetes updates and manually apply them to GKE clusters.

QUESTION 22

Your Kubernetes application requires a password for connecting to an external service. Currently, this password is hardcoded in the pod's deployment YAML. To follow Kubernetes security best practices, how should you manage this password?

A) Convert the password to a base64 encoded string and store it in the deployment YAML.
B) Store the password in a Kubernetes Secret and reference this Secret in the deployment YAML.
C) Place the password in a ConfigMap and reference it in the application deployment.
D) Write the password to a file, store it on a Persistent Volume, and mount it in the pod.

QUESTION 23

As part of your company's marketing efforts, you've uploaded several promotional PDF brochures to a Cloud Storage bucket. To provide a better user experience, you want these PDFs to be viewable in the browser instead of being downloaded when clicked. What configuration change is necessary?

A) Enable 'Share publicly' on each PDF brochure.
B) Set the Content-Disposition metadata of each PDF to 'inline'.
C) Set the Content-Type metadata of each PDF to 'application/pdf'.
D) Upload the PDFs to a new bucket with public access enabled.

QUESTION 24

For your financial analytics application, you need to run computation-heavy batch jobs every night. The jobs complete within 3 hours and can be interrupted. Which GCP service would be the most cost-efficient for this requirement?

A) Configure a persistent Compute Engine VM with high CPU and run the jobs nightly.
B) Use a Google Kubernetes Engine (GKE) cluster with autoscaling for the nightly jobs.
C) Implement the jobs in Cloud Functions for a serverless approach.
D) Utilize preemptible Compute Engine VMs for the batch processing.
E) Set up a nightly Dataproc cluster with high-compute machine types.
F) Run the jobs in a Cloud Run environment with increased concurrency.

QUESTION 25

You are configuring Compute Engine VMs for an application that requires high availability, especially during stock market hours. The VMs should not be affected by maintenance activities and must recover quickly from any downtime. What is the best setup for these VMs?

A) Utilize preemptible VMs and enable 'Automatic Restart'.
B) Enable 'Automatic Restart' and set 'On-host maintenance' to 'Migrate VM instance' in the VM settings.
C) Set up the VMs within a managed instance group with auto-scaling and auto-healing.
D) Deploy the VMs in multiple regions and enable 'Automatic Restart'.
E) Use standard VMs with 'Automatic Restart' disabled and 'On-host maintenance' set to 'Terminate VM instance'.
F) Configure each VM with a custom machine type and high-availability options.

QUESTION 26

For audit compliance, you must ensure that all instances of reading sensitive data from a specific Cloud Storage bucket are logged. Which GCP service should you configure to meet this requirement?

A) Set up detailed Stackdriver logs for every read request on the bucket.
B) Implement Cloud Identity and Access Management (IAM) audit logging for access requests.
C) Enable Cloud Storage Data Access audit logs in the Cloud Audit Logs.
D) Configure Cloud Data Loss Prevention (DLP) to log every access to the sensitive data.
E) Activate Access Transparency logs for the Cloud Storage bucket.
F) Use Cloud Endpoint Security to monitor and log data access.

QUESTION 27

To align with your company's request for direct billing of GCP charges, what step should you take for the Sports Score tracking application project currently billed to your personal account?

A) Configure the project to generate monthly cost reports for your company's finance team.
B) Assign a company finance team member the role of Billing Account Administrator.
C) Switch the payment method on your personal GCP account to the company's billing information.
D) Change the billing account associated with the project to your company's GCP billing account.
E) Contact GCP customer service to request a billing account transfer to the company.

F) Establish a company policy for regular reimbursement of GCP charges.

QUESTION 28

Your company is planning to deploy a highly available web application on Google Cloud. You want to ensure that traffic is distributed across multiple regions for redundancy. Which Google Cloud service should you use for global load balancing?

A) Google Cloud CDN
B) Google Cloud Storage
C) Global HTTP(S) Load Balancer
D) Google Kubernetes Engine (GKE)
E) Google Cloud VPN

QUESTION 29

Your company is running a machine learning workload on Google Cloud, and you want to optimize the costs by selecting the most cost-effective virtual machine type. Which GCP service can help you analyze the historical usage patterns and recommend the appropriate virtual machine type?

A) Google Cloud Monitoring
B) Google Cloud Profiler
C) Google Cloud Recommender
D) Google Cloud Security Scanner
E) Google Cloud Debugger

QUESTION 30

For seamless connectivity in a hybrid environment where GCP-hosted applications use an on-premises database, what method should you employ to handle the database IP address dynamically?

A) Implement a network peering between GCP and the on-premises network for IP management.
B) Use Cloud DNS forwarding to manage the on-premises database IP address.
C) Set up a Cloud DNS private zone to resolve the on-premises database hostname.
D) Configure a dedicated Compute Engine instance to relay database connections.
E) Create a custom script in GCP VMs to periodically update the database IP.
F) Utilize a GCP-based proxy server to manage connectivity to the on-premises database.

QUESTION 31

To collaborate with a partner company that requires access to certain BigQuery datasets in your GCP project, which approach ensures secure and specific access?

A) Grant the partner's GCP project IAM roles for direct access to your BigQuery datasets.
B) Have the partner create a Service Account in their project and assign access to your datasets.
C) Share your project's BigQuery credentials with the partner for direct dataset access.
D) Use BigQuery's cross-project data sharing capabilities to grant access to the datasets.
E) Duplicate the relevant datasets into a joint GCP project managed by both companies.
F) Set up a data replication process to the partner's BigQuery instance for dataset access.

QUESTION 32

In order to progressively roll out an update to a web application running on Cloud Run for Anthos to a select group of users, what should be your strategy?

A) Configure a set of HTTP routing rules to direct a subset of traffic to the new version.
B) Launch the updated version on a separate domain and gradually redirect users.
C) Create a new revision of your service with the update and adjust the traffic split to test with specific users.
D) Use a custom script to randomly redirect users to either the old or new version of the application.
E) Set up a Cloud Function to manage the distribution of users between the old and new versions.
F) Implement a third-party A/B testing tool to manage user access to different application versions.

QUESTION 33

What is the most efficient way to execute a Python function each time a new object is added to a Cloud Storage bucket?

A) Configure a Cloud Function to trigger on Cloud Storage events and run the Python function.
B) Set up a Cloud Run service that activates upon new object uploads in the Cloud Storage bucket.
C) Use a Compute Engine VM with a script to poll the bucket for new objects and execute the Python function.
D) Implement a Cloud Dataflow pipeline that processes new objects in the bucket using the Python function.
E) Deploy an App Engine service that continuously monitors the bucket and runs the Python function on new uploads.
F) Create a Cloud Scheduler job that periodically checks the bucket and executes the Python function on new files.

QUESTION 34

As part of a digital transformation initiative, your company plans to migrate a legacy monolithic application to GCP. The application is critical and requires high availability, scalability, and minimal downtime during migration. Additionally, the application must integrate with existing GCP services for logging and monitoring. What migration strategy and service selection would be most appropriate?

A) Refactoring the application into microservices, deploying on Kubernetes Engine, using Stackdriver for logging and monitoring, and migrating using a blue-green deployment strategy.
B) Migrating the application as-is to Compute Engine, implementing Cloud Monitoring and Cloud Logging, and using a canary deployment strategy for minimal downtime.
C) Replatforming the application on App Engine, integrating with Operations Suite for monitoring and logging, and employing a phased migration approach.
D) Lifting and shifting the application to Cloud Run, utilizing Cloud Operations for logging and monitoring, and adopting a rolling update deployment method.
E) Breaking down the application into serverless functions, deploying on Cloud Functions, using Cloud Trace for monitoring, and transitioning through a hybrid cloud setup.

QUESTION 35

To comply with industry regulations, your company needs to ensure that all access to sensitive documents stored in Cloud Storage is tracked and any unauthorized access is immediately reported. What is the best approach to meet this compliance requirement?

A) Configure Data Access Logs for Cloud Storage, analyze them using Cloud Logging, and set up Cloud Monitoring alerts.
B) Use Cloud IAM and Cloud Identity to manage and monitor access permissions to Cloud Storage.
C) Enable Access Transparency for Cloud Storage and integrate with Cloud Security Command Center.
D) Implement a VPC Service Control perimeter around Cloud Storage and monitor with Cloud Audit Logs.
E) Set up a custom application to monitor Cloud Storage access and report using Cloud Functions.

QUESTION 36

You need to run a series of gcloud commands in a script on a server that will interact with GCP resources. The server does not have a default service account with appropriate permissions. You have a service account key file for this purpose. What is the correct way to use this key file in your script?

A) Directly embed the service account key in your script as a variable.
B) Use the gcloud auth activate-service-account command at the start of your script and provide the key file path.
C) Set the key file path as an environment variable in your server's operating system.
D) Upload the key file to a secure location in Cloud Storage and reference it in your script.
E) Convert the service account key file to a base64 encoded string and use it in your script.

QUESTION 37

You are responsible for setting up a disaster recovery (DR) plan for your organization's critical applications running on GCP. Which GCP service or feature can help you achieve automated, cross-region failover and recovery?

A) Google Cloud Spanner
B) Google Cloud Storage
C) Google Cloud VPN
D) Google Cloud Pub/Sub
E) Google Cloud Monitoring and Alerting

QUESTION 38

Your organization is planning to set up a disaster recovery (DR) plan for its critical applications on Google Cloud Platform. Which GCP service or feature can help you achieve automated cross-region failover and recovery for your applications in case of a regional outage?

A) Utilize Google Cloud Memorystore for caching and load balancing for regional failover.
B) Implement Google Cloud VPN for secure connectivity and data replication across regions.
C) Use Google Cloud Deployment Manager to define and automate resource deployment across regions for cross-region failover.
D) Deploy Google Cloud Functions for event-driven disaster recovery.

E) Configure Google Cloud IAM (Identity and Access Management) for access control during DR scenarios.

QUESTION 39

Your team is responsible for optimizing cost management in a Google Cloud project that uses various GCP services. You want to identify opportunities for cost reduction and analyze resource usage. Which GCP service or feature can you use for cost optimization and resource usage analysis?

A) Implement Google Cloud Billing Reports for cost reduction and resource usage analysis.
B) Configure Google Cloud Monitoring for real-time cost tracking and analysis.
C) Utilize Google Cloud Cost Explorer for cost optimization and resource usage analysis.
D) Set up Google Cloud Security Command Center for cost management and resource usage analysis.
E) Deploy Google Cloud Audit Logging for cost reduction and resource tracking.

QUESTION 40

Your company is running a fleet of virtual machines (VMs) on Google Cloud Compute Engine. You want to ensure that each VM can access specific Google Cloud APIs based on their roles. What should you do to achieve this access control?

A) Assign the same service account to all VMs for uniform access.
B) Use instance metadata to define API access for each VM.
C) Create a custom IAM role for each VM instance.
D) Use service accounts to grant permissions to each VM instance.

QUESTION 41

Your team is responsible for optimizing cost management in a Google Cloud project that uses multiple GCP services. You want to identify opportunities for cost reduction and analyze resource usage. Which GCP service or feature can you use for cost optimization and resource usage analysis?

A) Google Cloud Billing Reports
B) Google Cloud Monitoring
C) Google Cloud Cost Explorer
D) Google Cloud Security Command Center

QUESTION 42

Your organization is planning to set up a multi-cloud strategy, including Google Cloud and another cloud provider. You want to ensure consistent identity management across both cloud environments. What should you use to achieve this goal?

A) Google Cloud IAM (Identity and Access Management)
B) Google Cloud Identity Platform
C) Google Cloud Directory Sync

D) Google Cloud Identity-Aware Proxy (IAP)

QUESTION 43

Your organization's data analysis pipeline relies on Cloud Storage for mission-critical data. Users are located in Bangalore, India, and require frequent and dynamic access to this data. What storage configuration will offer optimal performance and cost-effectiveness for users in Bangalore?

A) Configure regional storage with nearline storage class. B) Configure regional storage with standard storage class. C) Configure dual-regional storage with nearline storage class for the dual region closest to the users. D) Configure dual-regional storage with standard storage class for the dual region closest to the users.

QUESTION 44

Your organization needs to ensure high availability for your Kubernetes workloads on Google Cloud. Which Google Kubernetes Engine (GKE) feature allows you to achieve this by distributing your cluster across multiple zones within a region?

A) Node Pools
B) Cluster Autoscaler
C) Regional Clusters
D) Istio Service Mesh

QUESTION 45

Your organization is planning to establish a secure network connection between its on-premises data center and Google Cloud resources. You want to ensure data privacy and encryption over the network. Which Google Cloud service should you use to achieve this secure network connection?

A) Google Cloud Load Balancing
B) Google Cloud VPN
C) Google Cloud Interconnect
D) Google Cloud Identity and Access Management (IAM)

QUESTION 46

Your organization needs to securely manage and store cryptographic keys for its cloud-native applications running on Google Cloud. You want to choose a managed service that provides a Hardware Security Module (HSM) for key storage and management. Which Google Cloud service should you select for this key management requirement?

A) Google Cloud Identity and Access Management (IAM)
B) Google Cloud Key Management Service (KMS)
C) Google Cloud Security Command Center
D) Google Cloud Security Scanner

QUESTION 47

Your organization is implementing a disaster recovery plan for its Google Cloud resources. You want to ensure that your data is backed up regularly and can be restored quickly in case of a disaster. Which Google Cloud service can help you achieve this goal for your virtual machines?

A) Use Google Cloud Monitoring and Alerting for disaster recovery.
B) Implement Google Cloud Resource Manager for automated backup and restore.
C) Leverage Google Cloud Backup for virtual machine backups.
D) Set up regular snapshots using Google Cloud Compute Engine .

QUESTION 48

Your organization is planning to set up a disaster recovery (DR) solution for its Google Cloud resources. You want to ensure minimal data loss and rapid recovery in case of a disaster. Which GCP service can help you achieve this objective effectively?

A) Use Google Cloud VPN for secure communication between on-premises and Google Cloud resources.
B) Implement Google Cloud Interconnect for low-latency and high-bandwidth connectivity.
C) Set up Google Cloud Storage for offsite backups and data archiving.
D) Deploy Google Cloud's Disaster Recovery (DR) service for automated replication and failover.

QUESTION 49

Your team is responsible for implementing a scalable and reliable database solution for a new social media application. Cloud Spanner has been chosen for this purpose. What is the first step you should take in your GCP project to begin this implementation?

A) Assign Cloud Spanner Database Admin roles to your team members.
B) Enable the Cloud Spanner API in your GCP project.
C) Purchase additional quota for Cloud Spanner operations.
D) Start by designing the database tables and relationships in Cloud Spanner.

QUESTION 50

In your company's shift to using Cloud Identity, you find that some team members have personal Google Accounts using their work email addresses. What is the recommended method to handle this situation without disrupting their access to Google services?

A) Instruct the team members to manually migrate their data to newly created Cloud Identity accounts.
B) Request the team members to relinquish their personal Google Accounts in favor of company-provided accounts.
C) Use the administrative tools provided by Google to send invitations to users for transferring their personal accounts to Cloud Identity.
D) Allow team members to continue using their personal Google Accounts alongside their new Cloud Identity accounts.
E) Automatically delete the personal Google Accounts and replace them with Cloud Identity accounts.

SET 5 - ANSWERS ONLY

QUESTION 1

Answer - A) Cloud Pub/Sub, Dataflow, and BigQuery

A) Correct, Cloud Pub/Sub for real-time data ingestion, Dataflow for processing, and BigQuery for analysis provide a scalable, efficient solution for real-time data.
B) Incorrect, Bigtable is not the best choice for real-time data ingestion, and periodic batch processing may not provide timely insights.
C) Incorrect, while Compute Engine and Cloud Functions are viable, they may not offer the scalability and efficiency required for real-time processing.
D) Incorrect, Cloud IoT Core is ideal for device management but using Dataproc for real-time processing is less efficient compared to Dataflow.
E) Incorrect, Cloud SQL is not designed for high-volume real-time data ingestion, and this approach might not be scalable for real-time analysis.

QUESTION 2

Answer - A) Dataflow and BigQuery

A) Correct, Dataflow can process real-time streaming data, and BigQuery is ideal for real-time analytics.
B) Incorrect, Pub/Sub is for messaging, and Datastore is a NoSQL database, not specifically for real-time analytics.
C) Incorrect, Bigtable is for large-scale data storage, and Cloud Functions is a serverless execution environment but not specifically for real-time analytics.
D) Incorrect, Dataflow is suitable for data processing, but Cloud SQL is a relational database service and might not be optimal for real-time analytics.
E) Incorrect, BigQuery is for analytics, but Cloud Storage is for storing large amounts of unstructured data.
F) Incorrect, Dataproc is for running big data workloads, and Firestore is a NoSQL database, not specifically for real-time analytics.

QUESTION 3

Answer - A) Separate VPCs and VPC peering

A) Correct, separate VPCs for each application with VPC peering to a shared VPC for the database ensures isolation and secure communication.
B) Incorrect, using network tags in a single VPC may not provide the required isolation level.
C) Incorrect, Shared VPC is more suited for scenarios where multiple teams need access to common resources, not for complete application isolation.
D) Incorrect, separate subnets within a single VPC offer some isolation but may not be sufficient for complete application separation.
E) Incorrect, setting up VPN tunnels is more complex and may not be necessary for communication within GCP's network.

QUESTION 4

Answer - B) Cloud Spanner with multi-regional configuration

A) Incorrect, Cloud SQL with read replicas provides read scaling but not low-latency writes across multiple regions.
B) Correct, Cloud Spanner's multi-regional configuration offers global data distribution and low-latency read-write access, suitable for highly available applications.
C) Incorrect, managing a self-hosted MySQL database on VMs introduces complexity and may not achieve the desired low-latency multi-region access.
D) Incorrect, Cloud Bigtable is a NoSQL database and may not be suitable for applications requiring a relational database model.
E) Incorrect, Firestore in Datastore mode is primarily for NoSQL use cases and does not provide the same relational database features as Spanner.

QUESTION 5

Answer - A) App Engine with automatic scaling

A) Correct, App Engine standard environment provides automatic scaling which is cost-effective for variable traffic patterns, and can connect to Cloud SQL easily.
B) Incorrect, using custom machine types and manual scaling in Compute Engine is less efficient and cost-effective compared to App Engine.
C) Incorrect, while GKE offers scalability, it might be more complex and costly for this use case compared to App Engine.
D) Incorrect, Cloud Functions are ideal for event-driven applications but may not offer the same level of control or performance as App Engine for web applications.
E) Incorrect, managed instance groups provide scalability but App Engine offers a more integrated and cost-effective solution for this scenario.

QUESTION 6

Answer - B) Separate datasets with IAM roles

A) Incorrect, row-level security is complex and may not be necessary if data can be segregated at the dataset level.
B) Correct, creating separate datasets for each team and assigning appropriate IAM roles is an effective way to ensure data access segregation.
C) Incorrect, VPC Service Controls provide network-level isolation and are not specifically for data access control within BigQuery.
D) Incorrect, labels help in resource management but do not provide the level of access control needed for data segregation.
E) Incorrect, using different encryption keys for data access control is overly complex and not as straightforward as separate datasets with IAM roles.

QUESTION 7

Answer - B) roles/monitoring.viewer at the organization level

A) Incorrect, roles/viewer might provide access to view content within the resources.

B) Correct, roles/monitoring.viewer at the organization level allows viewing of resource usage and costs without access to the content within the resources.
C) Incorrect, roles/billing.viewer at the project level is too restrictive and focused only on billing.
D) Incorrect, roles/resourcemanager.folderViewer is limited to viewing folders, not resource usage and costs.
E) Incorrect, roles/cloudasset.viewer provides a broader scope of access than required for just viewing resource usage and costs.

QUESTION 8

Answer - A) Cloud Monitoring with uptime checks

A) Correct, Cloud Monitoring provides uptime checks and dashboards for monitoring the health and uptime of Compute Engine instances across projects.
B) Incorrect, implementing custom scripts is less efficient and scalable than using Cloud Monitoring.
C) Incorrect, relying solely on automatic email alerts is not proactive and lacks the granularity of Cloud Monitoring.
D) Incorrect, the metadata server is not intended for monitoring uptime and health of instances.
E) Incorrect, Cloud Trace is more focused on application performance analysis rather than instance uptime monitoring.

QUESTION 9

Answer - B) Budget in Cloud Billing for Cloud Storage

A) Incorrect, Cloud Monitoring alerts are more focused on operational metrics than billing thresholds.
B) Correct, creating a budget in Cloud Billing for Cloud Storage usage is the most direct way to monitor and receive notifications for usage limits.
C) Incorrect, using a Cloud Function for this purpose is more complex and not necessary.
D) Incorrect, Object Lifecycle Management is for managing object storage, not for monitoring usage costs.
E) Incorrect, Cloud Pub/Sub notifications are not designed to monitor usage costs directly.

QUESTION 10

Answer – A) Identity-Aware Proxy and Cloud IAM

A) Identity-Aware Proxy (IAP) and Cloud IAM provide robust access control and identity management, ensuring only authorized users access sensitive data.
B) VPC Service Controls and Cloud Endpoints are more about securing network boundaries and API management.
C) Cloud Armor and DLP are focused on external threats and data protection but do not directly manage access control.
D) Cloud Audit Logs and Security Scanner are for monitoring and vulnerability scanning, not direct access control.
E) Kubernetes Network Policies manage network access within clusters, not user access to data.
F) Cloud IAM is essential for access control, but KMS is more about encryption key management rather than access control.

QUESTION 11

Answer - C) Implement organization-level IAM policies for monitoring access.

A) Creates unnecessary complexity and user management overhead.
B) Service accounts are not primarily for user access management.
C) Correct, allows streamlined and secure access management at the organization level.
D) Too restrictive and not practical for teams needing access to monitoring data.

QUESTION 12

Answer - A) Use Cloud IoT Core to manage device connections and Pub/Sub for real-time data ingestion, combined with Dataflow for stream processing and analysis.

A) Correct. Cloud IoT Core, Pub/Sub, and Dataflow provide a robust, scalable, and efficient solution for real-time IoT data management and analysis.
B) Cloud Spanner is powerful but may not be the most straightforward solution for real-time data ingestion from IoT devices.
C) Compute Engine VMs would require extensive setup and management, not optimal for real-time data ingestion.
D) Cloud Storage is not designed for real-time data ingestion and processing, and this approach would introduce delays.

QUESTION 13

Answer - A) Provision a new GCP project and set up the AI Platform environment to mirror the development setup, then deploy the ML model.

A) Correctly follows organizational standards for operational separation and risk mitigation by establishing a new project for the production environment.
B) Does not meet the standard of having separate projects for development and production.
C) There is no specific AI Platform cloning tool that facilitates this process.
D) This approach does not conform to the requirement of having separate projects and may not leverage the full capabilities of AI Platform.

QUESTION 14

Answer - C) Assign the 'spanner.databaseUser' role to a new service account for the specific Spanner database.

C) This option correctly follows the principle of least privilege by assigning the necessary role to a new service account for the specific task, enhancing security and compliance.
A) The default service account should not be used for specific service interactions.
B) The 'spanner.databaseAdmin' role is more permissive than necessary for querying and writing data.
D) Granting project owner access is overly broad and against best practices for specific service interactions.

QUESTION 15

Answer - A) Cloud SQL Admin

A) Cloud SQL Admin role is the most appropriate as it specifically provides the necessary permissions for managing Cloud SQL instances, including creation and configuration, without extending beyond the scope of Cloud SQL.
B) Cloud SQL Editor is not a predefined role in GCP.
C) Project Editor provides broader access than required for managing Cloud SQL instances.
D) Database Admin is more relevant to database management within instances rather than the instances themselves.

QUESTION 16

Answer - B) Google Cloud Key Management Service (KMS)

Option B: This is the correct choice as Google Cloud KMS allows you to manage encryption keys for both at-rest and in-transit data encryption in Google Cloud Storage.
Option A: Google Cloud Storage encryption alone doesn't handle both at-rest and in-transit encryption.
Option C: Google Cloud IAP is for identity-based access control, not encryption.
Option D: Google Cloud Armor is a security service for DDoS protection, not encryption.

QUESTION 17

Answer - C) Google Cloud BigQuery

Option C: This is the correct choice as Google Cloud BigQuery is a fully managed, serverless data warehouse that is designed for running complex analytical queries on large datasets with high performance.
Option A: Google Cloud Bigtable is a NoSQL database and may not be suitable for complex analytical queries.
Option B: Google Cloud Datastore is a NoSQL database and may not provide the performance needed for analytical workloads.
Option D: Google Cloud Pub/Sub is a messaging service, not for data analytics.

QUESTION 18

Answer - A) Google Cloud IAM (Identity and Access Management).

Option A is the correct choice as Google Cloud IAM provides centralized access control and policy enforcement across all Google Cloud services, allowing you to define and manage access policies.
Option B focuses on user identity management, Option C is for threat detection, and Option D is for encryption key management.

QUESTION 19

Answer - D) Google Cloud Deployment Manager for infrastructure as code (IaC).

Option D is the correct choice because Google Cloud Deployment Manager allows you to define and deploy resources as code, making it a suitable choice for implementing a disaster recovery strategy to quickly restore infrastructure and services in case of a disaster. Options A, B, and C are not primarily designed for disaster recovery purposes.

QUESTION 20

Answer - C) Construct a new GCP project and replicate the App Engine application in an East Asian region.

C) Since App Engine applications are bound to the region they were first deployed in, the appropriate method is to create a new GCP project and replicate the application in the desired East Asian region.
 A) App Engine applications cannot be transferred to a different region once deployed.
 B) You cannot deploy multiple instances of an App Engine application in different regions within the same project.
 D) A Global Load Balancer does not address the issue of the original App Engine application's regional hosting constraints.

QUESTION 21

Answer - C) Implement GKE's Node Auto-Upgrades feature to ensure Kubernetes versions are always current.

C) Node Auto-Upgrades is the best practice to maintain up-to-date Kubernetes versions on GKE nodes, ensuring compliance with security standards without manual intervention.
 A) GKE requires specific configuration for updates, not just pulling and installing.
 B) Manual updates of the control plane can lead to inconsistencies and delays.
 D) Relying on a manual process for updates is less reliable and more labor-intensive compared to GKE's automated features.

QUESTION 22

Answer - B) Store the password in a Kubernetes Secret and reference this Secret in the deployment YAML.

B) Storing sensitive data like passwords in Kubernetes Secrets and referencing them in deployments is a secure and recommended practice. Secrets ensure that sensitive data is not exposed in plain text and is managed properly.
 A) Base64 encoding is not encryption and does not secure the password.
 C) ConfigMaps are not intended for sensitive data.
 D) Storing sensitive information on disk can be less secure and is less manageable than using Secrets.

QUESTION 23

Answer - C) Set the Content-Type metadata of each PDF to 'application/pdf'.

C) Setting the Content-Type metadata of PDF files to 'application/pdf' ensures that web browsers recognize the file type and display it inline, rather than prompting a download. This provides a smoother experience for users accessing the promotional materials.
 A) Public sharing makes the file accessible but does not control how it is displayed.
 B) While Content-Disposition can affect display, setting Content-Type to 'application/pdf' is more directly relevant to PDF viewing in browsers.
 D) The bucket's public access doesn't influence how files within it are displayed.

QUESTION 24

Answer - D) Utilize preemptible Compute Engine VMs for the batch processing.

D) Preemptible VMs offer a highly cost-effective solution for running interruptible, compute-heavy batch jobs, providing significant savings while meeting the job requirements.
A) A persistent VM leads to higher costs due to continuous resource usage.
B) GKE might be overkill for simple batch jobs and can be more expensive.
C) Cloud Functions are not designed for long-running, compute-intensive tasks.
E) Dataproc provides big data processing capabilities but may be more costly for simple batch jobs.
F) Cloud Run is optimized for stateless, scalable web applications, not batch processing.

QUESTION 25

Answer - B) Enable 'Automatic Restart' and set 'On-host maintenance' to 'Migrate VM instance' in the VM settings.

B) Enabling 'Automatic Restart' ensures that VMs recover from crashes, while setting 'On-host maintenance' to 'Migrate VM instance' guarantees continuous operation during maintenance, meeting the high availability requirement for the stock market application.
A) Preemptible VMs are not appropriate for high-availability scenarios.
C) Managed instance groups are useful but don't address specific VM settings for maintenance and recovery.
D) Deploying in multiple regions adds redundancy but doesn't specify maintenance and restart policies.
E) Disabling 'Automatic Restart' and setting maintenance to 'Terminate' contradicts high availability needs.
F) Custom machine types offer flexibility but don't inherently provide high availability.

QUESTION 26

Answer - C) Enable Cloud Storage Data Access audit logs in the Cloud Audit Logs.

C) Enabling Data Access audit logs for Cloud Storage in Cloud Audit Logs is the most direct and effective way to log every read request, ensuring compliance with the audit requirement.
A) Stackdriver provides monitoring, but its logs are not specific enough for detailed access logging.
B) IAM audit logging tracks changes to access policies, not individual data access events.
D) DLP is focused on discovering and protecting sensitive data, not on access logging.
E) Access Transparency logs are typically for Google's operations, not user access.
F) Endpoint Security monitors network security, not specific access to storage data.

QUESTION 27

Answer - D) Change the billing account associated with the project to your company's GCP billing account.

D) Changing the billing account for the project to the company's GCP billing account is the most straightforward solution. This adjustment ensures that all future project costs are billed directly to the company, aligning with their request for streamlined billing.
A) Generating cost reports is useful for analysis but doesn't change the billing process.
B) Assigning a role in billing administration helps manage the account but doesn't change who is billed.

C) Switching payment methods on a personal account doesn't transition the billing account.
E) Directly changing the billing account in GCP is more efficient than contacting customer service.
F) Continuing reimbursement is not in line with the company's request to streamline billing.

QUESTION 28

Answer - C) Global HTTP(S) Load Balancer

Option C - Global HTTP(S) Load Balancer can distribute traffic across multiple regions, providing high availability and redundancy.
Option A - Google Cloud CDN is a content delivery network, not a load balancer.
Option B - Google Cloud Storage is for object storage.
Option D - Google Kubernetes Engine (GKE) is a container orchestration platform, and
Option E - Google Cloud VPN is a virtual private network service.

QUESTION 29

Answer - C) Google Cloud Recommender

Option C - Google Cloud Recommender analyzes historical usage patterns and recommends appropriate resource configurations, helping you optimize costs and performance.
Option A - Google Cloud Monitoring is for monitoring and alerting, not resource recommendations.
Option B - Google Cloud Profiler is used for application profiling.
Option D - Google Cloud Security Scanner is for security scanning, and
Option E - Google Cloud Debugger is for debugging applications.

QUESTION 30

Answer - C) Set up a Cloud DNS private zone to resolve the on-premises database hostname.

C) A Cloud DNS private zone for the on-premises database allows for dynamic resolution of the database IP address using a hostname. When the database IP changes, you only need to update the DNS record in the private zone, and all applications will automatically connect to the new address without requiring configuration changes.
A) Network peering facilitates connectivity but doesn't manage dynamic IP addresses.
B) DNS forwarding is for outbound DNS queries, not for managing specific IPs.
D) A dedicated Compute Engine instance adds unnecessary complexity to the architecture.
E) Custom scripts are less efficient and reliable compared to DNS management.
F) A proxy server adds another layer but doesn't address dynamic IP management.

QUESTION 31

Answer - B) Have the partner create a Service Account in their project and assign access to your datasets.

B) This method is secure and effective for collaboration. The partner creating a Service Account in their own project allows them to manage their access credentials, while you can grant them specific permissions to access only the necessary datasets in your BigQuery. This approach maintains security and control over data access.
A) Granting IAM roles to another project can be less secure and might provide broader access than

necessary.
C) Sharing credentials is not secure and could compromise your project's integrity.
D) BigQuery's data sharing is an option but Service Accounts offer more precise control.
E) Creating a joint project adds complexity and might not be required for dataset access.
F) Data replication could lead to data redundancy and additional costs.

QUESTION 32

Answer - C) Create a new revision of your service with the update and adjust the traffic split to test with specific users.

C) The most straightforward and effective way to roll out an update to a subset of users is to create a new revision of the existing Cloud Run service and then use the platform's traffic splitting feature. This allows for a controlled, gradual rollout to a specified percentage of users, enabling you to gather valuable feedback and ensure stability before the full deployment.
A) HTTP routing rules are less precise than Cloud Run's built-in traffic splitting capabilities.
B) Launching on a separate domain does not provide the same control and can lead to inconsistency.
D) Custom scripts are less reliable and harder to manage compared to Cloud Run's native features.
E) Cloud Functions are not designed for traffic management between application versions.
F) Third-party A/B testing tools are unnecessary given Cloud Run's native traffic splitting feature.

QUESTION 33

Answer - A) Configure a Cloud Function to trigger on Cloud Storage events and run the Python function.

A) The most efficient and direct approach is to use Cloud Functions, as they offer built-in integration with Cloud Storage for event-driven triggers. By configuring a Cloud Function to trigger on new object uploads in the Cloud Storage bucket, the Python function will automatically execute each time a new object is added, ensuring immediate and seamless processing.
B) Cloud Run is a possible solution but requires more configuration than Cloud Functions for this specific task.
C) A Compute Engine VM with a polling script is less efficient and not real-time.
D) Dataflow is more complex and suited for large-scale data processing tasks.
E) App Engine requires constant monitoring and is less efficient for event-driven execution.
F) Cloud Scheduler is not designed for real-time, event-driven tasks like new file uploads.

QUESTION 34

Answer – A) Kubernetes Engine, Stackdriver, Blue-Green Deployment

A) Correct, refactoring into microservices and deploying on Kubernetes Engine with Stackdriver ensures scalability, high availability, and smooth migration with blue-green deployment.
B) Incorrect, migrating as-is to Compute Engine may not fully leverage cloud-native features and may not provide the required scalability.
C) Incorrect, while App Engine offers scalability, replatforming may not fully address the high availability and integration requirements.
D) Incorrect, Cloud Run is great for containerized apps but may not suit a large monolithic application without refactoring.
E) Incorrect, breaking down into serverless functions is a significant change and may not be feasible or

necessary for the legacy application.

QUESTION 35

Answer – A) Data Access Logs, Cloud Logging, Cloud Monitoring

A) Correct, Data Access Logs provide detailed access information, Cloud Logging for analysis, and Cloud Monitoring for immediate alerts.
B) Incorrect, IAM and Cloud Identity manage access but do not provide detailed tracking and alerting.
C) Incorrect, Access Transparency is for Google's operations, not user access.
D) Incorrect, VPC Service Controls add a layer of security but don't specifically track and report access.
E) Incorrect, a custom application is not as integrated or efficient as using native GCP services.

QUESTION 36

Answer – B) gcloud auth activate-service-account

A) Incorrect, embedding the key in the script is insecure.
B) Correct, this will authenticate the gcloud commands in your script using the provided service account.
C) Incorrect, setting as an environment variable is not the recommended approach for scripts.
D) Incorrect, storing keys in Cloud Storage is not secure.
E) Incorrect, encoding the key does not change the security implications of embedding it in the script.

QUESTION 37

Answer - E) Google Cloud Monitoring and Alerting (Correct)

Option A is incorrect because Cloud Spanner provides high availability but does not directly offer automated cross-region failover.
Option B is incorrect because Cloud Storage is an object storage service and not a DR solution.
Option C is incorrect because Cloud VPN is a network connectivity service, not a DR tool.
Option D is incorrect because Cloud Pub/Sub is a messaging service, not a DR solution.
Option E is correct because Google Cloud Monitoring and Alerting can be used to set up automated alerts and actions for cross-region failover and recovery in case of application failures.

QUESTION 38

Answer - C) Use Google Cloud Deployment Manager to define and automate resource deployment across regions for cross-region failover. (Correct)

Option A is incorrect because while Memorystore can be used for caching, it does not provide automated cross-region failover capabilities.
Option B is incorrect because Google Cloud VPN is for network connectivity and data replication but does not offer automated resource deployment and cross-region failover.
Option D is incorrect because Google Cloud Functions are for event-driven functions and may not be the best choice for automated disaster recovery.
Option E is incorrect because Google Cloud IAM is related to access control and not automated disaster

recovery planning.
Option C is correct because Google Cloud Deployment Manager allows you to define and automate the deployment and management of resources across regions, enabling automated cross-region failover and recovery in case of application failures or regional outages.

QUESTION 39

Answer - C) Utilize Google Cloud Cost Explorer for cost optimization and resource usage analysis. (Correct)

Option A is incorrect because Google Cloud Billing Reports are primarily for billing and invoice management, not for in-depth cost optimization and resource usage analysis.
Option B is incorrect because Google Cloud Monitoring provides real-time monitoring and alerting capabilities but does not specialize in cost optimization analysis.
Option D is incorrect because Google Cloud Security Command Center focuses on security-related aspects and does not directly address cost management and resource usage analysis.
Option E is incorrect because Google Cloud Audit Logging is designed for audit trails and compliance, not for cost reduction and resource tracking.
Option C is correct because Google Cloud Cost Explorer is a tool that allows you to analyze your Google Cloud spending, identify cost-saving opportunities, and gain insights into resource usage, making it a suitable choice for cost optimization and resource analysis in a GCP project.

QUESTION 40

Answer - D) Use service accounts to grant permissions to each VM instance. (Correct)

Option A is incorrect because assigning the same service account to all VMs may not allow for granular access control to specific Google Cloud APIs.
Option B is incorrect because using instance metadata to define API access is not a recommended method for access control and does not provide granularity.
Option C is incorrect because creating a custom IAM role for each VM instance can become cumbersome to manage and may not provide the necessary flexibility.
Using service accounts allows you to assign specific roles and permissions to each VM instance, ensuring fine-grained access control to Google Cloud APIs.

QUESTION 41

Answer - C) Google Cloud Cost Explorer

Option A, Google Cloud Billing Reports, primarily deals with billing and invoice management, not in-depth cost optimization and resource usage analysis. Option B, Google Cloud Monitoring, provides real-time monitoring and alerting but does not specialize in cost optimization analysis. Option D, Google Cloud Security Command Center, focuses on security-related aspects and does not directly address cost management and resource usage analysis. Option C, Google Cloud Cost Explorer, allows you to analyze Google Cloud spending, identify cost-saving opportunities, and gain insights into resource usage, making it a suitable choice for cost optimization and resource analysis in a GCP project.

QUESTION 42

Answer - D) Google Cloud Identity-Aware Proxy (IAP)

Option D suggests using Google Cloud Identity-Aware Proxy (IAP), which provides identity management and access control across different cloud environments, helping to achieve consistency.
 Option A (Google Cloud IAM) is for managing access within Google Cloud, not for multi-cloud identity management.
 Option B (Google Cloud Identity Platform) is focused on user identity and access within Google Cloud.
 Option C (Google Cloud Directory Sync) synchronizes on-premises directory services with Google Cloud Directory, not multi-cloud identity management.

QUESTION 43

Answer - D) Configure dual-regional storage with standard storage class for the dual region closest to the users.

Option A is incorrect because regional storage with nearline storage class may not provide the necessary performance for users in Bangalore.
Option B is incorrect because regional storage with standard storage class may not consider the proximity of users and could lead to latency issues.
Option C is incorrect because configuring dual-regional storage with nearline storage class may not strike the right balance between cost and performance for users in Bangalore.

QUESTION 44

Answer - C) Regional Clusters

Option C is correct because Regional Clusters in Google Kubernetes Engine (GKE) distribute the cluster control plane and nodes across multiple zones within a region. This configuration enhances high availability and fault tolerance.
Option A (Node Pools) allows you to create pools of nodes but does not inherently provide multi-zone distribution.
Option B (Cluster Autoscaler) automatically adjusts the size of your cluster but is not related to multi-zone distribution.
Option D (Istio Service Mesh) is a service mesh tool and not a GKE feature for multi-zone distribution.

QUESTION 45

Answer - B) Google Cloud VPN

Option B is correct because Google Cloud VPN (Virtual Private Network) allows you to establish a secure and encrypted network connection between your on-premises data center and Google Cloud resources, ensuring data privacy over the network.
Option A (Google Cloud Load Balancing) is for traffic distribution and does not provide network encryption.
Option C (Google Cloud Interconnect) provides dedicated connections but may not inherently encrypt data over the network.
Option D (Google Cloud IAM) is for access control and is not related to network encryption.

QUESTION 46

Answer - B) Google Cloud Key Management Service (KMS)

Option B is correct because Google Cloud Key Management Service (KMS) provides a managed HSM for secure key storage and management, making it suitable for cryptographic key management.
Option A (Google Cloud IAM) is for access control and not a key management service.
Option C (Google Cloud Security Command Center) is for security monitoring and incident response.
Option D (Google Cloud Security Scanner) is a security scanning tool and not a key management service.

QUESTION 47

Answer - D) Set up regular snapshots using Google Cloud Compute Engine

Option D is correct because Google Cloud Compute Engine allows you to create and manage regular snapshots of virtual machine disks, ensuring that your data is backed up regularly and can be restored quickly in case of a disaster.
Option A and B are not focused on virtual machine backups and disaster recovery but rather on monitoring and resource management.
Option C is not a recognized Google Cloud service for virtual machine backups.

QUESTION 48

Answer - D) Deploy Google Cloud's Disaster Recovery (DR) service for automated replication and failover

Option D is correct because Google Cloud's Disaster Recovery (DR) service is specifically designed for setting up a disaster recovery solution with minimal data loss and rapid recovery. It provides automated replication and failover capabilities for critical resources.
Option A and B focus on network connectivity and do not address data replication or recovery.
Option C is related to data storage but does not provide automated disaster recovery capabilities.

QUESTION 49

Answer – B) Enable the Cloud Spanner API

A) Incorrect, assigning roles is not the first step.
B) Correct, enabling the Cloud Spanner API is the necessary first step.
C) Incorrect, purchasing additional quota is not the initial action required.
D) Incorrect, designing database tables is a step after the initial setup.

QUESTION 50

Answer – C) Administrative tools, transfer invitations

A) Incorrect, manual data migration is not user-friendly and prone to data loss.
B) Incorrect, relinquishing personal accounts is not necessary and can lead to data loss.
C) Correct, using administrative tools to manage account transfers is efficient and minimizes disruption.
D) Incorrect, continuing to use both accounts does not resolve the conflict.
E) Incorrect, automatic deletion of accounts can result in data loss and user dissatisfaction.

SET 6 - QUESTIONS ONLY

QUESTION 1

Your company is running a high-traffic web application on GKE with multiple pods on n1-standard-4 nodes. A new service requiring AI capabilities is to be deployed on n2-highcpu-8 nodes, without impacting the live application. What steps should you take?

A) Modify the existing node pool to change the machine type to n2-highcpu-8 and redeploy all services.
B) Create a Node Pool for n2-highcpu-8, enable node auto-provisioning on the existing cluster, and deploy the new service.
C) Instantiate a separate GKE cluster with n2-highcpu-8 nodes, migrate all services to this new cluster, and decommission the old cluster.
D) Add a new Node Pool with n2-highcpu-8 nodes to the existing cluster, then use node selectors to deploy the new service on the appropriate nodes.
E) Use Vertical Pod Autoscaler on existing pods to accommodate the new service requirements on the n1-standard-4 nodes.
F) Implement a combination of Horizontal Pod Autoscaling and Cluster Autoscaler on the existing setup without adding new node types.

QUESTION 2

You are a cloud engineer at a media streaming company. Your video processing application is hosted on Compute Engine VMs in the europe-west1-b zone. You need to ensure high availability and load balancing with minimal additional cost. What approach would you recommend?

A) Deploy additional VMs in the europe-west1-c zone and use a regional HTTP(S) Load Balancer.
B) Create a single Managed Instance Group in europe-west1-b and enable autoscaling based on CPU utilization.
C) Migrate the application to Kubernetes Engine in europe-west1-b for better container management and scalability.
D) Implement a multi-zonal Kubernetes Engine cluster spanning europe-west1-b and europe-west1-c zones.
E) Set up a Cloud CDN for content delivery and deploy a network load balancer for traffic distribution.

QUESTION 3

You are overseeing the security infrastructure for a large e-commerce platform hosted on GCP. The platform utilizes several APIs and microservices, each requiring different API keys and credentials. What is the best practice for managing and rotating these credentials while ensuring minimal disruption to the services?

A) Store all API keys and credentials in a centralized Cloud SQL database with restricted access.
B) Utilize Secret Manager to store and manage the API keys and credentials, enabling automatic rotation where applicable.
C) Keep the credentials in a secure on-premises server and set up a VPN tunnel for services to access them.
D) Embed the credentials within the application code and use a private Git repository for version control

and access management.
E) Use Cloud Storage buckets with customer-managed encryption keys to store the credentials and share them with services.

QUESTION 4

You are optimizing the costs for a data processing job on GCP that can tolerate occasional interruptions. The job requires high computational resources for a limited duration each day. What strategy would you implement to minimize costs while meeting the job's requirements?

A) Use Compute Engine N1 standard VMs with committed use discounts.
B) Implement a managed instance group with autoscaling based on CPU utilization.
C) Deploy the job on preemptible VMs in a managed instance group.
D) Utilize Cloud Functions for on-demand data processing needs.
E) Schedule the job on regular N2 high-CPU VMs with scheduling for specific time windows.

QUESTION 5

Your multinational corporation is using Active Directory for managing user accounts and now wants to integrate these accounts with GCP services for unified access management. What is the most efficient way to synchronize your Active Directory accounts with GCP?

A) Manually create matching accounts in GCP for each Active Directory account.
B) Use Google Cloud Directory Sync (GCDS) to synchronize Active Directory accounts with GCP.
C) Implement a custom synchronization tool using Cloud Functions and Cloud Identity APIs.
D) Set up a VPN tunnel between your on-premises network and GCP, and extend Active Directory to GCP.
E) Export users from Active Directory to a CSV file and import them into GCP manually.

QUESTION 6

You are developing a web application on Ubuntu that integrates with various GCP services. To test your application's integration with Cloud Pub/Sub locally, what steps should you follow?

A) Use the gcloud pubsub topics create command to create topics for local testing.
B) Configure your application to connect to actual Cloud Pub/Sub resources in GCP for testing.
C) Install and use the Pub/Sub emulator available in the Google Cloud SDK.
D) Deploy a minimal version of your application to GCP to test Pub/Sub integration.
E) Set up a local MQTT broker to simulate Cloud Pub/Sub behavior.

QUESTION 7

As the head of data and security, you need to integrate your organization's Active Directory with GCP for user authentication and management. Which GCP service should you use to establish this integration for Single Sign-On (SSO)?

A) Use Cloud Identity to set up SSO with Active Directory as the identity provider.
B) Configure Cloud Directory Sync to synchronize Active Directory users with GCP.
C) Implement Cloud IAM custom roles for Active Directory users.

D) Set up Cloud VPN to connect Active Directory with GCP for user authentication.
E) Use Cloud Endpoints to create an interface between Active Directory and GCP services.

QUESTION 8

As a startup owner, you need to delegate the management of IAM policies across your GCP projects without granting overly broad permissions. Which role should you assign to the person responsible for this task?

A) roles/iam.securityAdmin
B) roles/owner
C) roles/resourcemanager.projectIamAdmin
D) roles/editor
E) roles/iam.roleAdmin

QUESTION 9

You are tasked with setting up a scalable and secure web application in GCP. The application requires both SQL and NoSQL databases and must automatically scale in response to traffic spikes. The solution should also incorporate effective load balancing and be resilient to single-zone failures. Given these requirements, which combination of GCP services and configurations would be most suitable?

A) Deploy Compute Engine instances with manual scaling, use Cloud SQL for SQL database, and Cloud Bigtable for NoSQL database. Implement Network Load Balancing and deploy instances in a single zone.
B) Utilize App Engine with automatic scaling, Cloud Spanner for both SQL and NoSQL requirements, and HTTP(S) Load Balancing. Ensure multi-regional deployment.
C) Configure Compute Engine instances with automatic scaling, use Cloud SQL and Firestore for databases, employ HTTP(S) Load Balancing, and distribute instances across multiple zones.
D) Implement Kubernetes Engine for containerized applications, Cloud SQL for SQL database, and Datastore for NoSQL database. Use TCP/UDP Network Load Balancing and deploy in a single region.
E) Use Cloud Functions for compute, Firestore for NoSQL database, and MemoryStore for SQL caching. Implement Internal Load Balancing and distribute functions across multiple regions.

QUESTION 10

You are implementing a data archival strategy using GCP Cloud Storage. Your requirement is to store data in a Nearline storage class for 30 days, then move it to Coldline for 365 days, and finally delete it. How should you configure the Object Lifecycle Management policy?

A) SetStorageClass to Coldline at 30 days, then Delete at 395 days.
B) SetStorageClass to Coldline at 30 days, then Delete at 365 days.
C) SetStorageClass to Nearline at 30 days, then Delete at 365 days.
D) SetStorageClass to Nearline at 30 days, then to Coldline at 365 days, and Delete at 395 days.

QUESTION 11

You are managing a suite of applications on GCP, spread across multiple projects. Your task involves setting up a CI/CD pipeline for a new service requiring access to Cloud SQL and Cloud Storage and automatic deployment to a managed Kubernetes cluster in GCP. Considering the need for security and efficiency, which approach is most appropriate?

A) Create a Cloud Build trigger and use Cloud Build for the CI/CD process, ensuring IAM roles for Cloud Build service account are properly configured for necessary access. Set up deployment to GKE using kubectl commands in the build steps.
B) Use a third-party CI/CD tool, manually manage service account keys for access to GCP resources, and script the deployment process to GKE using external tools.
C) Implement Cloud Functions for CI/CD, manually trigger deployments, and use Cloud IAM for fine-grained access control to Cloud SQL and Cloud Storage.
D) Rely on manual deployment processes for each service update, using individual gcloud commands for resource management and kubectl for GKE deployment.

QUESTION 12

You are leading a project to develop a mobile app for managing smart home devices, including an air conditioner. The app needs to process and store real-time usage data for analysis and control. Considering the need for real-time data processing, storage, and analysis, which combination of Google Cloud Platform services is most suitable?

A) Cloud Pub/Sub for data ingestion, Firestore for storage, and Cloud Dataflow for data processing and analysis.
B) Cloud IoT Core for device management, Cloud Bigtable for time-series data storage, and BigQuery for data analysis.
C) Firebase Realtime Database for data ingestion and storage, and Dataflow combined with BigQuery for data analysis.
D) Cloud Pub/Sub for data ingestion, Cloud Storage for storing data, and Dataflow combined with BigQuery for data analysis.

QUESTION 13

Your organization's application processes sensitive customer data and needs periodic reviews by compliance officers. How should you configure IAM access in Cloud Storage to facilitate this requirement, adhering to Google's recommended practices?

A) Assign the compliance officers group the 'storage.objectViewer' and 'logging.viewer' predefined IAM roles.
B) Give individual compliance officer accounts the project owner role for necessary access.
C) Assign the compliance officers group the project viewer role.
D) Grant individual compliance officer accounts the 'storage.objectViewer' and 'logging.viewer' roles.

QUESTION 14

In your financial services organization, sensitive transaction records are stored in a Cloud Storage bucket. To comply with regulatory standards, you need to monitor and audit file deletion activities by specific users. What is the most efficient way to achieve this using Google Cloud's tools?

A) Review the deletion activities in the Cloud Storage Audit logs within the GCP console.
B) Utilize Stackdriver logging to filter and analyze deletion logs.
C) Check the Cloud Storage activity tab in the GCP console for user actions.

D) Set up a Cloud Monitoring alert for file deletion activities in the Cloud Storage bucket.

QUESTION 15

Your e-commerce application is hosted on a Compute Engine Managed Instance Group and requires a load balancing solution that supports both HTTP and HTTPS, with SSL offloading. What is the most suitable Google Cloud load balancing configuration for this requirement?

A) Deploy an HTTP(S) Load Balancer with SSL termination at the load balancer and forwarding rules to the instance group.
B) Use a TCP Proxy Load Balancer with SSL passthrough to the instance group for handling HTTPS traffic.
C) Implement an SSL Proxy Load Balancer to terminate SSL and forward traffic to the managed instance group.
D) Configure an Internal Load Balancer for internal traffic management and SSL termination at the instance level.

QUESTION 16

You are tasked with designing a highly available and globally distributed application on Google Cloud. The application needs to ensure low-latency access for users across the world. Which Google Cloud service should you consider to achieve this goal?

A) Google Cloud Storage
B) Google Cloud Datastore
C) Google Cloud CDN
D) Google Cloud Endpoints
E) Google Cloud Spanner

QUESTION 17

You are designing a network architecture for a cloud-based application that requires separate environments for development and production. These environments should have isolated subnets but need to communicate over the internal IP network. Which VPC configuration should you choose?

A) Create a single custom VPC with two subnets in the same region, each with different CIDR ranges.
B) Create two custom VPCs, one for development and one for production, each with a single subnet in the same region and different CIDR ranges.
C) Create a single custom VPC with two subnets in different regions, each with the same CIDR range.
D) Create two custom VPCs, one for development and one for production, each with a single subnet in different regions and the same CIDR range.

QUESTION 18

Your organization is planning to implement data archiving and backup strategies for its Google Cloud resources. Which GCP service should you consider for long-term data retention, seamless data retrieval, and cost-effective storage management?

A) Google Cloud Storage.
B) Google Cloud Dataprep.

C) Google Cloud Dataflow.
D) Google Cloud Memorystore.

QUESTION 19

In Google Cloud Platform (GCP), you want to design a highly available architecture for a web application. Which load balancing service can distribute traffic across multiple regions?

A) Global HTTP(S) Load Balancer
B) Regional HTTP(S) Load Balancer
C) External HTTP(S) Load Balancer
D) Network Load Balancer
E) Internal TCP/UDP Load Balancer
F) Network TCP/UDP Load Balancer

QUESTION 20

Your company's financial analytics application uses Cloud Spanner for database operations. A new analytics team requires both read and write access to specific Cloud Spanner instances. What is the recommended approach to grant this access in GCP?

A) Assign individual users the 'spanner.databaseUser' role directly.
B) Create a Google Group for the analytics team and assign the 'spanner.databaseUser' role to this group.
C) Grant the 'spanner.viewer' role to individual users for read access and manually manage write permissions.
D) Assign the 'spanner.admin' role to the new team for full administrative access.

QUESTION 21

Your healthcare startup has accumulated a significant amount of patient data over the past year. You need to back up this data to a Google Cloud Storage Standard Bucket, with a file size of 50 GB. You have a 500 Mbps dedicated internet connection. What is the most efficient method to upload this large file?

A) Upload the file directly using the GCP console for simplicity.
B) Enable parallel composite uploads using gsutil to maximize upload speed.
C) Increase the TCP window size on the machine performing the upload.
D) Change the storage class of the bucket to Coldline to expedite the upload process.

QUESTION 22

You are working on a project called 'data-analytics' and need to access BigQuery datasets stored in another project called 'data-storage'. Your security team has provided a specific service account from 'data-storage' for this purpose. How should you configure access?

A) Add the service account from 'data-storage' as a member in 'data-analytics' with BigQuery User role.
B) Use the private key of the service account from 'data-storage' to authenticate API requests from 'data-analytics'.
C) In 'data-storage', grant the service account the IAM role of BigQuery Data Viewer.

D) Set up a cross-project service account in 'data-analytics' to access resources in 'data-storage'.

QUESTION 23

In a GCP managed instance group for a web application, new instances take approximately 4 minutes to initialize but are added to the load balancer too soon, leading to temporary resource strain. How should you optimize the scaling process?

A) Decrease the CPU utilization threshold for scaling.
B) Increase the initial delay of the health check to 240 seconds.
C) Reduce the maximum number of instances.
D) Switch from HTTP to TCP health checks.
E) Extend the cooldown period between scaling actions.

QUESTION 24

You suspect that your recent App Engine deployment using gcloud app deploy may have targeted an unintended GCP project. What is the first step you should take to confirm which project the app was deployed to?

A) Check the app.yaml file for project-specific settings.
B) Inspect the web-application.xml file for deployment details.
C) Use the Deployment Manager to review recent deployment activities.
D) Run gcloud config list to view the active GCP project configuration.
E) Look at the App Engine dashboard in the GCP Console.
F) Review the recent activity logs in Cloud Logging.

QUESTION 25

Your website hosted on a Compute Engine instance is experiencing high traffic, leading to memory constraints. You decide to upgrade the instance from 4 GB to 8 GB of memory. What steps should you follow?

A) Perform a live migration to a machine type with more memory.
B) Update the instance's metadata to reflect the new memory requirement.
C) Stop the VM, change its machine type to one with 8 GB of memory, and start the VM.
D) Directly edit the VM settings in the GCP Console to increase memory without stopping the VM.
E) Create a snapshot of the VM, then restore it to a new instance with increased memory.
F) Use gcloud command-line tool to increase the memory while the VM is running.

QUESTION 26

How can you safeguard your critical Compute Engine instances in GCP from accidental deletion by team members, following an incident where an intern mistakenly deleted a production instance?

A) Implement a custom script using Cloud Functions to prevent instance deletion.
B) Activate the 'Delete Protection' feature on all production instances.
C) Restrict instance deletion permissions using Cloud IAM roles.
D) Regularly backup instances using snapshots to enable quick restoration.

E) Configure an alert in Stackdriver to notify before any instance is deleted.
F) Use Deployment Manager to control and log instance deletion actions.

QUESTION 27

In your multi-tenant accounting software, you need to ensure that users can upload invoices and access them for only 30 minutes, and the invoices should be automatically deleted after 45 days. What two actions should you take to implement these requirements?

A) Set up a cron job to delete invoices older than 45 days.
B) Use Cloud Storage lifecycle policies to automatically delete objects after 45 days.
C) Implement signed URLs for user uploads with a 30-minute expiration.
D) Create a separate Cloud Storage bucket for each user.
E) Utilize Cloud IAM to manage time-based access to invoice data.
F) Develop a custom application function to manage file deletion based on timestamps.

QUESTION 28

Your social media startup is growing rapidly, and you have decided to use Infrastructure as Code (IaC) to manage your GCP infrastructure. How can you minimize the amount of repetitive code required for managing the environment?

A) Use Cloud Deployment Manager to develop templates for environments
B) Send a REST request to the relevant Google API for each individual resource using curl in a terminal.
C) Provision and manage all related resources using the Google Cloud Console.
D) Write a bash script with all required steps using gcloud commands.

QUESTION 29

How can you ensure maximum egress control for a sensitive financial application hosted on a Compute Engine instance in a new VPC, allowing minimal egress traffic?

A) Create a default high-priority rule to block all egress traffic and specific low-priority rules to allow necessary ports.
B) Establish a single high-priority rule allowing only the necessary egress ports.
C) Implement a low-priority rule blocking all egress and high-priority rules for required ports.
D) Use network tags to specify egress rules for each service within the application.
E) Configure a Cloud NAT instance to manage and restrict egress traffic.
F) Apply a VPC Service Controls perimeter around the project to limit egress flows.

QUESTION 30

For an internal tool that needs to run only during specific hours and have zero running costs when not in use, which deployment option on Google Cloud Platform is most suitable?

A) Deploy the containerized application on Google Kubernetes Engine with a cron job to scale down to zero nodes.
B) Use Cloud Run (fully managed) with the minimum number of instances set to zero.
C) Set up the application on Compute Engine with a script to stop instances outside of work hours.

D) Deploy on App Engine Standard Environment with automatic scaling.
E) Utilize Cloud Functions triggered by a scheduler to start and stop the application.
F) Implement the tool on App Engine Flexible Environment with autoscaling.

QUESTION 31

What is the best way to manage permissions for a DevOps team needing access to multiple production services in GCP projects, ensuring minimal access rights are granted?

A) Assign the Project Editor role to the DevOps team for each production project.
B) Grant the DevOps team the Project Owner role at the organizational level.
C) Create a custom role with specific required permissions for each production project.
D) Use the Security Admin role for the DevOps team across all production projects.
E) Implement a policy that auto-assigns necessary roles to the DevOps team based on project labels.
F) Set up a shared VPC for centralized network management and access.

QUESTION 32

How can you minimize storage costs for a file-sharing app that stores files on Cloud Storage, with frequent access for 30 days and a 3-year retention period?

A) Use Standard storage for 30 days, then transfer files to Coldline storage for the remainder of the 3 years.
B) Store files in Nearline storage initially, then move to Archive storage for the remaining period.
C) Keep files in Standard storage for the first 30 days, then shift to Archive storage for the 3-year duration.
D) Utilize Nearline storage for 30 days, followed by Coldline for 1 year, and Archive for the final 2 years.
E) Implement a lifecycle policy to automatically shift files from Standard to Coldline after 30 days, then to Archive after 1 year.
F) Start with Coldline storage, and then move files to Archive storage after 30 days.

QUESTION 33

How can you set up a backend for a multiplayer mobile game on Google Cloud that uses UDP packets and requires a single IP address for horizontal scaling?

A) Implement an HTTP(S) Load Balancer in front of the game servers.
B) Deploy an Internal TCP/UDP Load Balancer for the backend servers.
C) Use an SSL Proxy Load Balancer to manage the game's traffic.
D) Configure an External Network Load Balancer for the UDP traffic.
E) Set up a Global UDP Proxy Load Balancer to distribute traffic.
F) Create a Cloud VPN tunnel to route all game traffic through a single IP.

QUESTION 34

Your organization has a large collection of historical financial data stored in an on-premise database. You need to migrate this data to GCP for analysis while ensuring it is stored cost-effectively for occasional access. How would you design this solution?

A) Migrate data to Cloud SQL and use federated queries with BigQuery for analysis.
B) Transfer data to Cloud Storage using Transfer Service and set lifecycle policies to move data to Nearline or Coldline storage.
C) Use Cloud Dataflow to stream data into BigQuery for real-time analysis and long-term storage.
D) Implement a Datastore to Cloud Storage pipeline using Dataflow, and schedule regular batch jobs for data synchronization.
E) Sync data to Cloud Storage using gsutil, and use Bigtable for analysis due to its high throughput for read/write operations.

QUESTION 35

Your organization is deploying a new web application on Compute Engine and needs to provide secure administrative access to external developers. The developers do not have Google accounts. What is the best way to facilitate this access?

A) Configure IAM roles for external developers and use Cloud Identity for authentication.
B) Set up a VPN between the developers' network and your VPC, and use firewall rules to restrict access.
C) Create SSH key pairs for each developer and add their public keys to the VM instances.
D) Use Cloud Endpoints to expose a secure API for administrative tasks.
E) Enable Cloud IAP for VM instances and create temporary Google accounts for developers.

QUESTION 36

You are monitoring a critical application on GCP and want to be notified immediately if there's an unexpected spike in HTTP 500 errors from your application's load balancer. How can you set up this alert?

A) Use Cloud Monitoring to create an uptime check for HTTP 500 errors and set up an alert policy.
B) Configure a custom metric in Cloud Logging for HTTP 500 errors and use it in an Alerting Policy.
C) Create a Cloud Function to scan logs for HTTP 500 errors and send notifications.
D) Set up a log sink to BigQuery and analyze the logs periodically for HTTP 500 errors.
E) Use Cloud Trace to monitor all requests and set alerts for any HTTP 500 errors.

QUESTION 37

You are developing a cloud-native e-commerce platform using a microservices architecture. Each microservice is packaged in its own Docker container image. To deploy this application on Google Kubernetes Engine (GKE) while ensuring each microservice can scale independently, what is the recommended approach?

A) Use a single Kubernetes Deployment for all microservices.
B) Utilize a Google Cloud Function for each microservice.
C) Create a Google Kubernetes Engine (GKE) Deployment for each microservice.
D) Deploy all microservices using Google App Engine.

QUESTION 38

Your team is responsible for ensuring data security in a Google Cloud project that uses multiple GCP services. To enhance security, you want to implement centralized access control and fine-grained permissions management. Which GCP service or feature should you use for this purpose?

A) Utilize Google Cloud Identity-Aware Proxy (IAP) for centralized access control.
B) Implement Google Cloud Armor for fine-grained permissions management.
C) Set up Google Cloud IAM (Identity and Access Management) for centralized access control and fine-grained permissions management.
D) Configure Google Cloud Pub/Sub for access control and permissions management.
E) Deploy Google Cloud VPN for centralized access control.

QUESTION 39

You are responsible for managing a Google Cloud project with multiple team members. You want to ensure that each team member has appropriate access to project resources and services without granting unnecessary permissions. What should you do to achieve this access control?

A) Assign the Owner role to all team members for maximum access.
B) Use Google Groups to manage team member access efficiently.
C) Share your personal credentials with team members for resource access.
D) Grant the Editor role to all team members for collaboration.

QUESTION 40

Your company provides cloud services that help migrate other companies to GCP. Multiple teams at your Organization use Google Cloud services in their own separate projects. The marketing team is working on a new initiative and the GCP costs for this initiative will be borne by the Marketing department. How can you bill the Marketing team only for their Google Cloud services for the new initiative within their group?

A) Make sure you have the Billing Administrator IAM role for the company's Marketing department GCP project.
B) Create a new GCP project for the Marketing department's new initiative and link it to a Marketing Billing Account.
C) Make sure you have the Organization Administrator IAM role at the Organization level and create a new GCP project linked to a Marketing Billing Account.
D) Make sure you have the Billing Administrator IAM role for the company's Marketing department GCP project and set project labels to department:marketing.

QUESTION 41

You work as a senior cloud engineer at a premiere medical institute where your team is working on migrating the entire infrastructure of a legacy enterprise client to GCP Compute Engine. Some medical servers are accessible from the internet, others via the institute's internal intranet. All servers talk to each other over specific ports and protocols. You are studying the current network setup, and you have found that the public servers rely on a demilitarized zone (DMZ), and the private servers use the Local Area Network (LAN). How can you design the networking setup on GCP with these requirements?

A) Use a single VPC with two subnets: one for the DMZ and one for LAN.
B) Use a single VPC with two subnets: one for the DMZ and one for LAN.
C) Create two separate VPCs: one for the DMZ and one for LAN.
D) Create two separate VPCs: one for the DMZ and one for LAN.

QUESTION 42

You are tasked with deploying a third-party OTP application on a Compute Engine instance that will send OTPs to users during sign-up. The installation files for the application are stored in a Cloud Storage bucket. What is the most secure way to grant access to these files for the new instance only?

A) Select the default Compute Engine service account for the instance while creating it.
B) Select the default Compute Engine service account for the instance while creating it and copy the metadata from the Cloud Storage bucket to the instance's metadata.
C) Create a new service account and select the new service account while creating the new instance. Grant the service account permissions on Cloud Storage.
D) Create a new service account and select the new service account while creating the new instance. Copy the metadata from the Cloud Storage bucket to the metadata of the new instance.
E) Grant permissions directly to the instance's external IP address for the Cloud Storage bucket.

QUESTION 43

You are developing a medicine delivery web application on GCP, and one of your requirements is to test updates on a small portion of live users before rolling them out to everyone. What should be your GCP deployment strategy to achieve this?

A) Use App Engine to run your app. For each update, create a new version of the same service and send a small percentage of traffic to the new version using traffic splitting.
B) Use App Engine to run your app. For each update, create a new service and send a small percentage of traffic to the new version using traffic splitting.
C) Use Kubernetes Engine to run your app. For a new release, update the deployment to use the new version.
D) Use Kubernetes Engine to run your app. For a new release, create a new deployment for the new version and update the service to use the new deployment.

QUESTION 44

Your organization is planning to deploy a web application on Google Cloud that requires real-time data processing and analysis. You need a service that can ingest large volumes of streaming data, process it in real-time, and provide insights through dashboards. Which Google Cloud service should you use for this purpose?

A) Google Cloud Dataflow
B) Google Cloud Dataprep
C) Google Cloud Pub/Sub and Cloud Dataflow
D) Google Cloud Dataproc

QUESTION 45

Your organization requires a cost-effective solution for storing archival data securely. You want to choose a Google Cloud storage option that offers the lowest cost per gigabyte and is suitable for long-term storage. Which Google Cloud storage class should you select for this archival data?

A) Google Cloud Standard Storage
B) Google Cloud Nearline Storage
C) Google Cloud Coldline Storage
D) Google Cloud Multi-Regional Storage

QUESTION 46

Your organization needs to implement a highly available and scalable storage solution on Google Cloud for its critical data. The solution should provide object storage with strong durability and low latency access. Which Google Cloud storage service should you choose for this requirement?

A) Google Cloud Filestore
B) Google Cloud Storage
C) Google Cloud Persistent Disks
D) Google Cloud Bigtable

QUESTION 47

Your organization is implementing a microservices architecture on Google Cloud. Each microservice needs to communicate securely with others, and you want to ensure authentication and encryption between services. Which Google Cloud service can you use to manage identity and access control for microservices?

A) Deploy Google Cloud Identity Platform for microservice identity management.
B) Utilize Google Cloud Identity and Access Management (IAM) for microservice authentication.
C) Implement Google Cloud Endpoints for microservice identity and access control.
D) Create a custom authentication service using Google Kubernetes Engine (GKE).

QUESTION 48

Your organization is planning to set up a disaster recovery (DR) solution for its Google Cloud resources. You want to ensure minimal data loss and rapid recovery in case of a disaster. Which GCP service can help you achieve this objective effectively?

A) Use Google Cloud VPN for secure communication between on-premises and Google Cloud resources.
B) Implement Google Cloud Interconnect for low-latency and high-bandwidth connectivity.
C) Set up Google Cloud Storage for offsite backups and data archiving.
D) Deploy Google Cloud's Disaster Recovery (DR) service for automated replication and failover.

QUESTION 49

As a developer, you have containerized a web application and now need to deploy it on Google Kubernetes Engine. What steps should you follow to achieve this?

A) Upload the container image to Container Registry and create a Kubernetes Deployment in GKE.
B) Store the container image in Cloud Storage and set up a Compute Engine instance to run it.
C) Deploy the container directly onto a Compute Engine instance without using GKE.
D) Upload the container image to Artifact Registry and create a GKE service to run the image.
E) Save the container image as a Dockerfile and use Cloud Build to deploy it on GKE.

QUESTION 50

Your video streaming application has varying resource requirements for its microservices running on GKE. The video processing service demands high CPU, while other services require moderate resources. How should you optimize the cluster resource allocation?

A) Assign high CPU priority to the video processing service in the deployment configuration.
B) Create separate node pools, one with compute-optimized machines for video processing and another with general-purpose machines for other services.
C) Increase the CPU allocation for all services to match the requirement of the video processing service.
D) Use Vertical Pod Autoscaling to automatically adjust CPU and memory allocation based on usage.
E) Implement node affinity rules to ensure all microservices run on compute-optimized machines.

SET 6 - ANSWERS ONLY

QUESTION 1

Answer - D) Add a new Node Pool

A) Incorrect, as modifying the existing node pool would cause disruption to the running application and doesn't address the need for different machine types.
B) Incorrect, while adding a new Node Pool and enabling auto-provisioning is a viable approach, it does not ensure the specific deployment of the new service on n2-highcpu-8 nodes.
C) Incorrect, as creating a new cluster and migrating all services would lead to downtime and is not required for adding a new service.
D) Correct, adding a new Node Pool with the desired machine type and using node selectors for deployment ensures minimal disruption and meets the specific requirements of the new service.
E) Incorrect, Vertical Pod Autoscaler adjusts resources within existing pods but does not address the need for a different node type for the new service.
F) Incorrect, Horizontal Pod Autoscaling and Cluster Autoscaler help manage resources efficiently but don't solve the requirement of deploying a new service on a specific node type.

QUESTION 2

Answer - A) Deploy VMs in europe-west1-c

A) Correct, deploying VMs in another zone and using a regional HTTP(S) Load Balancer ensures high availability and load balancing at minimal cost.
B) Incorrect, a single Managed Instance Group in one zone doesn't provide high availability in case of zonal failure.
C) Incorrect, while Kubernetes offers scalability, it doesn't inherently provide zonal redundancy for high availability.
D) Incorrect, a multi-zonal Kubernetes cluster may increase costs and complexity beyond minimal requirements.
E) Incorrect, Cloud CDN is for content delivery and doesn't address high availability of the application's backend infrastructure.

QUESTION 3

Answer - B) Secret Manager

A) Incorrect, storing sensitive data in a Cloud SQL database, even with restricted access, is not as secure as using a dedicated secret management service.
B) Correct, Secret Manager provides a secure and centralized way to manage credentials, with features for automatic rotation.
C) Incorrect, storing credentials off-premises introduces unnecessary complexity and potential latency issues.
D) Incorrect, embedding credentials in application code, even in a private repository, is not a secure practice.

E) Incorrect, using Cloud Storage for credential storage lacks the specific security and management features needed for API keys and credentials.

QUESTION 4

Answer - C) Preemptible VMs in a managed instance group

A) Incorrect, while committed use discounts provide cost savings, they are less optimal for intermittent high-compute needs.
B) Incorrect, autoscaling helps manage the load but may not provide the best cost savings for short-duration high-compute tasks.
C) Correct, preemptible VMs offer significant cost savings for interruptible jobs and a managed instance group can manage these VMs efficiently.
D) Incorrect, Cloud Functions are suitable for lightweight, serverless tasks but may not meet the high computational requirements of the job.
E) Incorrect, scheduling regular VMs can reduce costs but is not as cost-effective as using preemptible VMs for interruptible tasks.

QUESTION 5

Answer - B) Google Cloud Directory Sync (GCDS)

A) Incorrect, manually creating accounts is time-consuming and prone to errors.
B) Correct, GCDS provides an efficient and automated way to synchronize Active Directory accounts with GCP.
C) Incorrect, developing a custom tool is resource-intensive and unnecessary given the existence of GCDS.
D) Incorrect, a VPN tunnel extends network connectivity but does not address account synchronization.
E) Incorrect, manually exporting and importing users is inefficient for a large multinational corporation.

QUESTION 6

Answer - C) Pub/Sub emulator in Google Cloud SDK

A) Incorrect, creating topics using gcloud command will create them in GCP, not locally.
B) Incorrect, connecting to actual Cloud Pub/Sub in GCP does not constitute local testing.
C) Correct, using the Pub/Sub emulator available in the Google Cloud SDK allows for local testing of Pub/Sub integration.
D) Incorrect, deploying to GCP is not a method for local testing.
E) Incorrect, MQTT broker is a different technology and does not accurately simulate Cloud Pub/Sub.

QUESTION 7

Answer - A) Cloud Identity with Active Directory as the identity provider

A) Correct, Cloud Identity can be used to set up SSO with Active Directory as the identity provider, integrating AD with GCP.
B) Incorrect, Cloud Directory Sync synchronizes users but does not set up SSO.
C) Incorrect, Cloud IAM custom roles manage access but do not integrate with Active Directory for

authentication.
D) Incorrect, Cloud VPN provides network connectivity, not user authentication integration.
E) Incorrect, Cloud Endpoints are used for API management, not for integrating Active Directory with GCP.

QUESTION 8

Answer - C) roles/resourcemanager.projectIamAdmin

A) Incorrect, roles/iam.securityAdmin is more focused on security settings than IAM policy management.
B) Incorrect, roles/owner grants full control over all aspects of the project, which is overly broad.
C) Correct, roles/resourcemanager.projectIamAdmin provides the necessary permissions to manage IAM policies without being overly broad.
D) Incorrect, roles/editor provides edit access to all resources but is not specific to IAM policy management.
E) Incorrect, roles/iam.roleAdmin is focused on creating and managing custom roles, not IAM policies in general.

QUESTION 9

Answer – C) Configure Compute Engine instances with automatic scaling, use Cloud SQL and Firestore for databases, employ HTTP(S) Load Balancing, and distribute instances across multiple zones.

Option C is the best fit for the given requirements. It provides a scalable solution using Compute Engine with automatic scaling and leverages both Cloud SQL and Firestore to handle SQL and NoSQL needs. HTTP(S) Load Balancing ensures efficient traffic distribution, and multi-zone deployment offers resilience against zone failures. Option A lacks automatic scaling and multi-zone resilience. Option B, while offering scalability and multi-regional deployment, uses Cloud Spanner, which might be an overkill for certain applications. Option D focuses on containerized applications but lacks the automatic scalability across multiple zones. Option E, utilizing Cloud Functions, may not provide the necessary control over the environment compared to Compute Engine instances and its use of Internal Load Balancing does not align with the public-facing nature of a web application.

QUESTION 10

Answer – A) SetStorageClass to Coldline at 30 days, then Delete at 395 days.

A) Correct. This policy moves data to Coldline after 30 days and then deletes it after a total of 395 days (30 + 365 days).
B) Incorrect because this deletes the data 365 days after moving to Coldline, not 365 days after Nearline.
C) Incorrect as it does not transition to Coldline.
D) Incorrect because it delays the deletion beyond the required 365 days in Coldline.

QUESTION 11

Answer - A) Create a Cloud Build trigger and use Cloud Build for the CI/CD process, ensuring IAM roles for Cloud Build service account are properly configured for necessary access. Set up deployment to GKE using kubectl commands in the build steps.

A) Correct. Leverages Cloud Build's integration with GCP services and IAM's role-based access control for efficiency and security.
B) Introduces complexity and security risks with manual key management.
C) Not optimal, as Cloud Functions are not designed for CI/CD workflows.
D) Lacks the automation and efficiency crucial for CI/CD.

QUESTION 12

Answer - B) Cloud IoT Core for device management, Cloud Bigtable for time-series data storage, and BigQuery for data analysis

A) Suitable for real-time applications but Firestore may not be optimal for time-series data.
B) Correct. Cloud IoT Core efficiently manages device connections, Cloud Bigtable is ideal for time-series data storage, and BigQuery excels in data analysis.
C) Firebase is effective for real-time applications, but combining Firestore with BigQuery is more complex for time-series data.
D) Does not provide optimal real-time data processing and storage for time-series data compared to Bigtable.

QUESTION 13

Answer - A) Assign the compliance officers group the 'storage.objectViewer' and 'logging.viewer' predefined IAM roles.

A) Correct. Grouping users with similar access needs and assigning predefined roles is a best practice for managing permissions efficiently and securely. 'storage.objectViewer' and 'logging.viewer' provide adequate access for reviewing data and logs.
B) Incorrect. Project owner role is too privileged for compliance officers.
C) The project viewer role might not provide specific access to logs.
D) Assigning roles to groups is preferable to individual accounts for easier management.

QUESTION 14

Answer - A) Review the deletion activities in the Cloud Storage Audit logs within the GCP console.

A) Audit logs provide detailed information about user actions including file deletions, making them suitable for compliance and monitoring purposes.
B) Stackdriver logging can be used, but audit logs in the GCP console are more direct and specific for this purpose.
C) The activity tab does not provide the detailed audit trail required for compliance.
D) Cloud Monitoring alerts are useful for real-time monitoring but not as effective for retrospective audit reviews.

QUESTION 15

Answer - A) Deploy an HTTP(S) Load Balancer with SSL termination at the load balancer and forwarding rules to the instance group.

A) This setup fulfills the requirement of supporting HTTP/HTTPS with SSL offloading at the load balancer,

providing efficient traffic management and security for the e-commerce application.
B) TCP Proxy Load Balancer does not support HTTP traffic and SSL offloading.
C) SSL Proxy Load Balancer does not support HTTP traffic, only SSL.
D) Internal Load Balancer is for internal traffic and does not provide SSL termination at the load balancer level.

QUESTION 16

Answer - E) Google Cloud Spanner

Option E: This is the correct choice as Google Cloud Spanner is a globally distributed and highly available database service that can ensure low-latency access for users across the world.
Option A: Google Cloud Storage is an object storage service and may not provide the required low-latency access for applications.
Option B: Google Cloud Datastore is a NoSQL database and may not have the global reach needed for low-latency access.
Option C: Google Cloud CDN is a content delivery network and can help with content delivery but may not address the database needs.
Option D: Google Cloud Endpoints is for creating and deploying APIs, not for database scalability and low-latency access.

QUESTION 17

Answer - A) Create a single custom VPC with two subnets in the same region, each with different CIDR ranges.

Option A: This is the correct choice as it meets the requirements of having separate, isolated subnets for development and production within the same VPC, allowing for internal IP communication.
Option B: Creating two separate VPCs is not necessary and may complicate network management.
Option C: Placing subnets in different regions with the same CIDR range may hinder network connectivity.
Option D: Similar to option C, placing subnets in different regions with the same CIDR range is not ideal for the required network architecture.

QUESTION 18

Answer - A) Google Cloud Storage.

Option A is the correct choice as Google Cloud Storage provides cost-effective and scalable object storage suitable for long-term data archiving and backup, along with features for seamless data retrieval and management.
Option B and Option C are for data processing, and Option D is for in-memory data caching.

QUESTION 19

Answer - A) Global HTTP(S) Load Balancer

Option A, "Global HTTP(S) Load Balancer," is the correct choice. It can distribute traffic across multiple regions, providing high availability. Regional load balancers (Option B) operate within a single region, and the other options are not designed for global distribution.

QUESTION 20

Answer - B) Create a Google Group for the analytics team and assign the 'spanner.databaseUser' role to this group.

B) This approach follows best practices by grouping users with similar access requirements and assigning the role to the group, ensuring both view and edit access while maintaining easier management and security.
  A) Assigning roles to individual users is less efficient and secure.
  C) The 'spanner.viewer' role does not provide edit access.
  D) The 'spanner.admin' role provides excessive permissions beyond the necessary scope.

QUESTION 21

Answer - B) Enable parallel composite uploads using gsutil to maximize upload speed.

B) Using parallel composite uploads with gsutil allows the large file to be divided into smaller chunks and uploaded simultaneously, making efficient use of the available bandwidth and speeding up the overall transfer.
  A) The GCP console is user-friendly but not optimized for large file transfers.
  C) TCP window size adjustments might not significantly impact upload efficiency.
  D) The storage class impacts cost and data retrieval, not upload speed.

QUESTION 22

Answer - C) In 'data-storage', grant the service account the IAM role of BigQuery Data Viewer.

C) This approach correctly assigns the necessary permissions to the service account from 'data-storage' to access its BigQuery datasets. It follows best practices by using existing service accounts and IAM roles for access control.
  A) Adding the service account as a member in 'data-analytics' doesn't grant it access to 'data-storage' resources.
  B) Using private keys for API requests is less secure and not recommended.
  D) Setting up a cross-project service account is unnecessary when a specific service account is provided.

QUESTION 23

Answer - B) Increase the initial delay of the health check to 240 seconds.

A) Decreasing the CPU threshold could trigger scaling even sooner, exacerbating the issue.
 B) Correct. Aligning the health check delay with initialization time prevents premature addition of instances to the load balancer.
 C) Reducing the maximum number of instances doesn't address the timing of health checks.
 D) Changing the health check type doesn't solve the premature scaling problem.
 E) Extending the cooldown period may reduce scaling frequency but doesn't align with initialization time.

QUESTION 24

Answer - D) Run gcloud config list to view the active GCP project configuration.

D) This command shows the current configuration settings, including the active project ID, which indicates where the App Engine application was deployed.
 A) The app.yaml file doesn't specify the target project for deployment.
 B) The web-application.xml file is not related to GCP project configurations.
 C) Deployment Manager is not typically used for App Engine deployments.
 E) The App Engine dashboard requires knowing the project in advance.
 F) Cloud Logging might not provide direct information about the deployment target without extensive searching.

QUESTION 25

Answer - C) Stop the VM, change its machine type to one with 8 GB of memory, and start the VM.

C) This is the correct approach to resize a VM in GCP. Stopping the VM allows you to change its machine type to one with the desired memory capacity, and then you can restart the VM with the new configuration.
 A) Live migration does not change the machine type or memory.
 B) Updating metadata does not affect the actual resources of the VM.
 D) Memory cannot be increased directly without stopping the VM first.
 E) Creating a snapshot is unnecessary for a simple resize operation.
 F) The gcloud command-line tool cannot increase memory of a running VM.

QUESTION 26

Answer - B) Activate the 'Delete Protection' feature on all production instances.

B) Enabling 'Delete Protection' on Compute Engine instances effectively prevents them from being accidentally or prematurely deleted, ensuring that critical instances remain operational.
 A) Custom scripts may not provide the same level of protection as built-in features.
 C) Restricting permissions is a good practice but may not prevent all accidental deletions.
 D) Snapshots are useful for recovery but don't prevent deletion.
 E) Alerts can notify about deletions but won't prevent them.
 F) Deployment Manager is for infrastructure deployment, not for real-time deletion prevention.

QUESTION 27

Answer - B) and C)

B) Lifecycle policies in Cloud Storage allow for automatic deletion of objects after a specified period, addressing the 45-day retention requirement.
 C) Signed URLs provide temporary access to Cloud Storage, enabling users to upload and access their invoices with a time limit, fulfilling the 30-minute access requirement.
 A) Cron jobs require manual setup and maintenance, less efficient than lifecycle policies.
 D) Separate buckets for each user are not necessary and can be complex to manage.
 E) Cloud IAM manages access control but not temporary access or auto-deletion.
 F) Custom functions for file deletion are less efficient compared to lifecycle policies.

QUESTION 28

Answer - A) Use Cloud Deployment Manager to develop templates for environments

Option A - Using Cloud Deployment Manager to develop templates allows you to define and manage your infrastructure using reusable templates, minimizing repetitive code.
 Option B - Sending REST requests individually for each resource using curl is not efficient and leads to a lot of repetitive code.
 Option C - Managing resources through the Google Cloud Console involves manual intervention and does not align with Infrastructure as Code principles.
 Option D - Writing a bash script with gcloud commands results in repetitive code for each resource, making it less efficient for IaC.

QUESTION 29

Answer - C) Implement a low-priority rule blocking all egress and high-priority rules for required ports.

C) Setting a low-priority rule to block all egress traffic ensures that by default no data leaves the network. Then, creating specific high-priority rules to allow only essential egress ports ensures that only necessary traffic is permitted. This approach provides strict control over egress traffic, which is critical for a highly sensitive application.
 A) Default high-priority rules to block all traffic may override more specific rules to allow necessary traffic.
 B) A single rule might not be flexible enough for different egress needs.
 D) Network tags are useful but less specific than firewall rules for controlling egress.
 E) Cloud NAT manages outbound traffic but doesn't provide specific port control.
 F) VPC Service Controls add a layer of security but don't specifically manage egress ports.

QUESTION 30

Answer - B) Use Cloud Run (fully managed) with the minimum number of instances set to zero.

B) Cloud Run (fully managed) is ideal for this use case as it allows the application to scale down to zero instances when not in use, incurring no costs during downtime. This meets the requirement of having zero running costs outside of designated hours.
 A) Google Kubernetes Engine doesn't scale down to zero nodes automatically.
 C) Compute Engine requires manual intervention for stopping and starting instances.
 D) App Engine Standard Environment scales down but not to zero instances.
 E) Cloud Functions are for event-driven applications, not continuous applications like a note-taking tool.
 F) App Engine Flexible Environment does not scale down to zero instances.

QUESTION 31

Answer - C) Create a custom role with specific required permissions for each production project.

C) Creating a custom role with specific required permissions and granting it to the DevOps team for each production project is the best practice. This approach ensures the DevOps team has only the necessary permissions to perform their tasks, adhering to the principle of least privilege and reducing security risks.
 A) The Project Editor role might grant more permissions than necessary.
 B) The Project Owner role at the organizational level is too broad and risky.

D) The Security Admin role might not provide appropriate access for DevOps tasks.
E) Auto-assigning roles based on labels might still result in broader access than needed.
F) A shared VPC focuses on network access, not specific project service permissions.

QUESTION 32

Answer - C) Keep files in Standard storage for the first 30 days, then shift to Archive storage for the 3-year duration.

C) This strategy optimizes cost while accommodating usage patterns. Using Standard storage for the initial 30 days supports frequent access needs. After 30 days, moving files to Archive storage, which offers the lowest cost for infrequently accessed data, aligns with the 3-year retention requirement and further reduces costs.
A) Coldline storage for 3 years may incur higher costs than necessary after the initial frequent access period.
B) Nearline storage is less cost-effective than Standard for the first 30 days of frequent access.
D) The transition from Nearline to Coldline, then Archive, adds complexity and may not be cost-effective.
E) Shifting from Standard to Coldline and then to Archive may result in higher costs compared to directly moving to Archive.
F) Starting with Coldline is not optimal for the initial frequent access period.

QUESTION 33

Answer - D) Configure an External Network Load Balancer for the UDP traffic.

D) An External Network Load Balancer is the ideal solution for this scenario. It supports UDP traffic and provides a single external IP address that can be used to distribute traffic across multiple VMs. This setup enables horizontal scaling of the game servers while maintaining consistent external access for players.
A) HTTP(S) Load Balancers are designed for HTTP/HTTPS traffic, not UDP.
B) Internal TCP/UDP Load Balancers are used within a private network and don't expose a public IP.
C) SSL Proxy Load Balancers are intended for SSL-encrypted traffic, not UDP.
E) Global UDP Proxy Load Balancer is not a standard product in Google Cloud.
F) Cloud VPN is for secure network connections, not suitable for distributing game traffic.

QUESTION 34

Answer – B) Transfer to Cloud Storage, Nearline/Coldline

A) Incorrect, Cloud SQL is not cost-effective for large-scale historical data.
B) Correct, it provides a cost-effective storage solution with lifecycle management for occasional access.
C) Incorrect, Dataflow to BigQuery is more suited for real-time data processing.
D) Incorrect, overly complex for the requirement.
E) Incorrect, Bigtable is overkill for occasional access and analysis.

QUESTION 35

Answer – C) SSH key pairs

A) Incorrect, IAM roles require Google accounts for authentication.
B) Incorrect, a VPN provides network access but not specific VM access control.
C) Correct, SSH key pairs allow secure, individual access without needing Google accounts.
D) Incorrect, Cloud Endpoints is for API management, not VM administration.
E) Incorrect, creating temporary Google accounts may not align with the organization's security policies.

QUESTION 36

Answer – B) Custom metric in Cloud Logging, Alerting Policy

A) Incorrect, uptime checks are for availability, not specific error monitoring.
B) Correct, creating a custom metric for HTTP 500 errors in Cloud Logging and setting an alert is the most direct and efficient way.
C) Incorrect, while possible, this method is less efficient and more complex.
D) Incorrect, this method lacks real-time alerting.
E) Incorrect, Cloud Trace is not primarily used for error monitoring and alerting.

QUESTION 37

Answer - C) Create a Google Kubernetes Engine (GKE) Deployment for each microservice. (Correct)

Option A is incorrect because using a single Kubernetes Deployment for all microservices would limit the ability to scale each microservice independently.
Option B is incorrect because Google Cloud Functions are designed for serverless execution of functions and may not be suitable for deploying and managing containerized microservices.
Option D is incorrect because Google App Engine is a platform-as-a-service (PaaS) offering and does not provide the fine-grained control and flexibility required for deploying microservices in individual containers on GKE.
Option C is correct because creating a GKE Deployment for each microservice is the recommended approach to allow individual scaling and management of microservices within a Kubernetes cluster. This approach provides flexibility and isolation for each microservice.

QUESTION 38

Answer - C) Set up Google Cloud IAM (Identity and Access Management) for centralized access control and fine-grained permissions management. (Correct)

Option A is incorrect because Google Cloud Identity-Aware Proxy (IAP) primarily focuses on identity verification and access control for web applications and does not provide fine-grained permissions management.
Option B is incorrect because Google Cloud Armor is a DDoS protection service and does not offer fine-grained permissions management.
Option D is incorrect because Google Cloud Pub/Sub is a messaging service and not designed for access control and permissions management at the project level.
Option E is incorrect because Google Cloud VPN is for network connectivity and does not provide centralized access control and fine-grained permissions management.
Option C is correct because Google Cloud IAM (Identity and Access Management) allows for centralized

access control and fine-grained permissions management at the project level, enhancing data security across multiple GCP services.

QUESTION 39

Answer - B) Use Google Groups to manage team member access efficiently. (Correct)

Option A is incorrect because assigning the Owner role to all team members would grant them maximum access and may lead to over-privileged accounts.
Option C is incorrect because sharing personal credentials is a security violation and should never be done.
Option D is incorrect because granting the Editor role to all team members may provide excessive permissions and is not the most efficient way to manage access.
Using Google Groups allows you to efficiently manage access control by assigning specific roles to groups of team members, ensuring appropriate permissions.

QUESTION 40

Answer - A) Make sure you have the Billing Administrator IAM role for the company's Marketing department GCP project.

Option B is incorrect because it suggests creating a new GCP project without mentioning the role required to manage billing. Option C is incorrect because it involves unnecessary roles and does not specifically address billing the Marketing team. Option D is incorrect because it adds unnecessary steps and project labels without directly addressing the billing requirement. Option A is correct because having the Billing Administrator role for the Marketing department's GCP project allows you to manage billing specifically for that project, ensuring that the costs for the new initiative are billed to the Marketing team's billing account.

QUESTION 41

Answer - A) Use a single VPC with two subnets: one for the DMZ and one for LAN.

Option B is a duplicate of Option A. Options C and D suggest creating two separate VPCs, which would not allow for the required communication between the DMZ and LAN servers. Option A is correct because it recommends using a single VPC with two subnets to separate the DMZ (Demilitarized zone) and LAN (Local Area Network) servers, allowing control of traffic between them using firewall rules and enabling public ingress traffic for the DMZ servers.

QUESTION 42

Answer - C) Create a new service account and select the new service account while creating the new instance. Grant the service account permissions on Cloud Storage.

Option A is incorrect because selecting the default Compute Engine service account grants access to all other instances using the same service account, which does not fulfill the requirement of restricting access to the new instance.
Option B is incorrect because copying the metadata from the Cloud Storage bucket to the instance's

metadata does not provide adequate access control, as other already-configured instances could still access the files.
Option D is incorrect for the same reasons as option B.
Option E is incorrect because granting permissions to an external IP address does not ensure secure access control to the Cloud Storage bucket.

QUESTION 43

Answer - A) Use App Engine to run your app. For each update, create a new version of the same service and send a small percentage of traffic to the new version using traffic splitting.

Option A is correct because it aligns with your goal of A/B testing. Using App Engine, you can create new versions of the same service and use traffic splitting to test updates on a small portion of live users while keeping the rest on the live version.
Option B is incorrect because creating a new service for each update would result in multiple instances of the app running simultaneously, which is not suitable for A/B testing.
Option C is incorrect because updating the deployment in Kubernetes Engine would direct all traffic to the new version, which does not allow for controlled A/B testing.
Option D is incorrect because creating a new deployment and updating the service would also direct all traffic to the new deployment, making it unsuitable for A/B testing.

QUESTION 44

Answer - C) Google Cloud Pub/Sub and Cloud Dataflow

Option C is correct because Google Cloud Pub/Sub can ingest large volumes of streaming data, and Google Cloud Dataflow can process and analyze this data in real-time. Together, they provide a robust solution for real-time data processing and dashboard generation.
Option A (Google Cloud Dataflow) is a data processing service but requires a data ingestion service like Pub/Sub for streaming data.
Option B (Google Cloud Dataprep) is a data preparation tool and not designed for real-time data processing.
Option D (Google Cloud Dataproc) is for batch and stream processing using Apache Spark and Hadoop and may not provide real-time insights.

QUESTION 45

Answer - C) Google Cloud Coldline Storage

Option C is correct because Google Cloud Coldline Storage is designed for archival data with the lowest cost per gigabyte among storage classes. It provides secure, long-term storage for data that is accessed infrequently.
Option A (Google Cloud Standard Storage) is for frequently accessed data and may not be cost-effective for archival data.
Option B (Google Cloud Nearline Storage) is for data accessed less frequently than standard storage but is not as cost-effective as Coldline Storage for long-term archival.
Option D (Google Cloud Multi-Regional Storage) is for frequently accessed data with high availability and may not be suitable for low-cost archival.

QUESTION 46

Answer - B) Google Cloud Storage

Option B is correct because Google Cloud Storage provides highly available and scalable object storage with strong durability and low-latency access, making it suitable for critical data storage.
Option A (Google Cloud Filestore) is a managed NFS file storage service and may not be the best fit for object storage.
Option C (Google Cloud Persistent Disks) is block storage and not primarily designed for object storage.
Option D (Google Cloud Bigtable) is a NoSQL database service and is not intended for general-purpose object storage.

QUESTION 47

Answer - C) Implement Google Cloud Endpoints for microservice identity and access control

Option C is correct because Google Cloud Endpoints is designed for managing identity and access control for microservices. It provides authentication, authorization, and encryption capabilities for microservices, ensuring secure communication between them.
Option A is incorrect because Google Cloud Identity Platform is more focused on user identity and access management, not specifically designed for microservices.
Option B is not the best choice because Google Cloud IAM is primarily used for managing access to Google Cloud resources, not for securing communication between microservices.
Option D is not the recommended approach because creating a custom authentication service using GKE would require additional development and maintenance, which is not necessary when Google Cloud offers dedicated services for this purpose.

QUESTION 48

Answer - D) Deploy Google Cloud's Disaster Recovery (DR) service for automated replication and failover

Option D is correct because Google Cloud's Disaster Recovery (DR) service is specifically designed for setting up a disaster recovery solution with minimal data loss and rapid recovery. It provides automated replication and failover capabilities for critical resources.
Option A and B focus on network connectivity and do not address data replication or recovery.
Option C is related to data storage but does not provide automated disaster recovery capabilities.

QUESTION 49

Answer – A) Container Registry, Kubernetes Deployment

A) Correct, uploading to Container Registry and creating a Kubernetes Deployment is the standard workflow for deploying containerized apps on GKE.
B) Incorrect, Cloud Storage is not used for storing container images for GKE.
C) Incorrect, this does not utilize GKE which is crucial for container orchestration.
D) Incorrect, while Artifact Registry can be used, Kubernetes Deployment is the correct resource, not a service.
E) Incorrect, Dockerfile is for building images, not directly deploying them.

QUESTION 50

Answer – B) Separate node pools

A) Incorrect, assigning priority doesn't address specific resource needs.
B) Correct, creating separate node pools for different resource requirements ensures efficient resource utilization.
C) Incorrect, increasing CPU for all services is inefficient and costly.
D) Incorrect, Vertical Pod Autoscaling is useful but doesn't address the fundamental need for different machine types.
E) Incorrect, running all services on compute-optimized machines may be overkill for non-CPU-intensive services.

SET 7 - QUESTIONS ONLY

QUESTION 1

You need to ensure high availability for a stateful application hosted on Compute Engine, which experiences variable load. How should you architect this?

A) Utilize managed instance groups with autoscaling based on CPU utilization, combined with regional persistent disks.
B) Deploy the application on a single high-memory VM instance with periodic snapshot backups.
C) Implement a zonal managed instance group with preemptible VMs and standard persistent disks.
D) Use unmanaged instance groups across multiple zones with manual scaling and local SSDs.
E) Configure a regional managed instance group with custom machine types and snapshot-based autoscaling.
F) Implement a global HTTP(S) load balancer with backend services running on Compute Engine VMs in multiple regions.

QUESTION 2

As a cloud architect in a fintech company, you need to design a solution for a high-performance computing (HPC) workload that requires both computational power and high network throughput. Your solution must balance performance with cost-effectiveness. What is the best approach to provision resources on GCP for this need?

A) Utilize custom machine types with high CPU and RAM in a single zone, combined with premium tier network service.
B) Deploy VMs using Compute Engine's predefined n1-highcpu machine types across multiple zones with standard network service.
C) Implement a combination of preemptible VMs and regular VMs in a Managed Instance Group, ensuring cost-effectiveness and performance.
D) Choose n2-highcpu machine types for computational needs and use Cloud Interconnect for enhanced network performance.
E) Leverage sole-tenant nodes with custom VM configurations and regional Persistent Disks for data storage.

QUESTION 3

As the DevOps lead in a financial technology company, you are tasked with implementing a reliable and efficient deployment strategy for a set of microservices on GCP. The microservices need to be deployed with zero downtime and should support quick rollbacks in case of failures. Which deployment strategy would you recommend?

A) Use GKE with rolling updates for the microservices and configure readiness and liveness probes for health checks.
B) Deploy the microservices on App Engine with traffic splitting, gradually increasing traffic to new versions.

C) Implement blue-green deployments using Compute Engine VMs and manually switch traffic between versions.
D) Set up a CI/CD pipeline with Cloud Build and Spinnaker, using canary deployments to slowly roll out changes.
E) Utilize Cloud Functions for the microservices, ensuring automatic scaling and versioning for quick rollbacks.

QUESTION 4

As a cloud engineer, you are responsible for a GCP environment that hosts various web applications. To improve the performance and reduce the latency of these applications, what should you prioritize in your network configuration?

A) Set up a multi-regional Cloud CDN to cache static content closer to the users.
B) Implement Cloud Interconnect for dedicated network connectivity.
C) Use Cloud VPN to securely connect the applications with on-premises data centers.
D) Configure regional external HTTP(S) Load Balancers for the applications.
E) Optimize the network routes using custom routes and network tags.

QUESTION 5

As a cloud engineer, you are tasked with ensuring that only employees of specific departments have access to certain GCP resources. Your company uses Active Directory for user management. Which combination of GCP and Active Directory features should you use to achieve this?

A) Utilize IAM Conditional Roles in GCP and map them to Active Directory Groups.
B) Configure VPC Service Controls in GCP and integrate them with Active Directory organizational units.
C) Set up Identity-Aware Proxy for resource access in GCP and use Active Directory groups for access control.
D) Implement Cloud Identity and synchronize it with Active Directory groups, applying IAM roles based on group membership.
E) Use Access Context Manager in GCP to define access levels and link them with Active Directory user attributes.

QUESTION 6

As a part of your development process on Ubuntu, you need to ensure that your application can interact with Cloud Storage without deploying it to GCP. What tool or component should you use to facilitate local testing for Cloud Storage integration?

A) Configure your application to use a locally mounted network file system that simulates Cloud Storage.
B) Use the gsutil command-line tool to interact with Cloud Storage buckets for testing purposes.
C) Install and configure the Cloud Storage emulator from the Google Cloud SDK.
D) Create a local instance of MinIO as a stand-in for Google Cloud Storage during development.
E) Directly connect to Cloud Storage from your application using the Google Cloud client libraries.

QUESTION 7

You are tasked with ensuring that your organization's GCP resources are only accessible to users authenticated through the organization's Active Directory. What configuration is necessary to enforce this policy?

A) Set up IAM policies in GCP to restrict access to users authenticated via Active Directory.
B) Configure Security Assertion Markup Language (SAML) SSO integration between GCP and Active Directory.
C) Implement a network policy to allow access to GCP resources only from the organization's network.
D) Use VPC Service Controls to create a security perimeter that includes Active Directory for authentication.
E) Create a custom application in App Engine to manage GCP access for Active Directory authenticated users.

QUESTION 8

In your financial services startup, you want to ensure that the new team member managing service accounts can create and manage keys for these accounts. What is the most appropriate role to grant them?

A) roles/iam.serviceAccountKeyAdmin
B) roles/iam.serviceAccountAdmin
C) roles/iam.serviceAccountUser
D) roles/iam.securityReviewer
E) roles/cloudkms.admin

QUESTION 9

As a GCP architect, you are designing a data processing solution for a financial services company. The system must process large volumes of transactional data daily, requiring robust data warehousing and real-time analytics capabilities. The solution should also ensure data encryption, both at rest and in transit, and comply with financial industry regulations. Which combination of services and configurations would best meet these criteria?

A) Use BigQuery for data warehousing and Dataflow for real-time processing. Implement VPC Service Controls for security and enable Customer-Managed Encryption Keys (CMEK) for all data.
B) Deploy Cloud SQL as the data warehouse and utilize Pub/Sub with DataProc for real-time processing. Implement Identity-Aware Proxy for secure access and use default encryption settings.
C) Implement Cloud Bigtable for data warehousing and DataPrep for real-time processing. Utilize Cloud Armor for security and enable default encryption for data at rest.
D) Utilize BigQuery for data warehousing, Stream Analytics for real-time processing, ensure the use of Dedicated Interconnect for secure data transfer, and apply default encryption methods.
E) Choose Datastore for data warehousing and Cloud Functions for real-time processing. Employ Cloud Endpoints for secure data exchange and use Google-managed keys for encryption.

QUESTION 10

For a project, you need to frequently access data for the first 60 days, occasionally for the next 300 days, and rarely thereafter. The data should be deleted after 3 years. How should you configure the lifecycle policy in GCP Cloud Storage?

A) Use Standard for 60 days, then Nearline for 300 days, Coldline thereafter, and Delete after 1095 days.
B) Use Standard for 60 days, Coldline for 300 days, then Archive, and Delete after 1095 days.
C) Use Nearline for 60 days, then Coldline for 300 days, Archive thereafter, and Delete after 1095 days.
D) Use Standard for 360 days, then move to Archive, and Delete after 1095 days.

QUESTION 11

Your organization is planning to migrate a large database from an on-premises data center to Google Cloud. The database is critical for your operations, and the migration should minimize downtime and data loss. Considering these requirements, which migration strategy should you adopt?

A) Utilize Cloud SQL's import functionality to migrate data directly from a backup file.
B) Implement a lift-and-shift approach using VM migration to Compute Engine, then transfer data to a GCP database service.
C) Set up a temporary replication from the on-premises database to a Cloud SQL instance, switch over once replication is consistent.
D) Manually export data from the on-premises database and use gsutil to transfer data to Cloud Storage, then import into Cloud SQL.

QUESTION 12

Your team is tasked with enhancing the efficiency of a cloud-based system that manages temperature and energy data from various smart AC units installed in homes and offices. The system should be able to handle large-scale data ingestion, provide real-time analytics, and store data for historical analysis. What is the most appropriate GCP service combination for this scenario?

A) Use Cloud Dataflow for processing incoming data streams, store data in Cloud Spanner for scalability, and utilize Looker for real-time analytics.
B) Implement Cloud Pub/Sub for data ingestion, use Dataflow for stream processing, store processed data in Bigtable, and analyze with BigQuery.
C) Deploy Firebase Realtime Database for data ingestion and storage, with Cloud Functions for processing, and integrate with BigQuery for analytics.
D) Set up a Kubernetes Engine cluster to process data, store in Cloud SQL for transactional data handling, and use Data Studio for analytics.

QUESTION 13

As part of regulatory compliance, your healthcare application needs to be audited regularly. You need to set up IAM access for external auditors to review data in Cloud Healthcare API. What is the best approach to configure this access?

A) Create a group for auditors and assign them the 'healthcare.datasetViewer' and 'logging.viewer' roles.
B) Assign the auditors individual user accounts the project owner role for full access.
C) Give the auditors group the 'healthcare.admin' role for comprehensive access.
D) Allocate individual auditor accounts the 'healthcare.datasetViewer' and 'logging.viewer' roles.

QUESTION 14

As part of a security audit for your healthcare application, you need to verify which users accessed specific patient records stored in Cloud Storage. Your focus is on read and download activities over the past month. What is the best approach to gather this information?

A) Examine the read and download activities in the Cloud Storage Audit logs in the GCP console.
B) Filter for access logs in Stackdriver logging for the specific time period.
C) Review the access history in the Cloud Storage metadata section in the GCP console.
D) Implement a BigQuery data transfer service to analyze Cloud Storage access logs.

QUESTION 15

For a high-traffic web application on GCP, you need a load balancing solution that can handle millions of HTTPS requests and provide SSL offloading. The solution should also route requests based on the content of the HTTP(S) headers. Which GCP service should you choose?

A) Utilize HTTP(S) Load Balancer with URL maps for content-based routing and SSL termination capabilities.
B) Implement Global SSL Proxy Load Balancer for handling high-traffic HTTPS requests and SSL offloading.
C) Deploy Network Load Balancer to distribute traffic across regions and handle SSL decryption on backend instances.
D) Set up TCP Proxy Load Balancer with an SSL certificate for SSL termination and custom routing based on IP addresses.

QUESTION 16

Your company wants to create automated backups of important data stored in Google Cloud Storage. You need to set up a solution that allows regular backups to a different region for disaster recovery purposes. What GCP service or feature would you use to automate this process?

A) Google Cloud Storage Transfer Service
B) Google Cloud Dataflow
C) Google Cloud Pub/Sub
D) Google Cloud Storage Object Versioning
E) Google Cloud Storage Lifecycle policies

QUESTION 17

Your organization is planning to deploy a critical application on Google Cloud, and high availability is a top priority. Which Google Cloud service or feature should you leverage to ensure high availability for your application?

A) Google Cloud Storage for data backup.
B) Google Cloud Load Balancer for traffic distribution.
C) Google Cloud Pub/Sub for event-driven processing.
D) Google Cloud VPN for secure network connections.

QUESTION 18

Your project involves real-time analysis of streaming data from various sources, and you need a service that can ingest, process, and analyze data at scale. Which GCP service should you choose to handle real-time data streaming, data transformation, and analytics efficiently?

A) Google Cloud Pub/Sub.
B) Google Cloud Bigtable.
C) Google Cloud Dataflow.
D) Google Cloud Spanner.

QUESTION 19

You need to optimize your Google Kubernetes Engine (GKE) cluster's performance by ensuring that pods always run on nodes with sufficient resources. Which GKE feature should you configure for this purpose?

A) Horizontal Pod Autoscaling
B) Vertical Pod Autoscaling
C) Node Auto-Provisioning
D) Pod Disruption Budgets
E) Cluster Autoscaler

QUESTION 20

A project management team in your organization needs to periodically review data from a Cloud Spanner instance but should not have edit permissions. How should you configure their access?

A) Directly assign the 'spanner.viewer' role to each team member.
B) Create a Google Group for the team and grant the 'spanner.viewer' role to the group.
C) Grant the team the 'spanner.databaseUser' role for combined view and edit access.
D) Provide the team with 'spanner.admin' role for full access to the Cloud Spanner instance.

QUESTION 21

For a marketing analysis project, your company needs to transfer a 40 GB dataset to a Google Cloud Storage Standard Bucket. Your office has a 750 Mbps connection. To optimize the data transfer speed, which approach should you adopt?

A) Upload the dataset via the GCP console to utilize its built-in optimization.
B) Utilize gsutil with parallel composite uploads to enhance upload efficiency.
C) Compress the dataset before uploading to reduce file size.
D) Upgrade the bucket to a Multi-Regional storage class for faster uploads.

QUESTION 22

Your team needs to perform routine maintenance on VMs located in a project named 'prod-infra'. A dedicated service account from a management project named 'infra-mgmt' is provided for these tasks. How should you proceed to use this service account in 'prod-infra'?

A) Download the service account's private key and use it to authenticate maintenance scripts in 'prod-infra'.
B) In 'prod-infra', assign the Compute Instance Admin role to the service account from 'infra-mgmt'.
C) Create a new service account in 'prod-infra' and replicate the permissions from the 'infra-mgmt'

service account.

D) Use the 'infra-mgmt' service account to generate temporary access tokens for VMs in 'prod-infra'.

QUESTION 23

Your GCP managed instance group for an e-commerce platform experiences inefficient scaling during peak times. The application start-up time is about 5 minutes. What change can improve scaling efficiency?

A) Increase the CPU utilization threshold.
B) Decrease the initial health check delay to 60 seconds.
C) Increase the initial health check delay to 300 seconds.
D) Decrease the minimum number of instances.
E) Implement a more aggressive scaling policy.

QUESTION 24

After deploying an App Engine application, you realize it might be in the wrong GCP project. How can you quickly verify the project to which the application was deployed?

A) Navigate to the App Engine section in the GCP Console and check the listed applications.
B) Check the environment variables in the app.yaml file for project identifiers.
C) Run gcloud app describe to see the details of the deployed application.
D) Execute gcloud config list in the Cloud Shell to see the current project settings.
E) Review the web.xml file in your application source code.
F) Access Deployment Manager and look for recent App Engine deployments.

QUESTION 25

You have a Compute Engine instance that needs more memory due to increased traffic. Currently, it has 4 GB of RAM and you want to upgrade it to 8 GB. What is the best way to do this?

A) Use the gcloud command-line tool to dynamically allocate more memory to the running instance.
B) Stop the instance, modify its machine type to one with higher memory, and restart it.
C) Apply a memory-scaling policy to the instance for automatic memory adjustment.
D) Migrate the instance to a different zone where instances have more memory by default.
E) Increase the memory allocation from the VM's operating system settings.
F) Add more virtual CPUs, which will automatically increase the memory.

QUESTION 26

After experiencing downtime due to an accidental deletion of a Compute Engine instance by a team member, what measure can you take to prevent such incidents in the future?

A) Set the instances as 'Preemptible' to avoid accidental long-term use.
B) Enable 'Deletion Protection' on all critical Compute Engine instances.
C) Change the instances to a different machine type that doesn't allow deletion.
D) Apply network tags to critical instances to restrict deletion operations.
E) Create a Cloud Function that triggers a warning when an instance is set for deletion.

F) Use the gcloud command-line tool to lock the instance against deletion.

QUESTION 27

You are developing software where users can upload invoices with limited-time access and automatic deletion after a certain period. Which two GCP features should you utilize to meet these requirements?

A) Implement Cloud Functions to delete files after 45 days.
B) Use Object Versioning in Cloud Storage for file retention control.
C) Configure lifecycle management in Cloud Storage for automatic deletion.
D) Create signed URLs with an expiration of 30 minutes for file uploads.
E) Set up a Data Loss Prevention (DLP) policy for invoice data.
F) Utilize Cloud Pub/Sub for triggering deletion events based on timestamps.

QUESTION 28

You are tasked with optimizing a Google Kubernetes Engine (GKE) cluster's resource utilization. Which GKE feature can automatically adjust the CPU and memory requests and limits for pods based on their usage?

A) Horizontal Pod Autoscaler (HPA)
B) Vertical Pod Autoscaler (VPA)
C) Cluster Autoscaler
D) Pod Disruption Budgets
E) GKE Node Pool Scaling

QUESTION 29

In setting up a secure web application for a financial institution on Compute Engine, you need to tightly control the egress traffic. What firewall configuration should you use for effective egress control in a new VPC?

A) Configure a high-priority rule to allow only essential egress ports and a default rule to deny all other traffic.
B) Set up a VPC firewall with a low-priority rule to block all egress and specific rules with higher priority to allow necessary ports.
C) Use Cloud Armor to create policies that restrict egress traffic to only specific ports.
D) Create network tags for each service, associating them with specific egress rules.
E) Employ a custom route in the VPC to direct all egress traffic through a security inspection service.
F) Implement a Cloud IDS to monitor and control egress traffic based on predefined security rules.

QUESTION 30

To minimize costs for a containerized internal application that's only used during work hours, what's the most cost-effective deployment strategy on GCP?

A) Deploy the application on Compute Engine with scheduled instance shutdowns.
B) Utilize Cloud Run with the configuration to scale to zero instances when idle.
C) Set up the application in a Google Kubernetes Engine cluster with horizontal pod autoscaling.

D) Implement the application on App Engine Flexible Environment with manual scaling.
E) Use Cloud Scheduler to trigger the application's start and stop on Cloud Functions.
F) Configure App Engine Standard Environment to use automatic scaling.

QUESTION 31

To ensure a DevOps team has appropriate access to production services in GCP projects without unnecessary privileges, what permission management strategy should be employed?

A) Assign the Compute Admin role to the DevOps team in all production projects.
B) Give the DevOps team Project Viewer access in all projects and add specific roles as needed.
C) Create a custom role tailored to the DevOps team's needs for each production project.
D) Use predefined roles like Storage Admin and Network Admin for the DevOps team.
E) Grant Organization Admin role to the DevOps team for centralized management.
F) Implement IAM conditional roles based on the DevOps team's usage patterns.

QUESTION 32

For a free file-sharing app using Cloud Storage, with files accessed frequently for 30 days and retained for 3 years, what is the most cost-effective storage management approach?

A) Use Standard storage for ongoing access and transition to Nearline storage after 30 days.
B) Initially store files in Coldline storage, then move them to Archive storage after 30 days.
C) Start with Nearline storage, then switch to Coldline after 30 days, and finally to Archive after a year.
D) Keep files in Standard storage for the first 30 days, followed by a transition to Archive storage for 3 years.
E) Maintain files in Coldline storage for the first 30 days, then transfer to Archive storage for the long-term.
F) Utilize a lifecycle policy to automatically move files from Standard to Coldline, and then to Archive over 3 years.

QUESTION 33

For a mobile multiplayer game using UDP packets and hosted on Google Cloud, which option is best for exposing the backend with a single IP while allowing horizontal scaling?

A) Set up an SSL Proxy Load Balancer in front of the game servers.
B) Configure an External HTTP(S) Load Balancer for the backend.
C) Use a Global TCP Proxy Load Balancer for traffic management.
D) Implement an External Network Load Balancer for UDP traffic.
E) Deploy an Internal UDP Load Balancer with a public IP.
F) Create an External TCP/UDP Load Balancer for unified traffic handling.

QUESTION 34

You are designing a cloud solution for a media company that requires a scalable video processing system. Videos uploaded to an on-premise server need to be processed and stored in GCP. What is the most efficient architecture for this requirement?

A) Utilize Cloud Storage FUSE to mount a bucket directly on the on-premise server, and use Cloud Functions for processing upon upload.
B) Write a script using gsutil for transferring videos to Cloud Storage, then process them using Cloud Dataprep and store in Cloud SQL.
C) Deploy a Kubernetes Engine cluster with a custom video processing service, and sync videos using Cloud Storage Transfer Service.
D) Implement an App Engine application to handle video uploads, process them using Cloud Video Intelligence API, and store in Cloud Storage.
E) Set up a Dataflow job to transfer and process videos, using Pub/Sub for triggering processing tasks, and archive processed videos in Cloud Storage.

QUESTION 35

You are managing a set of Compute Engine instances that need to be accessed by a remote monitoring tool. The tool requires network-level access to these VMs for health checks but does not support Google Cloud authentication mechanisms. How should you configure access?

A) Enable VPC Flow Logs to monitor VMs and share logs with the monitoring tool.
B) Set up a Cloud VPN and create specific firewall rules to allow traffic from the monitoring tool.
C) Implement a Cloud Interconnect and use IAM policies to regulate the tool's access.
D) Create a dedicated service account and use its credentials for the monitoring tool's authentication.
E) Use Network Tags to identify VMs and configure firewall rules to allow access from the tool's IP range.

QUESTION 36

As an SRE, you need to ensure that any increase in latency over a certain threshold for your GCP-hosted API is quickly identified and addressed. What is the best approach to achieve this?

A) Implement Stackdriver Profiler to continuously analyze API performance and set up email alerts.
B) Use Cloud Endpoints to monitor API performance and configure an alert in Cloud Monitoring for latency thresholds.
C) Set up a dedicated VM that pings the API at regular intervals and logs response times.
D) Create a log-based metric in Cloud Logging for high latency and set an alert policy.
E) Configure a Cloud Scheduler job to test API latency and report any increases.

QUESTION 37

Your organization is developing a machine learning model that requires large-scale data processing on Google Cloud Platform. Which GCP service is best suited for this task, allowing you to scale resources based on the workload?

A) Google Cloud Storage
B) Google Cloud Pub/Sub
C) Google BigQuery
D) Google Cloud Dataprep
E) Google Cloud Dataproc

QUESTION 38

Your organization is migrating its on-premises data center to Google Cloud, and you need to set up a hybrid cloud architecture to facilitate the migration. You want to maintain a private connection between your on-premises network and Google Cloud. Which Google Cloud networking solution should you choose to establish this private connection?

A) Deploy Google Cloud VPN for secure hybrid connectivity.
B) Implement Google Cloud Direct Peering for direct on-premises-to-cloud communication.
C) Set up Google Cloud Interconnect for dedicated, private network connections.
D) Configure Google Cloud VPC Peering for network isolation.
E) Utilize Google Cloud CDN for hybrid cloud communication.

QUESTION 39

Your company is migrating its existing on-premises servers to Google Cloud. You need to ensure that the migrated servers have a public IP address to facilitate external access. What should you configure in Google Cloud to enable this public IP assignment during migration?

A) Disable external IP addresses in the Google Cloud project.
B) Enable Cloud NAT for private server communication.
C) Create a firewall rule to block external access for security.
D) Set up an external IP address reservation for the migrated servers.

QUESTION 40

Your company is planning to set up a multi-tier web application on Google Cloud Platform (GCP). The architecture includes a web server, an application server, and a database server. To ensure high availability and fault tolerance, which GCP service or feature should you use for the web server and application server instances?

A) Use Google Cloud Load Balancing to distribute traffic across multiple instances in different zones.
B) Deploy a single instance in a single zone to minimize complexity.
C) Utilize Google Cloud CDN to cache content and improve performance.
D) Enable auto-healing for the instances to automatically replace failed ones.

QUESTION 41

You are working on a project that involves processing a large amount of data using Google Cloud services. To optimize costs, you want to minimize data egress charges when transferring data out of Google Cloud Storage to the public internet. Which Google Cloud service should you use to achieve this optimization?

A) Google Cloud Pub/Sub
B) Google Cloud Dataflow
C) Google Cloud Transfer Appliance
D) Google Cloud CDN

QUESTION 42

You have multiple Compute Engine instances in your project, and you need to grant access to a specific Cloud Storage bucket for one instance only to install a third-party OTP application. Which approach should you follow to achieve this?

A) Grant permissions directly to the instance's external IP address for the Cloud Storage bucket.
B) Grant permissions to the default Compute Engine service account for the instance.
C) Create a new service account and select it while creating the new instance. Grant the service account permissions on Cloud Storage.
D) Grant permissions to all Compute Engine instances in the project for the Cloud Storage bucket.
E) Use a shared access key for the Compute Engine instance to access the Cloud Storage bucket.

QUESTION 43

You are developing a web application on GCP, and you want to perform A/B testing by testing updates on a small portion of live users before rolling them out to everyone. Which GCP deployment strategy should you choose to achieve this goal effectively?

A) Use App Engine to run your app. For each update, create a new version of the same service and send a small percentage of traffic to the new version using traffic splitting.
B) Use App Engine to run your app. For each update, create a new service and send a small percentage of traffic to the new version using traffic splitting.
C) Use Kubernetes Engine to run your app. For a new release, update the deployment to use the new version.
D) Use Kubernetes Engine to run your app. For a new release, create a new deployment for the new version and update the service to use the new deployment.

QUESTION 44

Your organization is looking to implement a disaster recovery strategy for its critical data stored in Google Cloud Storage. You want to ensure data resilience and availability in the event of data corruption or accidental deletion. What should you do to achieve this?

A) Enable versioning for the Google Cloud Storage bucket
B) Create multiple Google Cloud Storage buckets for redundancy.
C) Set up daily backups to an on-premises data center.
D) Use Google Cloud Transfer Service to replicate data to another region.

QUESTION 45

Your organization is planning to set up a private, dedicated connection between its data center and Google Cloud. You require a high-bandwidth connection that offers low-latency and is suitable for large data transfers. Which Google Cloud networking option should you choose for this dedicated connection?

A) Google Cloud VPN
B) Google Cloud Interconnect (Dedicated)
C) Google Cloud CDN
D) Google Cloud DNS

QUESTION 46

Your organization wants to implement a managed Kubernetes service on Google Cloud for deploying containerized applications. You need a service that provides auto-scaling, managed control plane, and integration with Google Cloud monitoring and logging. Which Google Cloud service should you choose for managed Kubernetes?

A) Google Kubernetes Engine (GKE)
B) Google Cloud Compute Engine
C) Google Cloud Run
D) Google App Engine

QUESTION 47

Your organization is building a web application on Google Cloud Platform (GCP) that needs to scale automatically based on user traffic. You want to ensure that the application can handle sudden spikes in traffic without manual intervention. Which GCP service should you use for this purpose?

A) Utilize Google Cloud Load Balancing for traffic management.
B) Implement Google Cloud Auto Scaling for managing virtual machine instances.
C) Leverage Google Cloud App Engine for automatic scaling of web applications.
D) Use Google Cloud Functions for serverless event-driven scaling.

QUESTION 48

Your organization is using Google Kubernetes Engine (GKE) to deploy containerized applications. You want to automate the scaling of your application based on custom metrics and conditions. Which GKE feature allows you to achieve this level of automation?

A) Implement GKE's Horizontal Pod Autoscaling (HPA) for scaling based on CPU and memory metrics.
B) Use GKE's Cluster Autoscaler for automatically resizing the GKE cluster based on resource demands.
C) Configure GKE's Node Pools for granular control of node scaling.
D) Leverage GKE's Persistent Disk Autoscaler for dynamically adjusting disk capacity.

QUESTION 49

Your team has developed a microservice that is packaged as a Docker container. You are tasked with deploying this microservice on Google Kubernetes Engine. What should be your first step in this deployment process?

A) Upload the Docker container image to Container Registry.
B) Write a Kubernetes YAML configuration file for the microservice.
C) Create a GKE cluster to host the microservice.
D) Configure a CI/CD pipeline to automate the deployment process.
E) Set up a Cloud SQL database for the microservice to use.

QUESTION 50

In a GKE cluster hosting a complex application, one microservice requires significantly more memory than others. How can you ensure efficient resource utilization across the cluster?

A) Utilize Horizontal Pod Autoscaling to scale the memory-intensive microservice based on memory usage.

B) Configure all microservices with equal memory and CPU requests to ensure uniform resource allocation.

C) Create a dedicated node pool with memory-optimized machine types for the memory-intensive microservice.

D) Apply resource limits on the Kubernetes deployment configuration for the memory-intensive microservice.

E) Set up a Cluster Autoscaler to automatically adjust the number of nodes based on memory requirements.

SET 7 - ANSWERS ONLY

QUESTION 1

Answer - A) Utilize managed instance groups

A) Correct, managed instance groups with autoscaling and regional persistent disks provide high availability and handle variable load efficiently.
B) Incorrect, a single VM instance does not ensure high availability, and periodic snapshots do not address variable load.
C) Incorrect, preemptible VMs are cost-effective but not suitable for high-availability due to their ephemeral nature.
D) Incorrect, unmanaged instance groups lack the autoscaling feature, and manual scaling is less efficient.
E) Incorrect, snapshot-based autoscaling is not a standard feature, and custom machine types may not be necessary.
F) Incorrect, while a global HTTP(S) load balancer provides high availability, it doesn't address the stateful nature of the application.

QUESTION 2

Answer - C) Preemptible VMs and regular VMs

A) Incorrect, custom machine types in a single zone may not offer the best cost-effectiveness.
B) Incorrect, predefined machine types may not optimally balance computational power and cost.
C) Correct, a combination of preemptible and regular VMs balances performance and cost, suitable for HPC workloads.
D) Incorrect, n2-highcpu machines are powerful but may be more costly; Cloud Interconnect focuses on connectivity rather than computational throughput.
E) Incorrect, sole-tenant nodes provide dedicated hardware but might exceed the required budget for cost-effectiveness.

QUESTION 3

Answer - A) GKE with rolling updates

A) Correct, GKE with rolling updates and health checks ensures zero downtime and supports quick rollbacks.
B) Incorrect, while App Engine's traffic splitting is effective, it may not provide the granularity needed for microservices deployment.
C) Incorrect, blue-green deployments are reliable but may not be as efficient as automated rolling updates in GKE.
D) Incorrect, canary deployments are effective but can be complex to set up and may not be necessary for all microservices.
E) Incorrect, Cloud Functions is ideal for serverless workloads but may not offer the control needed for complex microservices deployments.

QUESTION 4

Answer - A) Multi-regional Cloud CDN

A) Correct, Cloud CDN caches content closer to users, reducing latency and improving performance for web applications.
B) Incorrect, Cloud Interconnect is more about providing reliable and secure connectivity between on-premises and GCP, not reducing latency for web applications.
C) Incorrect, Cloud VPN secures connectivity between different networks but does not inherently improve application performance or reduce latency.
D) Incorrect, while load balancers distribute traffic, they don't cache content or reduce latency in the same way as a CDN.
E) Incorrect, optimizing network routes can improve efficiency, but it's not as impactful for latency and performance as a CDN.

QUESTION 5

Answer - D) Cloud Identity and Active Directory synchronization

A) Incorrect, IAM Conditional Roles are used for defining access conditions but don't directly integrate with Active Directory.
B) Incorrect, VPC Service Controls provide network-level isolation and do not manage user access based on Active Directory.
C) Incorrect, Identity-Aware Proxy controls access to web applications but is not specifically for integrating with Active Directory groups.
D) Correct, synchronizing Cloud Identity with Active Directory groups and applying IAM roles based on group membership ensures that only specific departments have access to certain resources.
E) Incorrect, Access Context Manager is more for defining access policies based on user context and location, not direct integration with Active Directory.

QUESTION 6

Answer - D) Local instance of MinIO

A) Incorrect, a locally mounted file system does not fully simulate Cloud Storage's behavior or API.
B) Incorrect, gsutil interacts with actual Cloud Storage buckets in GCP, not a local environment.
C) Incorrect, there is no official Cloud Storage emulator in the Google Cloud SDK.
D) Correct, setting up a local instance of MinIO can simulate Cloud Storage for development purposes.
E) Incorrect, connecting directly to Cloud Storage is not a method for local testing.

QUESTION 7

Answer - B) SAML SSO integration

A) Incorrect, IAM policies control access but don't enforce authentication methods.
B) Correct, configuring SAML SSO integration between GCP and Active Directory ensures that GCP resources are accessible only to users authenticated through Active Directory.
C) Incorrect, network policies control network access but do not specify authentication methods.
D) Incorrect, VPC Service Controls create security perimeters for data but do not enforce specific authentication methods.

E) Incorrect, developing a custom App Engine application for this purpose is unnecessary and overly complex.

QUESTION 8

Answer - A) roles/iam.serviceAccountKeyAdmin

A) Correct, roles/iam.serviceAccountKeyAdmin is specifically designed for creating and managing keys for service accounts.
B) Incorrect, roles/iam.serviceAccountAdmin allows service account management but does not specifically include key management.
C) Incorrect, roles/iam.serviceAccountUser allows using service accounts but not managing their keys.
D) Incorrect, roles/iam.securityReviewer is for viewing security configurations, not for managing service account keys.
E) Incorrect, roles/cloudkms.admin is related to Cloud Key Management Service and not directly to service account key management.

QUESTION 9

Answer – A) Use BigQuery for data warehousing and Dataflow for real-time processing. Implement VPC Service Controls for security and enable Customer-Managed Encryption Keys (CMEK) for all data.

Option A is the most suitable solution for the requirements. BigQuery is ideal for large-scale data warehousing, and Dataflow supports robust real-time analytics. VPC Service Controls enhance security by ensuring that data does not leave a secure perimeter, and CMEK provides the necessary encryption controls for compliance. Option B, while offering real-time processing capabilities, does not leverage an optimal data warehousing solution for large volumes of data. Option C's choice of Cloud Bigtable is not ideal for data warehousing purposes. Option D does not specify an appropriate real-time analytics tool and relies on default encryption, which might not meet the stringent compliance needs. Option E, using Datastore and Cloud Functions, does not provide the required scalability and control over encryption for a financial services data processing system.

QUESTION 10

Answer – A) Use Standard for 60 days, then Nearline for 300 days, Coldline thereafter, and Delete after 1095 days.

A) Correct. This aligns with the access pattern: Standard for frequent access, Nearline for occasional, Coldline for rare, and deletion after 3 years.
B) Incorrect due to premature use of Coldline.
C) Incorrect as Nearline is not optimal for the initial frequent access period.
D) Incorrect as it does not match the specified access frequencies and timelines.

QUESTION 11

Answer - C) Set up a temporary replication from the on-premises database to a Cloud SQL instance, switch over once replication is consistent.

A) Not suitable for large databases and can cause significant downtime.

B) Involves unnecessary steps and potential compatibility issues.
C) Correct. Minimizes downtime and ensures data consistency through replication.
D) Can result in considerable downtime and potential data consistency issues.

QUESTION 12

Answer - B) Implement Cloud Pub/Sub for data ingestion, use Dataflow for stream processing, store processed data in Bigtable, and analyze with BigQuery.

A) Offers scalability but Spanner may not be the best fit for time-series data. Looker is more for business intelligence than real-time analytics.
B) Correct. Cloud Pub/Sub and Dataflow provide efficient real-time data processing, Bigtable is ideal for time-series data storage, and BigQuery allows for complex data analytics.
C) Firebase is suitable for real-time applications but not for large-scale data ingestion and processing.
D) Kubernetes Engine and Cloud SQL are not the most efficient choices for real-time data processing and time-series data storage in this context.

QUESTION 13

Answer - A) Create a group for auditors and assign them the 'healthcare.datasetViewer' and 'logging.viewer' roles.

A) This approach is in line with best practices for IAM, allowing auditors to access necessary data and logs without excessive permissions.
B) Too broad and risky as it provides full project access.
C) The 'healthcare.admin' role is overly permissive for auditing purposes.
D) Managing individual accounts is less efficient than using groups.

QUESTION 14

Answer - A) Examine the read and download activities in the Cloud Storage Audit logs in the GCP console.

A) Using audit logs is the most direct and efficient way to track specific user activities, such as reading or downloading files from Cloud Storage.
B) While Stackdriver logging can be used, audit logs provide a more focused approach for this specific requirement.
C) The metadata section does not provide detailed user access logs.
D) BigQuery can be used for analysis but is not necessary for simply reviewing access logs.

QUESTION 15

Answer - A) Utilize HTTP(S) Load Balancer with URL maps for content-based routing and SSL termination capabilities.

A) HTTP(S) Load Balancer with URL maps is ideal for content-based routing and supports SSL offloading, handling high traffic efficiently.
B) SSL Proxy Load Balancer does not support HTTP header-based routing.
C) Network Load Balancer does not support SSL offloading and operates at a lower level without HTTP awareness.

D) TCP Proxy Load Balancer does not provide content-based routing and operates at the TCP level, not HTTP(S).

QUESTION 16

Answer - A) Google Cloud Storage Transfer Service

Option A: This is the correct choice as Google Cloud Storage Transfer Service allows you to automate data transfers, including backups, to different regions for disaster recovery.
Option B: Google Cloud Dataflow is a data processing service and not primarily used for automating backups.
Option C: Google Cloud Pub/Sub is a messaging service and not designed for automated backups.
Option D: Google Cloud Storage Object Versioning helps with versioning but does not automate backups to different regions.
Option E: Google Cloud Storage Lifecycle policies are used for data lifecycle management but may not fully automate cross-region backups.

QUESTION 17

Answer - B) Google Cloud Load Balancer for traffic distribution.

Option B: This is the correct choice as Google Cloud Load Balancer is designed to distribute traffic across multiple instances or regions, ensuring high availability and redundancy.
Option A: Google Cloud Storage is for data storage and backup, not for ensuring high availability of applications.
Option C: Google Cloud Pub/Sub is a messaging service, not specifically for high availability of applications.
Option D: Google Cloud VPN provides secure network connections but doesn't directly address high availability of applications.

QUESTION 18

Answer - C) Google Cloud Dataflow.

Option C is the correct choice as Google Cloud Dataflow is a fully managed stream and batch data processing service that can handle real-time data streaming, data transformation, and analytics efficiently.
Option A is for messaging, Option B is for NoSQL storage, and Option D is for globally distributed databases.

QUESTION 19

Answer - E) Cluster Autoscaler

Option E, "Cluster Autoscaler," is the correct choice. It automatically adjusts the size of the GKE cluster, ensuring that there are enough nodes with sufficient resources to accommodate the pods. Horizontal and Vertical Pod Autoscaling (Options A and B) deal with pod resource management but not node scaling. Node Auto-Provisioning (Option C) is related to creating new node pools, and Pod Disruption Budgets (Option D) define pod disruption constraints.

QUESTION 20

Answer - B) Create a Google Group for the team and grant the 'spanner.viewer' role to the group.

B) This method is efficient and follows best practices, granting the necessary view-only access without the complexity of managing individual user permissions.
 A) Assigning roles to individuals is less manageable.
 C) The 'spanner.databaseUser' role provides unnecessary edit access.
 D) The 'spanner.admin' role grants excessive privileges that are not needed for review purposes.

QUESTION 21

Answer - B) Utilize gsutil with parallel composite uploads to enhance upload efficiency.

B) Parallel composite uploads with gsutil split the dataset into smaller parts, allowing for faster and more efficient uploads that better utilize the available high-speed connection.
 A) The GCP console doesn't offer the same level of upload optimization as gsutil.
 C) While compression reduces file size, it may not optimize upload speed as effectively as parallel uploads.
 D) Storage class affects storage cost and redundancy, not upload speed.

QUESTION 22

Answer - B) In 'prod-infra', assign the Compute Instance Admin role to the service account from 'infra-mgmt'.

B) Assigning the necessary IAM role to the service account from the 'infra-mgmt' project in 'prod-infra' is the appropriate way to grant it permissions to perform maintenance tasks on VMs. This approach follows the principle of least privilege and does not involve sharing private keys.
 A) Downloading and using private keys is not recommended for security reasons.
 C) Creating a new service account is unnecessary and complicates permission management.
 D) Generating temporary access tokens is not required and adds complexity.

QUESTION 23

Answer - C) Increase the initial health check delay to 300 seconds.

A) Increasing the CPU threshold might delay necessary scaling during high traffic.
 B) Decreasing the health check delay could cause even more premature scaling.
 C) Correct. Matching the health check delay with the start-up time ensures new instances are ready before being checked.
 D) Decreasing the minimum number of instances does not address the issue of health check timing.
 E) A more aggressive scaling policy could lead to more frequent, unnecessary scaling.

QUESTION 24

Answer - D) Execute gcloud config list in the Cloud Shell to see the current project settings.

D) This command will display the current gcloud configuration, including the project ID, which indicates the default project for deployments.

A) This method requires access to the correct GCP project, which might be unknown.
B) Environment variables in app.yaml typically do not include project identifiers.
C) gcloud app describe can be useful but requires specifying the project.
E) The web.xml file does not contain information about GCP project deployments.
F) Deployment Manager is not used for standard App Engine deployments.

QUESTION 25

Answer - B) Stop the instance, modify its machine type to one with higher memory, and restart it.

B) Stopping the instance and changing its machine type to one with the desired memory (and possibly vCPU) configuration is the correct way to upgrade a VM's memory in GCP.
A) The gcloud tool cannot dynamically allocate more memory to a running instance.
C) GCP does not offer an automatic memory-scaling policy.
D) Migrating zones does not affect the machine type or memory of an instance.
E) Memory allocation for a VM must be done through GCP, not the OS.
F) Adding more CPUs does not automatically increase memory; it's a separate configuration.

QUESTION 26

Answer - B) Enable 'Deletion Protection' on all critical Compute Engine instances.

B) 'Deletion Protection' is a specific feature designed to prevent accidental or unintended deletion of Compute Engine instances, which directly addresses the issue faced.
A) Making instances 'Preemptible' doesn't prevent deletion; it affects instance lifespan and availability.
C) Changing machine types does not impact the ability to delete instances.
D) Network tags are used for network access control, not for preventing deletion.
E) A Cloud Function can alert but may not prevent the deletion process.
F) The gcloud tool does not offer a direct command to lock an instance against deletion.

QUESTION 27

Answer - C) and D)

C) Cloud Storage lifecycle management automates the deletion of files after a specified duration (45 days in this case), simplifying maintenance.
D) Signed URLs with a 30-minute expiration time control user access to their uploaded files, ensuring they can only access or upload invoices for a limited duration.
A) Cloud Functions for deletion is more complex and less efficient than lifecycle policies.
B) Object Versioning does not directly address the specified time-based requirements.
E) DLP is for data security and privacy, not for access control or auto-deletion.
F) Cloud Pub/Sub is more suited for event-driven applications, not for direct file management.

QUESTION 28

Answer - B) Vertical Pod Autoscaler (VPA)

Option B - Vertical Pod Autoscaler (VPA) automatically adjusts the CPU and memory requests and limits for pods based on their actual resource usage, optimizing resource allocation.

Option A - Horizontal Pod Autoscaler (HPA) scales the number of pod replicas, not resource allocation.
Option C - Cluster Autoscaler manages node scaling, not pod resource limits.
Option D - Pod Disruption Budgets set constraints on pod disruptions, and
Option E - GKE Node Pool Scaling is related to the cluster's node pool size.

QUESTION 29

Answer - B) Set up a VPC firewall with a low-priority rule to block all egress and specific rules with higher priority to allow necessary ports.

B) This configuration effectively restricts all egress traffic by default, while higher priority rules selectively permit traffic through only the necessary ports. This granular control is essential for a secure financial web application.
A) High-priority rules to allow traffic might not adequately prevent other unwanted egress traffic.
C) Cloud Armor is primarily used for ingress protection, not egress.
D) Network tags are helpful but need to be combined with specific firewall rules for effective control.
E) Custom routes control traffic flow but don't inherently restrict egress ports.
F) Cloud IDS is for intrusion detection, not for specific egress traffic control.

QUESTION 30

Answer - B) Utilize Cloud Run with the configuration to scale to zero instances when idle.

B) Cloud Run is the most suitable option as it can automatically scale down to zero instances, ensuring that you are only billed for the time the application is in use. This aligns perfectly with the requirement to minimize costs during off-hours.
A) Compute Engine requires manual scheduling for shutdowns, which is less efficient.
C) Google Kubernetes Engine doesn't naturally scale to zero and incurs costs even when idle.
D) App Engine Flexible with manual scaling does not automatically scale to zero.
E) Cloud Scheduler with Cloud Functions is more suited for occasional tasks, not continuous applications.
F) App Engine Standard Environment does not scale to zero, leading to ongoing costs.

QUESTION 31

Answer - C) Create a custom role tailored to the DevOps team's needs for each production project.

C) A custom role specifically tailored to the DevOps team's responsibilities in each production project is the most secure and efficient method. It allows precise control over the permissions granted, ensuring they have access only to what is necessary for their job, thereby following the principle of least privilege.
A) The Compute Admin role might be too broad for specific DevOps tasks.
B) Project Viewer is too restrictive and may not allow necessary access for DevOps operations.
D) Predefined roles like Storage and Network Admin may not align precisely with DevOps needs.
E) Organization Admin grants excessively broad access and increases security risks.
F) IAM conditional roles can be complex to manage and may not be as precise as custom roles.

QUESTION 32

Answer - D) Keep files in Standard storage for the first 30 days, followed by a transition to Archive storage for 3 years.

D) This method is cost-effective and aligns with the app's usage pattern. Standard storage is ideal for the initial 30-day frequent access period, and transitioning to Archive storage afterwards provides the most economical solution for long-term retention of 3 years, minimizing costs while ensuring data availability.
A) Nearline storage after 30 days is less cost-effective compared to Archive for long-term retention.
B) Starting with Coldline is not ideal for frequent access in the initial 30 days.
C) This multiple-transition approach is less efficient and may increase costs.
E) Coldline for the initial 30 days is not suitable for frequent file access.
F) Moving from Standard to Coldline and then to Archive may incur unnecessary costs.

QUESTION 33

Answer - D) Implement an External Network Load Balancer for UDP traffic.

D) An External Network Load Balancer is the most suitable for this requirement. It effectively handles UDP traffic and allows exposing the backend servers through a single external IP address. This enables efficient load balancing and horizontal scaling of the game servers to accommodate varying player traffic.
A) SSL Proxy Load Balancers do not support UDP traffic.
B) External HTTP(S) Load Balancers are for HTTP/HTTPS traffic, not suitable for UDP.
C) Global TCP Proxy Load Balancers are for TCP traffic, not UDP.
E) Internal UDP Load Balancers do not provide external IP addresses for internet exposure.
F) External TCP/UDP Load Balancers as described do not exist in Google Cloud Platform.

QUESTION 34

Answer – E) Dataflow, Pub/Sub, Cloud Storage

A) Incorrect, FUSE is not ideal for heavy processing tasks.
B) Incorrect, Cloud SQL isn't suited for large video files.
C) Incorrect, overly complex and not the most efficient.
D) Incorrect, App Engine isn't ideal for heavy processing like video files.
E) Correct, leverages GCP's strengths in data transfer, processing, and storage.

QUESTION 35

Answer – E) Network Tags, firewall rules

A) Incorrect, VPC Flow Logs are for monitoring network traffic, not for providing access.
B) Correct, Cloud VPN and firewall rules provide a secure way to allow specific network-level access.
C) Incorrect, Cloud Interconnect is more for high-volume data transfer, not specific tool access.
D) Incorrect, service accounts are for internal GCP services, not external tools.
E) Correct, Network Tags and firewall rules can be used to selectively allow traffic from the tool's IP range.

QUESTION 36

Answer – B) Cloud Endpoints, Cloud Monitoring alert

A) Incorrect, Stackdriver Profiler is for CPU and memory profiling, not latency monitoring.
B) Correct, Cloud Endpoints for monitoring and Cloud Monitoring for alerting is a seamless integration for this requirement.
C) Incorrect, using a VM for pinging is less efficient and scalable.
D) Incorrect, log-based metrics are less suitable for real-time latency monitoring.
E) Incorrect, Cloud Scheduler is not ideal for continuous monitoring.

QUESTION 37

Answer - E) Google Cloud Dataproc (Correct)

Option A is incorrect because Google Cloud Storage is an object storage service and does not provide the data processing capabilities needed for large-scale data processing.
Option B is incorrect because Google Cloud Pub/Sub is a messaging service and not designed for data processing.
Option C is incorrect because while Google BigQuery is a powerful data warehouse and analytics service, it may not provide the scalability required for large-scale data processing jobs.
Option D is incorrect because Google Cloud Dataprep is a data preparation tool, not a data processing service.
Option E is correct because Google Cloud Dataproc is a managed Apache Hadoop and Apache Spark service that allows you to process large volumes of data with the ability to scale resources dynamically based on the workload.

QUESTION 38

Answer - C) Set up Google Cloud Interconnect for dedicated, private network connections. (Correct)

Option A is incorrect because while Google Cloud VPN provides secure connectivity, it may not offer the same level of dedicated, private network connections as Google Cloud Interconnect.
Option B is incorrect because Google Cloud Direct Peering focuses on direct internet-based communication and may not provide the private connection needed for hybrid cloud architecture.
Option D is incorrect because Google Cloud VPC Peering is used for network isolation within GCP, not for connecting on-premises networks.
Option E is incorrect because Google Cloud CDN is for content delivery and not for establishing private connections between on-premises and cloud networks.
Option C is correct because Google Cloud Interconnect is designed for dedicated, private network connections, making it suitable for maintaining a private connection between on-premises networks and Google Cloud in a hybrid cloud architecture.

QUESTION 39

Answer - D) Set up an external IP address reservation for the migrated servers. (Correct)

Option A is incorrect because disabling external IP addresses in the Google Cloud project would prevent public IP assignment, which is required for external access.
Option B is incorrect because enabling Cloud NAT is for providing internet access to private instances,

not for assigning public IP addresses.
Option C is incorrect because creating a firewall rule to block external access contradicts the goal of enabling public IP addresses for external access.
Setting up an external IP address reservation allows you to assign public IPs to the migrated servers, facilitating external access during migration.

QUESTION 40

Answer - A) Use Google Cloud Load Balancing to distribute traffic across multiple instances in different zones.

Option B is incorrect because deploying a single instance in a single zone does not provide high availability or fault tolerance. Option C is incorrect because Google Cloud CDN is primarily used for content caching and does not directly address instance availability. Option D is incorrect because enabling auto-healing alone does not distribute traffic across multiple instances or zones. Option A is correct because using Google Cloud Load Balancing allows you to distribute traffic across multiple instances in different zones, providing both high availability and fault tolerance for the web and application servers.

QUESTION 41

Answer - D) Google Cloud CDN

Option A, Google Cloud Pub/Sub, is a messaging service and not related to data egress charges. Option B, Google Cloud Dataflow, is used for data processing and not specifically for minimizing data egress charges. Option C, Google Cloud Transfer Appliance, is a physical appliance used for data transfer, but it is not a service for optimizing egress charges. Option D, Google Cloud CDN (Content Delivery Network), can help optimize costs by caching and delivering content from Google Cloud Storage closer to the user, reducing data egress charges when transferring data to the public internet.

QUESTION 42

Answer - C) Create a new service account and select it while creating the new instance. Grant the service account permissions on Cloud Storage.

Option A is incorrect because granting permissions to an external IP address does not provide the necessary access control and isolates access to a specific instance.
Option B is incorrect because using the default service account may lead to unintended access by other instances using the same account.
Option D is incorrect because granting permissions to all instances in the project does not isolate access to the specific instance that needs it.
Option E is incorrect because using a shared access key may not provide the required security and granularity of access control.

QUESTION 43

Answer - A) Use App Engine to run your app. For each update, create a new version of the same service and send a small percentage of traffic to the new version using traffic splitting.

Option A is correct because it aligns with your goal of A/B testing. Using App Engine, you can create new versions of the same service and use traffic splitting to test updates on a small portion of live users while keeping the rest on the live version.
Option B is incorrect because creating a new service for each update would result in multiple instances of the app running simultaneously, which is not suitable for A/B testing.
Option C is incorrect because updating the deployment in Kubernetes Engine would direct all traffic to the new version, which does not allow for controlled A/B testing.
Option D is incorrect because creating a new deployment and updating the service would also direct all traffic to the new deployment, making it unsuitable for A/B testing.

QUESTION 44

Answer - A) Enable versioning for the Google Cloud Storage bucket

Option A is correct because enabling versioning for a Google Cloud Storage bucket allows you to retain and recover previous versions of objects in case of data corruption or accidental deletion, ensuring data resilience and availability.
Option B suggests creating multiple buckets for redundancy, which may increase complexity and costs without guaranteeing data recovery.
Option C proposes daily backups to an on-premises data center, which may not provide real-time recovery and is not the most efficient approach.
Option D mentions replication but does not specifically address data resilience and versioning.

QUESTION 45

Answer - B) Google Cloud Interconnect (Dedicated)

Option B is correct because Google Cloud Interconnect (Dedicated) provides a private, high-bandwidth, and low-latency connection between on-premises data centers and Google Cloud, making it suitable for large data transfers and dedicated connections.
Option A (Google Cloud VPN) offers secure connections but may not provide the same high bandwidth and low latency as Dedicated Interconnect.
Option C (Google Cloud CDN) is for content delivery and does not provide dedicated connections.
Option D (Google Cloud DNS) is for domain name resolution and does not provide dedicated network connections.

QUESTION 46

Answer - A) Google Kubernetes Engine (GKE)

Option A is correct because Google Kubernetes Engine (GKE) is a managed Kubernetes service that offers auto-scaling, a managed control plane, and seamless integration with Google Cloud monitoring and logging, making it ideal for deploying containerized applications.
Option B (Google Cloud Compute Engine) is an Infrastructure-as-a-Service (IaaS) offering and does not provide a fully managed Kubernetes environment.
Option C (Google Cloud Run) is a serverless platform for containerized applications, but it does not provide full Kubernetes capabilities.
Option D (Google App Engine) is a platform-as-a-service (PaaS) offering and is not Kubernetes-based.

QUESTION 47

Answer - C) Leverage Google Cloud App Engine for automatic scaling of web applications

Option C is correct because Google Cloud App Engine is a fully managed platform-as-a-service (PaaS) that offers automatic scaling of web applications based on user traffic. It ensures that your application can handle sudden traffic spikes without manual intervention.
Option A is not the most suitable choice because Google Cloud Load Balancing focuses on distributing traffic to backend instances but does not handle the automatic scaling of application instances.
Option B is not the best choice for web applications because Google Cloud Auto Scaling is primarily used for managing virtual machine instances, not for web application platforms.
Option D is not the recommended choice for web applications, as Google Cloud Functions are more focused on serverless event-driven functions rather than scaling entire web applications.

QUESTION 48

Answer - A) Implement GKE's Horizontal Pod Autoscaling (HPA) for scaling based on CPU and memory metrics

Option A is correct because GKE's Horizontal Pod Autoscaling (HPA) allows you to automate the scaling of your application pods based on custom metrics, including CPU and memory utilization. It provides fine-grained control over application scaling based on application-specific requirements.
Option B focuses on cluster-level scaling and is not as granular as HPA for application pod scaling.
Option C is related to node pool management and does not directly address application scaling.
Option D is specifically for adjusting disk capacity and does not handle application scaling.

QUESTION 49

Answer – A) Upload to Container Registry

A) Correct, before deploying, the container image should be uploaded to Container Registry, which is the standard repository for Docker images in GCP.
B) Incorrect, writing a YAML file is a subsequent step after the image is available.
C) Incorrect, creating a GKE cluster is necessary but not the first step.
D) Incorrect, setting up CI/CD is part of automation, not the initial deployment step.
E) Incorrect, setting up a database is part of the application setup, not the container deployment.

QUESTION 50

Answer – C) Dedicated node pool

A) Incorrect, Horizontal Pod Autoscaling scales the number of pods, not memory allocation.
B) Incorrect, uniform resource allocation can lead to inefficiency.
C) Correct, a dedicated node pool for memory-intensive tasks allows for targeted resource optimization.
D) Incorrect, setting resource limits does not address the need for more memory capacity.
E) Incorrect, Cluster Autoscaler adjusts node count, not individual node specs.

SET 8 - QUESTIONS ONLY

QUESTION 1

A company needs to analyze large datasets with minimal latency. Which GCP solution should you recommend?

A) Deploy BigQuery with partitioned tables and enable BigQuery BI Engine for faster analysis.
B) Utilize Cloud SQL with read replicas in different regions for distributed data analysis.
C) Implement Dataflow for real-time data processing, storing results in Cloud Storage.
D) Set up a Hadoop cluster on Compute Engine with high-memory instances and SSDs.
E) Use Cloud Spanner for its global distribution and strong consistency, combined with Data Studio for visualization.
F) Leverage Bigtable for large-scale NoSQL data storage and analysis, with integration to Cloud Dataproc for processing.

QUESTION 2

Your company hosts a critical database on Cloud SQL in the us-east1 region. To enhance disaster recovery capabilities, you need to design a strategy that ensures data durability and minimal downtime in case of regional outages. Which of the following approaches would best achieve this objective?

A) Set up a read replica of the Cloud SQL instance in another region, such as europe-west1, and use it for failover.
B) Regularly export database snapshots to Cloud Storage in a multi-regional bucket and restore when needed.
C) Implement a cross-region Cloud SQL instance with automatic failover enabled.
D) Use Cloud Spanner for its built-in replication and multi-regional configuration capabilities.
E) Create a custom backup and restore solution using Cloud Functions and Cloud Pub/Sub to trigger and manage backups.

QUESTION 3

Your organization is developing a new IoT application to be deployed on GCP. This application will collect data from various sensors and devices. For security and scalability, each device needs a unique identity and credentials for authenticating to GCP services. What approach should you adopt for managing these identities and credentials?

A) Assign individual IAM roles to each device and manage credentials through IAM policies.
B) Use Cloud IoT Core for device management, utilizing its built-in device identity and authentication features.
C) Create a custom service account for each device and distribute the service account keys for authentication.
D) Store device credentials in a secure Cloud SQL instance and validate each device's identity through an application API.
E) Implement a third-party device management solution integrated with GCP for handling device

identities and credentials.

QUESTION 4

You are managing a large-scale video processing application on GCP. The application needs to store and retrieve large video files frequently. Which storage solution would you recommend for optimal performance and cost-effectiveness?

A) Use Cloud SQL with large instance sizes for the database and storage.
B) Implement Cloud Storage with multi-regional buckets for easy access and redundancy.
C) Deploy Filestore for high-performance file storage and sharing.
D) Utilize Cloud Bigtable for its scalability and large-object storage capabilities.
E) Store video files in Persistent Disks attached to Compute Engine VMs for quick access.

QUESTION 5

Your organization is migrating to GCP and plans to integrate existing on-premises Active Directory with GCP for managing user accounts and access. What should be your primary consideration to ensure a seamless integration and maintenance of security standards?

A) Choose an appropriate identity federation mechanism between GCP and Active Directory.
B) Ensure that network connectivity between on-premises Active Directory and GCP is constantly maintained.
C) Regularly export user data from Active Directory and import it into GCP's Cloud Identity.
D) Set up a dedicated interconnect between the on-premises network and GCP for enhanced security.
E) Create duplicate user accounts in GCP and establish a process for keeping them synchronized with Active Directory.

QUESTION 6

You're tasked with setting up a local development environment on Ubuntu for testing an application that interacts with Cloud Spanner. What approach should you take to emulate Cloud Spanner locally for development and testing?

A) Use the gcloud spanner instances create command to set up a test instance of Cloud Spanner.
B) Install and configure the Cloud Spanner emulator from the Google Cloud SDK.
C) Deploy a lightweight SQL database locally to simulate Cloud Spanner behavior.
D) Connect your application to a test Cloud Spanner instance in GCP with restricted access.
E) Use a containerized version of Cloud Spanner running locally in Docker.

QUESTION 7

As part of enhancing security, your organization wants to ensure that Active Directory remains the primary source of truth for user access management, and any changes in AD user status are reflected in GCP access. What approach should you adopt?

A) Regularly export user data from Active Directory and import it into GCP's IAM.
B) Use Cloud Identity and Group Sync to synchronize Active Directory with GCP IAM.
C) Configure a custom script to update GCP IAM roles based on Active Directory changes.

D) Manually update GCP IAM roles whenever there are changes in Active Directory.
E) Implement a third-party identity management tool that integrates with both Active Directory and GCP.

QUESTION 8

You want to assign permissions to a team member to view audit logs for all GCP projects in your startup without granting them any additional privileges. Which role should you provide to this team member?

A) roles/logging.viewer
B) roles/logging.privateLogViewer
C) roles/logging.logWriter
D) roles/logging.admin
E) roles/monitoring.viewer

QUESTION 9

Your company requires a disaster recovery plan for a critical application hosted in GCP. The application is data-intensive and utilizes GCP's storage and compute resources extensively. The recovery plan must ensure minimal downtime and data loss in the event of a regional outage. Which disaster recovery strategy and GCP services would you recommend to meet these requirements?

A) Implement a cold disaster recovery strategy using Nearline Storage for backups and Compute Engine instances in another region for recovery.
B) Use a warm disaster recovery strategy with Regional Persistent Disks for data replication and preemptible VMs in a secondary region for cost-effective recovery.
C) Opt for a hot disaster recovery strategy with synchronous data replication using Multi-Regional Storage and automatically scaling Compute Engine instances in an alternative region.
D) Adopt a pilot light disaster recovery approach, maintaining minimal critical functionalities using Cloud Functions in a secondary region and Cloud Storage for backups.
E) Deploy a backup and restore strategy, utilizing Coldline Storage for periodic backups and dedicated GKE clusters in a separate region for recovery operations.

QUESTION 10

You are managing a video processing application on GCP, where videos are processed and stored in Cloud Storage. Processed videos are frequently accessed for the first 10 days and infrequently thereafter. Videos should be archived after 6 months and retained for 2 years. What lifecycle management strategy should you apply?

A) Store in Standard class for 10 days, then Nearline, move to Archive after 180 days, and delete after 730 days.
B) Store in Standard class for 180 days, then move to Nearline and delete after 730 days.
C) Store in Nearline class for 10 days, then move to Coldline, and Archive after 180 days, delete after 730 days.
D) Store in Standard class for 10 days, move to Coldline, then Archive after 180 days, and delete after 730 days.

QUESTION 11

You are tasked with designing a disaster recovery strategy for a critical application hosted on GCP, which has a strict RTO and RPO. The application uses a mix of Compute Engine instances and Cloud SQL databases. What is the best approach to ensure business continuity in case of a regional outage?

A) Regularly create snapshots of Compute Engine instances and use Cloud SQL's automated backup feature, storing them in multi-regional storage. Implement an automation script to recreate the environment in another region.
B) Use a GKE cluster with multi-regional deployment for Compute Engine instances and Cloud SQL cross-region replication.
C) Rely solely on GCP's live migration feature to handle any regional outages automatically.
D) Configure Compute Engine instances for preemptible VMs to reduce costs and enable Cloud SQL's high availability configuration with failover replicas in another region.

QUESTION 12

You are architecting a solution on GCP to handle a large influx of data from numerous IoT sensors. The data includes time-stamped metrics which need to be analyzed for real-time decision-making and later stored for historical analysis. Which GCP services should be used to build this pipeline most effectively?

A) Cloud Pub/Sub for data ingestion, Dataflow for real-time processing, BigQuery for analysis, and Cloud Storage for long-term data archival.
B) Cloud IoT Core for device management, Cloud Spanner for storing time-series data, and Looker for real-time analytics.
C) Firebase Realtime Database for data collection, Dataflow for processing, Cloud Bigtable for storage, and BigQuery for analysis.
D) Cloud Functions for handling data input, Firestore for data storage, and Data Studio for analysis and visualization.

QUESTION 13

You are preparing for an external security audit of a project that involves sensitive data processing on Cloud Spanner. The auditors require access to audit logs and database schemas. What is the recommended way to configure their IAM access?

A) Assign the auditors group 'spanner.databaseReader' and 'logging.viewer' IAM roles.
B) Grant each auditor individual user accounts the 'spanner.admin' role.
C) Provide the auditor group with the 'project.viewer' role for necessary access.
D) Allocate 'spanner.databaseViewer' and 'logging.viewer' roles to individual auditor accounts.

QUESTION 14

You are managing a project where sensitive project designs are stored in Cloud Storage. To enhance security, you want to audit all instances where project members modify the sharing settings of these files. What method should you use to monitor these activities?

A) Access the Audit logs in the GCP console to review changes in sharing settings.
B) Use Stackdriver logging to create filters that detect changes in file permissions.
C) Monitor file permission changes through the Cloud Storage file metadata in the GCP console.

D) Set up a custom script to periodically check and report any changes in file permissions in Cloud Storage.

QUESTION 15

You are setting up a video streaming service on GCP that requires global distribution and SSL offloading for HTTPS traffic. The service must also handle WebSocket connections. What is the most effective load balancing configuration for these requirements?

A) Configure an HTTP(S) Load Balancer with SSL offloading and support for WebSocket connections.
B) Implement a Global TCP Proxy Load Balancer with SSL certificates for handling global traffic and WebSocket connections.
C) Use a Global SSL Proxy Load Balancer for SSL termination and WebSocket support.
D) Deploy a Network Load Balancer with regional forwarding rules and handle SSL in backend servers.

QUESTION 16

You are tasked with optimizing the cost of running virtual machines in Google Cloud. The workload requires flexibility in CPU and memory allocation based on demand. Which Google Cloud service should you choose to achieve cost optimization while maintaining performance?

A) Google Compute Engine
B) Google Kubernetes Engine (GKE)
C) Google App Engine
D) Google Cloud Functions
E) Google Cloud Run

QUESTION 17

You need to set up a secure connection between your on-premises data center and Google Cloud. The connection should provide a private and dedicated link with high bandwidth. Which Google Cloud networking product should you choose for this requirement?

A) Google Cloud VPN for encrypted site-to-site connections.
B) Google Cloud Interconnect for dedicated and high-bandwidth connections.
C) Google Cloud DNS for domain name resolution.
D) Google Cloud CDN for content delivery acceleration.

QUESTION 18

Your organization requires a secure and highly available DNS (Domain Name System) service for its web applications deployed on Google Cloud. Which GCP service should you use to ensure reliable DNS resolution, DDoS protection, and integration with GCP resources?

A) Google Cloud CDN.
B) Google Cloud DNS.
C) Google Cloud Load Balancing.
D) Google Cloud Armor.

QUESTION 19

You want to grant permissions to a user to create and manage Google Cloud Storage buckets and objects within a specific project. Which IAM role should you assign to the user at the project level?

A) Storage Object Viewer
B) Storage Object Creator
C) Storage Object Admin
D) Storage Admin
E) Project Editor
F) Project Owner

QUESTION 20

Your organization's Cloud Spanner instance contains sensitive user data. A data security team requires access to monitor this data without the ability to modify it. What is the best practice to grant access to this team in GCP?

A) Assign the 'spanner.viewer' role to each member of the data security team.
B) Set up a Google Group for the data security team and allocate the 'spanner.viewer' role to this group.
C) Provide the 'spanner.databaseUser' role to the team for monitoring and potential edits.
D) Grant the 'spanner.admin' role to the team for comprehensive monitoring and management.

QUESTION 21

As part of your company's disaster recovery plan, you are tasked with backing up 60 GB of critical data to a Google Cloud Storage Nearline Bucket. The company's internet connection is 1 Gbps. Which method would optimize the backup process?

A) Conduct the backup through the GCP console for ease of use.
B) Implement gsutil with parallel composite uploads for efficient data transfer.
C) Split the data into smaller files and upload them sequentially.
D) Switch to a Google Cloud Storage Standard Bucket for faster upload speeds.

QUESTION 22

In your organization, VM instances in the 'dev-env' project require periodic backups managed by a service account from the 'backup-services' project. What is the best practice to enable this functionality?

A) Export the service account key from 'backup-services' and import it into each VM in 'dev-env'.
B) In 'dev-env', grant the necessary IAM roles to the service account from 'backup-services' for performing backups.
C) Create a new service account in 'dev-env' with similar permissions to the 'backup-services' account.
D) Configure the VMs in 'dev-env' to use the service account from 'backup-services' as their primary account.

QUESTION 23

Managing a GCP managed instance group for a video processing service, you find that new instances are replaced before being ready, which takes about 3 minutes. How should you adjust the settings for optimal functionality?

A) Set the health check initial delay to 180 seconds.
B) Decrease the health check initial delay to 30 seconds.
C) Increase the maximum instances allowed.
D) Switch autoscaling from CPU to disk I/O.
E) Manually add instances during peak times.

QUESTION 24

To determine where your App Engine application has been deployed, you need to identify the active project in your gcloud configuration. What command should you use to find this information?

A) gcloud app instances list to list all instances of the deployed app.
B) gcloud projects list to see all available GCP projects.
C) gcloud app describe to get the details of the App Engine application.
D) gcloud config list to check the current configuration settings.
E) Inspect the Dockerfile for any project-specific instructions.
F) Look at the app.yaml file for deployment project details.

QUESTION 25

Your Compute Engine instance, currently configured with 4 GB of RAM, is facing performance issues due to a surge in web traffic. You need to upgrade the RAM to 8 GB. Which action should you take to achieve this?

A) Dynamically allocate additional RAM to the instance from the GCP Console without stopping it.
B) Reconfigure the existing instance type to a higher memory specification through the GCP Console.
C) Stop the VM, select a new machine type with 8 GB of RAM, and restart the VM.
D) Attach an additional RAM disk to the VM instance to increase its memory.
E) Utilize Cloud Functions alongside the VM to handle the extra load.
F) Migrate the VM to a machine type with more memory using live migration.

QUESTION 26

To avoid a repeat of the incident where a vital Compute Engine instance was deleted accidentally, which option should you choose to enhance the security of your instances?

A) Enable the 'Require OS Login' feature for all instances.
B) Set up 'Deletion Protection' for your essential Compute Engine instances.
C) Configure instance snapshots to be taken every hour.
D) Assign instances to a secure VPC network to control access.
E) Implement a custom IAM policy that audits instance deletion actions.
F) Use Stackdriver to monitor and alert on instance deletion activities.

QUESTION 27

In building a cloud-based accounting application, you need to ensure users can upload their invoices and have write access for only 30 minutes, with invoices being deleted automatically after 45 days. What are the best two approaches to achieve this in GCP?

A) Use Cloud Spanner to set time-to-live (TTL) for invoice data.
B) Create a custom script in the application to delete invoices after 45 days.
C) Enable a lifecycle rule in Cloud Storage to delete objects after 45 days.
D) Use signed URLs in Cloud Storage with a 30-minute expiration for uploads.
E) Implement a custom IAM policy for time-limited access to data.
F) Configure Cloud SQL to automatically purge data older than 45 days.

QUESTION 28

Your company is planning to deploy a highly available web application on Google Cloud. You want to ensure that traffic is distributed across multiple regions for redundancy. Which Google Cloud service should you use for global load balancing?

A) Google Cloud CDN
B) Google Cloud Storage
C) Global HTTP(S) Load Balancer
D) Google Kubernetes Engine (GKE)
E) Google Cloud VPN

QUESTION 29

For a high-security banking application on GCP, you need to ensure that the Compute Engine instances in your VPC only allow minimal and necessary egress traffic. What is the best approach to configure the VPC firewall?

A) Set a default egress rule to deny all traffic, with high-priority rules to allow specific necessary ports.
B) Implement a blanket rule to allow all egress traffic and rely on internal application controls for security.
C) Create a low-priority rule to block all egress and override it with higher-priority rules for essential traffic.
D) Use a GCP Cloud VPN to funnel all egress traffic through a secure, monitored channel.
E) Apply a high-priority egress rule for each specific service within the application.
F) Configure a third-party firewall appliance within the VPC to manage egress traffic.

QUESTION 30

Your team needs to deploy a budget-friendly, containerized internal application on GCP that should incur no costs when not in use. What deployment method should you choose?

A) Configure a Compute Engine instance group with an autoscaler and schedule-based scaling.
B) Use Cloud Run (fully managed) set to scale the number of instances to zero when idle.
C) Set up the application on App Engine Flexible Environment with autoscaling.
D) Deploy the application in a Google Kubernetes Engine (GKE) cluster with a cluster autoscaler.
E) Implement the containerized app on Cloud Functions, triggered based on usage.
F) Use App Engine Standard Environment with the scaling set to basic.

QUESTION 31

How can you effectively manage permissions for a DevOps team that requires access to production services across multiple GCP projects, while adhering to security best practices?

A) Provide the DevOps team with the Project Editor role across all projects.
B) Set up individual user accounts for each team member with specific roles in each project.
C) Use a group-based IAM policy with a custom role designed for the DevOps team's tasks.
D) Assign the DevOps team a combination of predefined roles like Network Admin and Compute Admin.
E) Grant the DevOps team Service Account User role for greater flexibility.
F) Establish an organization-wide policy giving the DevOps team broad access to all resources.

QUESTION 32

What is the best storage strategy for a file-sharing application on Cloud Storage, where files are frequently accessed for 30 days and need to be retained for a total of 3 years?

A) Begin with files in Standard storage, then move to Nearline after 30 days, and finally to Archive after 1 year.
B) Store files in Archive storage from the start, as it is the most cost-effective for long-term retention.
C) Use Coldline storage for the initial 30 days, followed by transferring files to Archive storage for the remainder.
D) Keep files in Standard storage for 30 days, then shift to Archive storage for the remaining 3-year period.
E) Implement a lifecycle policy to transition files from Nearline to Coldline and then to Archive at specified intervals.
F) Start with Coldline storage, moving to Nearline after 30 days, and finally to Archive storage after 6 months.

QUESTION 33

What is the best approach to provide a single IP address for a Google Cloud-hosted multiplayer game backend that receives UDP packets and needs to scale horizontally?

A) Utilize an External HTTP(S) Load Balancer for the game servers.
B) Implement an External Network Load Balancer for handling UDP traffic.
C) Set up a Global UDP Proxy Load Balancer to manage traffic.
D) Use an SSL Proxy Load Balancer to direct traffic to the servers.
E) Configure an Internal UDP Load Balancer with external access.
F) Create a Cloud DNS setup to route traffic through a single IP.

QUESTION 34

A healthcare organization wants to implement a system on GCP to analyze patient data stored in various formats and generate insights. The system must comply with healthcare regulations and provide secure, scalable storage and analysis capabilities. Which combination of services would you recommend?

A) Store data in Cloud Healthcare API, use BigQuery for analysis, and manage access with Cloud IAM, ensuring HIPAA compliance.
B) Migrate data to Cloud SQL, use Dataflow for data transformation, and employ Cloud DLP for securing

patient data.
C) Use Cloud Storage for data archival, Bigtable for real-time analysis, and Cloud KMS for encryption, ensuring compliance.
D) Implement Firestore for data storage, utilize AI Platform for generating insights, and secure data with VPC Service Controls.
E) Transfer data to Cloud Spanner, analyze using Looker, and maintain security and compliance with Cloud Identity and Access Management (IAM).

QUESTION 35

As part of a security upgrade, your company requires that all SSH access to Compute Engine VMs be logged and auditable. Which combination of GCP tools and services should you use to ensure compliance?

A) Enable OS Login on VMs and integrate with Cloud Audit Logs.
B) Use custom metadata scripts on VMs to log SSH access and export logs to Cloud Logging.
C) Implement IAP Tunneling for SSH and configure logging with Stackdriver.
D) Activate Cloud Identity-Aware Proxy (IAP) and use its logs for auditing SSH access.
E) Configure VMs to use IAM roles and track SSH access through Admin Activity logs.

QUESTION 36

Your GCP project experiences intermittent outages, and you need to be notified whenever the number of virtual machine restarts exceeds a normal range. What should you do to set up this notification?

A) Create a Cloud Monitoring dashboard to manually check VM restarts.
B) Use Cloud Logging to monitor for VM restart events and create an email alert for high numbers of restarts.
C) Set up a custom metric in Cloud Monitoring for VM restarts and configure an alert based on this metric.
D) Implement a script using the Compute Engine API to count VM restarts and send notifications.
E) Rely on the default Compute Engine notifications for any VM restarts.

QUESTION 37

Your company operates globally, and you need to ensure low-latency content delivery for your web application. Which Google Cloud service should you choose to set up a global content delivery network (CDN) with edge caching?

A) Google Cloud Load Balancing
B) Google Cloud Storage
C) Google Cloud CDN
D) Google Cloud Functions
E) Google Cloud Pub/Sub

QUESTION 38

Your team is responsible for optimizing cost management in a Google Cloud project that uses various

GCP services. You want to identify opportunities for cost reduction and analyze resource usage. Which GCP service or feature can you use for cost optimization and resource usage analysis?

A) Implement Google Cloud Billing Reports for cost reduction and resource usage analysis.
B) Configure Google Cloud Monitoring for real-time cost tracking and analysis.
C) Utilize Google Cloud Cost Explorer for cost optimization and resource usage analysis.
D) Set up Google Cloud Security Command Center for cost management and resource usage analysis.
E) Deploy Google Cloud Audit Logging for cost reduction and resource tracking.

QUESTION 39

Your organization is building a web application that requires low-latency access to a large dataset. The dataset is stored in Google Cloud Storage, and you want to optimize access performance. What should you use to achieve low-latency access to the dataset?

A) Utilize Google Cloud Pub/Sub for real-time data access.
B) Implement Google Cloud Datastore for low-latency data retrieval.
C) Choose Google Cloud Bigtable and use the HBase API for low-latency access.
D) Deploy Google Cloud SQL for efficient dataset access.

QUESTION 40

Your organization has multiple development teams working on different Google Cloud projects. Each team manages its own set of resources within their projects. To ensure resource isolation and minimize the risk of accidental deletion, which IAM best practice should you follow?

A) Grant the Organization Administrator role to all developers for centralized control.
B) Use a single Google Cloud project for all development teams to ensure uniform resource management.
C) Assign IAM roles at the project level, giving each team access only to their respective projects.
D) Share a single service account across all projects for consistent access control.

QUESTION 41

Your organization has multiple development teams working on different Google Cloud projects. Each team manages its own set of resources within their projects. To ensure resource isolation and minimize the risk of accidental deletion, which IAM best practice should you follow?

A) Grant the Organization Administrator role to all developers for centralized control.
B) Use a single Google Cloud project for all development teams to ensure uniform resource management.
C) Assign IAM roles at the project level, giving each team access only to their respective projects.
D) Share a single service account across all projects for consistent access control.

QUESTION 42

You want to deploy a third-party OTP application on a Compute Engine instance and access installation files stored in Cloud Storage. You need to ensure that the other already-configured instances do not have access to these files. Which approach should you take for securing access to the installation files?

A) Grant permissions directly to the instance's external IP address for the Cloud Storage bucket.
B) Use the same service account for all instances in the project and grant it permissions on Cloud Storage.
C) Create a new service account and select it while creating the new instance. Grant the service account permissions on Cloud Storage.
D) Use the default Compute Engine service account for the instance and restrict access in the Cloud Storage bucket ACL.
E) Grant permissions to all Compute Engine instances in the project for the Cloud Storage bucket.

QUESTION 43

Your project involves developing a web application on GCP, and you need to implement a deployment strategy that enables A/B testing by testing updates on a small portion of live users. What GCP deployment approach should you take for this purpose?

A) Use App Engine to run your app. For each update, create a new version of the same service and send a small percentage of traffic to the new version using traffic splitting.
B) Use App Engine to run your app. For each update, create a new service and send a small percentage of traffic to the new version using traffic splitting.
C) Use Kubernetes Engine to run your app. For a new release, update the deployment to use the new version.
D) Use Kubernetes Engine to run your app. For a new release, create a new deployment for the new version and update the service to use the new deployment.

QUESTION 44

Your team is tasked with optimizing costs for a Google Cloud project. You want to identify underutilized virtual machines to rightsize them for cost savings. Which Google Cloud service or feature can help you achieve this?

A) Google Cloud Billing reports and Cost Explorer
B) Google Cloud Pub/Sub
C) Google Cloud Identity and Access Management (IAM)
D) Google Cloud Composer

QUESTION 45

Your organization is developing a web application that requires a globally distributed, fully managed, and serverless NoSQL database service. You want to choose a Google Cloud database option that provides automatic scaling, high availability, and a flexible schema-less data model. Which Google Cloud database service should you select for this web application?

A) Google Cloud Firestore
B) Google Cloud Bigtable
C) Google Cloud SQL for PostgreSQL
D) Google Cloud Spanner

QUESTION 46

Your organization needs to ensure that your Google Cloud resources are compliant with industry-specific regulations and standards. You want to implement automated compliance checks and enforce policies for resources. Which Google Cloud service should you use for this compliance and policy enforcement?

A) Google Cloud Security Command Center
B) Google Cloud Identity and Access Management (IAM)
C) Google Cloud Key Management Service (KMS)
D) Google Cloud Monitoring

QUESTION 47

Your organization is migrating its existing on-premises SQL Server databases to Google Cloud. You want to ensure minimal downtime during the migration and keep the databases in sync during the transition. Which Google Cloud service can help you achieve this goal?

A) Use Google Cloud Storage to export and import SQL Server database backups.
B) Implement Google Cloud Database Migration Service (DMS) for real-time database replication.
C) Manually copy the database files to Google Cloud Compute Engine instances.
D) Leverage Google Cloud Dataprep for ETL-based data migration.

QUESTION 48

Your organization is running a critical application on Google Cloud Compute Engine virtual machines (VMs). You need to ensure high availability and redundancy for the application in case of VM failures. Which GCP feature can help you achieve this goal?

A) Configure GCP's Regional Managed Instance Groups (MIGs) for distributing VMs across multiple zones within a region .
B) Use GCP's Virtual Private Cloud (VPC) for network isolation and security.
C) Implement GCP's Shared VPC for resource sharing across multiple projects.
D) Leverage GCP's Identity-Aware Proxy (IAP) for secure remote access to VMs.

QUESTION 49

For a new project, you have created a set of Docker containers that need to be deployed on Google Kubernetes Engine. How would you proceed with the deployment?

A) Directly deploy the Docker containers on a GKE cluster without uploading them.
B) First upload the containers to Cloud Storage, then deploy them on GKE.
C) Upload the Docker container images to Container Registry, then create a Kubernetes Deployment in GKE.
D) Use Cloud Build to create the container images and automatically deploy to GKE.
E) Configure Cloud Endpoints to manage the deployment of the containers on GKE.

QUESTION 50

For your GKE-based application, one microservice requires intensive data processing, while others are lightweight. How would you configure the cluster for optimal performance?

A) Increase the CPU and memory allocation equally across all microservices.
B) Implement a custom scheduler to allocate resources based on microservice requirements.
C) Create a node pool with high-performance CPUs for the data-intensive microservice, and use standard machines for the rest.
D) Use preemptible VMs for all microservices to reduce costs and optimize resource usage.
E) Configure anti-affinity rules to distribute the microservices evenly across the cluster.

SET 8 - ANSWERS ONLY

QUESTION 1

Answer - A) Deploy BigQuery

A) Correct, BigQuery with partitioned tables and the BI Engine offers fast analysis of large datasets.
B) Incorrect, Cloud SQL is suitable for relational data but may not offer the minimal latency required for large datasets.
C) Incorrect, Dataflow is ideal for real-time processing but does not inherently minimize latency in data analysis.
D) Incorrect, a Hadoop cluster provides scalability but may not be the most efficient in terms of latency.
E) Incorrect, Cloud Spanner and Data Studio are powerful tools but may not offer the lowest latency for large dataset analysis.
F) Incorrect, while Bigtable and Dataproc are powerful, they may not offer the minimal latency required for this scenario.

QUESTION 2

Answer - C) Cross-region Cloud SQL instance

A) Incorrect, while read replicas provide some level of redundancy, they may not be sufficient for minimal downtime requirements.
B) Incorrect, manual restoration from Cloud Storage snapshots can result in significant downtime.
C) Correct, a cross-region Cloud SQL instance with automatic failover ensures data durability and minimal downtime.
D) Incorrect, migrating to Cloud Spanner may be an over-implementation for this requirement and could introduce unnecessary complexity.
E) Incorrect, a custom solution might not provide the same level of reliability and quick failover as a built-in cross-region feature.

QUESTION 3

Answer - B) Cloud IoT Core

A) Incorrect, managing individual IAM roles for each device is impractical and does not scale well.
B) Correct, Cloud IoT Core provides device management with built-in identity and authentication, suitable for IoT applications.
C) Incorrect, using individual service accounts for each device is not scalable and can become unmanageable.
D) Incorrect, storing credentials in Cloud SQL is not as secure or efficient as using a dedicated IoT management service.
E) Incorrect, while third-party solutions can be effective, Cloud IoT Core offers integrated features that are more efficient for GCP.

QUESTION 4

Answer - B) Cloud Storage with multi-regional buckets

A) Incorrect, Cloud SQL is not designed for storing and retrieving large files like videos.
B) Correct, Cloud Storage with multi-regional buckets offers the necessary scalability, performance, and redundancy for large video files.
C) Incorrect, while Filestore provides high performance, it may not be as cost-effective as Cloud Storage for large video files.
D) Incorrect, Cloud Bigtable is optimized for high-volume, real-time data, not for large file storage.
E) Incorrect, using Persistent Disks for large video file storage is less efficient and more costly than Cloud Storage.

QUESTION 5

Answer - A) Identity federation mechanism

A) Correct, choosing an appropriate identity federation mechanism is crucial for seamless integration and maintaining security standards.
B) Incorrect, while network connectivity is important, it is not the primary consideration for Active Directory integration.
C) Incorrect, regularly exporting and importing user data is not efficient and does not maintain real-time synchronization.
D) Incorrect, a dedicated interconnect enhances network connectivity but does not address the integration of identity management systems.
E) Incorrect, creating duplicate accounts is inefficient and can lead to synchronization and security issues.

QUESTION 6

Answer - B) Cloud Spanner emulator from Google Cloud SDK

A) Incorrect, this command creates a real instance in GCP, not a local emulator.
B) Correct, the Cloud Spanner emulator in the Google Cloud SDK allows for local testing without connecting to GCP.
C) Incorrect, a lightweight SQL database does not fully replicate Cloud Spanner's features or API behavior.
D) Incorrect, this approach involves testing in GCP, not locally.
E) Incorrect, there is no official containerized version of Cloud Spanner for local emulation.

QUESTION 7

Answer - B) Cloud Identity and Group Sync

A) Incorrect, exporting and importing data manually is inefficient and error-prone.
B) Correct, using Cloud Identity and Group Sync ensures that changes in Active Directory are automatically reflected in GCP.
C) Incorrect, custom scripting is less reliable and more complex compared to using built-in synchronization tools.
D) Incorrect, manual updates are not feasible for maintaining real-time synchronization and are prone to errors.

E) Incorrect, a third-party tool is unnecessary when GCP provides built-in solutions for this purpose.

QUESTION 8

Answer - A) roles/logging.viewer

A) Correct, roles/logging.viewer allows viewing logs, including audit logs, without additional privileges.
B) Incorrect, roles/logging.privateLogViewer is for viewing logs that include sensitive data.
C) Incorrect, roles/logging.logWriter is for writing logs, not viewing them.
D) Incorrect, roles/logging.admin provides broader permissions than necessary for just viewing logs.
E) Incorrect, roles/monitoring.viewer is for viewing monitoring data, not logs.

QUESTION 9

Answer – C) Opt for a hot disaster recovery strategy with synchronous data replication using Multi-Regional Storage and automatically scaling Compute Engine instances in an alternative region.

Option C offers the most effective disaster recovery strategy for the scenario. A hot disaster recovery approach, with its synchronous data replication and immediate failover capabilities, ensures minimal downtime and data loss. Multi-Regional Storage provides durable and accessible storage across regions, and automatically scaling Compute Engine instances offer immediate resource availability in the event of a regional outage. Option A's cold disaster recovery strategy, while cost-effective, would result in significant downtime and data loss. Option B's warm strategy offers a middle ground but may not meet the minimal downtime requirement. Option D's pilot light approach maintains basic functionality but may not scale quickly enough in a disaster scenario. Option E, focusing on backup and restore, also poses a risk of considerable downtime and potential data loss, not aligning with the critical nature of the application.

QUESTION 10

Answer – D) Store in Standard class for 10 days, move to Coldline, then Archive after 180 days, and delete after 730 days.

A) Incorrect due to early archiving.
B) Incorrect as it does not account for the change in access frequency after 10 days.
C) Incorrect, as Nearline is not optimal for the initial frequent access period.
D) Correct. It aligns with access patterns and retention requirements: Standard for initial frequent access, Coldline for less frequent access, and Archive for long-term storage.

QUESTION 11

Answer - B) Use a GKE cluster with multi-regional deployment for Compute Engine instances and Cloud SQL cross-region replication.

A) Offers some protection but may not meet strict RTO and RPO requirements due to manual intervention needed.
B) Correct. Provides automatic failover and high availability, meeting strict RTO and RPO needs.
C) Live migration is not sufficient for full disaster recovery planning.
D) Preemptible VMs are not suitable for critical applications and may not guarantee availability during

regional outages.

QUESTION 12

Answer - A) Cloud Pub/Sub for data ingestion, Dataflow for real-time processing, BigQuery for analysis, and Cloud Storage for long-term data archival.

A) Correct. This setup provides a comprehensive solution for real-time processing, analytics, and storage, tailored for IoT scenarios.
B) Spanner is not the optimal choice for time-series data compared to Bigtable.
C) Firebase is not designed for large-scale IoT data ingestion.
D) Firestore and Cloud Functions are not the best fit for large-scale, real-time IoT data scenarios.

QUESTION 13

Answer - A) Assign the auditors group 'spanner.databaseReader' and 'logging.viewer' IAM roles.

A) Correct. This gives auditors access to the database schemas and logs while adhering to the principle of least privilege.
B) Incorrect. The 'spanner.admin' role provides unnecessary administrative permissions.
C) May not grant specific access to Spanner database schemas.
D) Using groups is more efficient than individual accounts for permission management.

QUESTION 14

Answer - A) Access the Audit logs in the GCP console to review changes in sharing settings.

A) Audit logs are specifically designed to track such changes in Cloud Storage, making them the most efficient tool for this purpose.
B) Stackdriver logging can track such changes but is less direct than using audit logs.
C) File metadata in the console does not provide a comprehensive audit trail.
D) A custom script is less efficient and may not capture all changes compared to using built-in audit logs.

QUESTION 15

Answer - A) Configure an HTTP(S) Load Balancer with SSL offloading and support for WebSocket connections.

A) HTTP(S) Load Balancer is ideal for global distribution and supports SSL offloading. It also supports WebSocket, which is crucial for video streaming services.
B) TCP Proxy Load Balancer does not support SSL offloading.
C) SSL Proxy Load Balancer does not support HTTP(S) traffic, necessary for a video streaming service.
D) Network Load Balancer does not provide SSL offloading and is not optimized for global traffic distribution.

QUESTION 16

Answer - B) Google Kubernetes Engine (GKE)

Option B: This is the correct choice as Google Kubernetes Engine (GKE) allows you to optimize costs by scaling CPU and memory allocation based on demand while maintaining performance.

Option A: Google Compute Engine provides virtual machines with fixed configurations and may not offer the same level of flexibility.

Option C: Google App Engine abstracts infrastructure and may not provide fine-grained control over CPU and memory allocation.

Option D: Google Cloud Functions is a serverless compute service, but it's not designed for fine-grained control over VM resources.

Option E: Google Cloud Run is a managed container platform, but GKE offers more control over resource allocation.

QUESTION 17

Answer - B) Google Cloud Interconnect for dedicated and high-bandwidth connections.

Option B: This is the correct choice as Google Cloud Interconnect provides dedicated and high-bandwidth connections between on-premises data centers and Google Cloud, meeting the requirement for a private and high-speed link.

Option A: Google Cloud VPN offers encrypted site-to-site connections but may not provide the same level of dedicated bandwidth.

Option C: Google Cloud DNS is for domain name resolution and doesn't address the need for a dedicated and high-bandwidth connection.

Option D: Google Cloud CDN accelerates content delivery but is not designed for private, dedicated links between data centers.

QUESTION 18

Answer - B) Google Cloud DNS.

Option B is the correct choice as Google Cloud DNS is a scalable and highly available DNS service that ensures reliable DNS resolution, DDoS protection, and seamless integration with GCP resources.

Option A is for content delivery, Option C is for load balancing, and Option D is for DDoS protection.

QUESTION 19

Answer - F) Project Owner

Option F, "Project Owner," is the correct choice. It grants broad permissions at the project level, including the ability to create and manage Google Cloud Storage resources. Options A, B, C, and D are related to object-level permissions and do not provide project-level management. Options E and F are project-level roles, but Option F provides more extensive permissions.

QUESTION 20

Answer - B) Set up a Google Group for the data security team and allocate the 'spanner.viewer' role to this group.

B) Grouping the team and assigning the 'spanner.viewer' role is the most secure and manageable approach, providing the necessary permissions for monitoring without edit capabilities.

A) Directly assigning roles to individuals is less efficient.

C) The 'spanner.databaseUser' role would allow data modification, which is not required.
D) The 'spanner.admin' role is too permissive for just monitoring.

QUESTION 21

Answer - B) Implement gsutil with parallel composite uploads for efficient data transfer.

B) Parallel composite uploads with gsutil are ideal for large data transfers, allowing multiple parts of the file to be uploaded concurrently, thus maximizing the use of the available 1 Gbps connection.
A) The GCP console is less efficient for large data uploads.
C) Sequential uploads do not make full use of the bandwidth.
D) The bucket type primarily affects cost and data access frequency, not upload speed.

QUESTION 22

Answer - B) In 'dev-env', grant the necessary IAM roles to the service account from 'backup-services' for performing backups.

B) Granting the appropriate IAM roles to the existing service account from 'backup-services' in the 'dev-env' project is the most efficient and secure way to manage backups. It ensures that the service account has the necessary permissions without compromising security.
A) Exporting and importing service account keys is not a secure practice.
C) Creating a new service account is unnecessary and can lead to redundant and fragmented access management.
D) Changing the primary service account of VMs is not required and could disrupt existing configurations.

QUESTION 23

Answer - A) Set the health check initial delay to 180 seconds.

A) Correct. This aligns with the service's initialization time, reducing premature scaling.
B) This would exacerbate the problem by marking instances unhealthy too soon.
C) Increasing max instances doesn't address the premature health check issue.
D) Changing the scaling metric does not impact the timing of health checks.
E) Manual scaling is less efficient and doesn't solve the health check timing problem.

QUESTION 24

Answer - D) gcloud config list to check the current configuration settings.

D) This command is the most direct way to view the current configuration, including the active project, which will indicate where the application was deployed.
A) Listing app instances requires knowing the project in advance.
B) This lists all projects but doesn't indicate which one is currently active.
C) gcloud app describe requires specifying a project to be useful.
E) The Dockerfile typically doesn't contain GCP project information.
F) The app.yaml file doesn't usually specify the deployment project.

QUESTION 25

Answer - C) Stop the VM, select a new machine type with 8 GB of RAM, and restart the VM.

C) To upgrade the memory of a Compute Engine instance, you must stop the VM, change its machine type to one with the desired memory capacity, and then restart it. This process ensures the VM is resized correctly.
A) It's not possible to dynamically allocate additional RAM to a running instance in GCP.
B) The machine type of a running VM cannot be reconfigured without stopping it first.
D) Attaching a RAM disk does not increase the actual RAM of the VM.
E) Cloud Functions are for serverless computing and do not add RAM to a VM.
F) Live migration does not change the machine type or allocated resources.

QUESTION 26

Answer - B) Set up 'Deletion Protection' for your essential Compute Engine instances.

B) Setting up 'Deletion Protection' is the most effective way to prevent accidental or unauthorized deletion of Compute Engine instances, ensuring they remain intact and operational.
A) 'Require OS Login' secures SSH access but does not prevent instance deletion.
C) Regular snapshots are good for data recovery but don't prevent instance deletion.
D) A secure VPC network controls network access but not instance management actions like deletion.
E) Custom IAM policies can manage permissions but may not provide real-time protection against deletion.
F) Monitoring with Stackdriver can alert on deletions but does not actively prevent them.

QUESTION 27

Answer - C) and D)

C) A lifecycle rule in Cloud Storage for automatic deletion after 45 days ensures that invoices are not stored longer than necessary, meeting compliance and data retention policies.
D) Signed URLs with a 30-minute expiration limit provide a secure and time-bound way for users to upload their invoices, aligning with the specified access requirement.
A) Cloud Spanner TTL is not a feature for managing file storage and deletion in Cloud Storage.
B) Custom scripts are less efficient and require more maintenance than built-in lifecycle rules.
E) IAM policies manage access but do not offer temporary access control or auto-deletion features.
F) Cloud SQL's data management doesn't directly apply to file storage in Cloud Storage.

QUESTION 28

Answer - C) Global HTTP(S) Load Balancer

Option C - Global HTTP(S) Load Balancer can distribute traffic across multiple regions, providing high availability and redundancy.
Option A - Google Cloud CDN is a content delivery network, not a load balancer.
Option B - Google Cloud Storage is for object storage.
Option D - Google Kubernetes Engine (GKE) is a container orchestration platform, and
Option E - Google Cloud VPN is a virtual private network service.

QUESTION 29

Answer - C) Create a low-priority rule to block all egress and override it with higher-priority rules for essential traffic.

C) Establishing a low-priority rule to block all egress traffic ensures a secure default state. Specific higher-priority rules can then be used to selectively allow egress through necessary ports, providing tight control over the network traffic for the banking application.
A) Default deny rules should be low-priority to ensure they don't override specific allow rules.
B) Allowing all egress traffic by default is not secure for a high-security application.
D) Cloud VPN controls traffic channels but doesn't specify egress port control.
E) Individual high-priority rules for each service could be less efficient and harder to manage.
F) Third-party appliances add complexity and may not be necessary with GCP's firewall capabilities.

QUESTION 30

Answer - B) Use Cloud Run (fully managed) set to scale the number of instances to zero when idle.

B) Cloud Run (fully managed) is the most cost-effective choice for this scenario as it allows the application to automatically scale down to zero instances, ensuring you are not charged when the application is not in use. This meets the requirement of no costs during non-operational hours.
A) Compute Engine autoscaling doesn't scale down to zero and incurs ongoing costs.
C) App Engine Flexible Environment does not scale to zero, leading to continuous costs.
D) GKE's cluster autoscaler minimizes but doesn't eliminate costs during idle times.
E) Cloud Functions are not designed for continuous application hosting.
F) App Engine Standard's basic scaling doesn't fully scale down to zero.

QUESTION 31

Answer - C) Use a group-based IAM policy with a custom role designed for the DevOps team's tasks.

C) Implementing a group-based IAM policy where you create a custom role with specific permissions tailored to the DevOps team's responsibilities is the most secure approach. This method ensures that the team has access to only what they need, without unnecessary broadening of permissions, and simplifies management by using group-based assignment.
A) Project Editor may grant unnecessary broad permissions.
B) Individual user accounts can be hard to manage at scale.
D) Predefined roles may not align perfectly with the specific needs of the DevOps team.
E) Service Account User role may not provide the necessary specific access for DevOps tasks.
F) An organization-wide policy with broad access contradicts security best practices.

QUESTION 32

Answer - D) Keep files in Standard storage for 30 days, then shift to Archive storage for the remaining 3-year period.

D) This approach balances cost and accessibility. Using Standard storage for the first 30 days addresses the need for frequent access. After that, moving to Archive storage is the most cost-efficient for the 3-year retention period, as it is designed for long-term storage of data that is rarely accessed, thus reducing costs significantly.

A) Transitioning through multiple storage classes may not be as cost-effective as directly moving to Archive.
B) Archive storage is not suitable for frequent access in the initial 30 days.
C) Coldline storage is less optimal for frequent access in the first 30 days.
E) Multiple transitions through storage classes can be less efficient in terms of cost.
F) Starting with Coldline is not suitable for the initial frequent access period.

QUESTION 33

Answer - B) Implement an External Network Load Balancer for handling UDP traffic.

B) The External Network Load Balancer is the optimal choice for this use case. It supports UDP traffic, which is essential for the game's server communication, and provides a single external IP address that can be used for horizontal scaling of the backend infrastructure. This setup ensures efficient load distribution among servers and maintains the necessary scaling flexibility.
A) External HTTP(S) Load Balancers are not designed for UDP traffic.
C) Global UDP Proxy Load Balancer is not a standard offering in Google Cloud.
D) SSL Proxy Load Balancers are not suitable for UDP traffic.
E) Internal UDP Load Balancers do not provide the needed external exposure.
F) Cloud DNS does not handle traffic distribution or load balancing.

QUESTION 34

Answer – A) Cloud Healthcare API, BigQuery, Cloud IAM

A) Correct, integrates GCP's healthcare-specific solutions with BigQuery for analysis, focusing on compliance and security.
B) Incorrect, Cloud SQL may not handle various data formats efficiently.
C) Incorrect, Bigtable is not ideal for complex analytical queries.
D) Incorrect, Firestore is not the best choice for large-scale healthcare data.
E) Incorrect, Cloud Spanner and Looker might not be the most efficient for this specific healthcare scenario.

QUESTION 35

Answer – A) OS Login, Cloud Audit Logs

A) Correct, OS Login integrates with IAM and Cloud Audit Logs for centralized management and auditing of SSH access.
B) Incorrect, custom scripts may not be reliable for comprehensive logging and auditing.
C) Incorrect, IAP Tunneling is for secure access, but doesn't specifically log SSH sessions.
D) Incorrect, Cloud IAP is not primarily used for SSH logging.
E) Incorrect, IAM roles do not directly track SSH access on VMs.

QUESTION 36

Answer – C) Custom metric in Cloud Monitoring, Alert

A) Incorrect, dashboards are for manual monitoring, not automatic alerts.

B) Incorrect, Cloud Logging is not the most efficient for monitoring VM restart events.
C) Correct, a custom metric for VM restarts and an alert in Cloud Monitoring is a proactive approach to this issue.
D) Incorrect, writing a custom script is less efficient and more error-prone.
E) Incorrect, default notifications may not cover specific thresholds for restarts.

QUESTION 37

Answer - C) Google Cloud CDN (Correct)

Option A is incorrect because Google Cloud Load Balancing provides load balancing but not CDN capabilities.
Option B is incorrect because Google Cloud Storage is an object storage service and does not offer edge caching for content delivery.
Option D is incorrect because Google Cloud Functions are designed for serverless functions, not for setting up a CDN.
Option E is incorrect because Google Cloud Pub/Sub is a messaging service and not related to CDN functionality.
Option C is correct because Google Cloud CDN provides a global CDN with edge caching, allowing for low-latency content delivery worldwide.

QUESTION 38

Answer - C) Utilize Google Cloud Cost Explorer for cost optimization and resource usage analysis. (Correct)

Option A is incorrect because Google Cloud Billing Reports are primarily for billing and invoice management, not for in-depth cost optimization and resource usage analysis.
Option B is incorrect because Google Cloud Monitoring provides real-time monitoring and alerting capabilities but does not specialize in cost optimization analysis.
Option D is incorrect because Google Cloud Security Command Center focuses on security-related aspects and does not directly address cost management and resource usage analysis.
Option E is incorrect because Google Cloud Audit Logging is designed for audit trails and compliance, not for cost reduction and resource tracking.
Option C is correct because Google Cloud Cost Explorer is a tool that allows you to analyze your Google Cloud spending, identify cost-saving opportunities, and gain insights into resource usage, making it a suitable choice for cost optimization and resource analysis in a GCP project.

QUESTION 39

Answer - C) Choose Google Cloud Bigtable and use the HBase API for low-latency access. (Correct)

Option A is incorrect because Google Cloud Pub/Sub is a messaging service, not a direct data access solution, and it does not provide low-latency access to datasets.
Option B is incorrect because Google Cloud Datastore may not provide the same level of low-latency access as Google Cloud Bigtable with the HBase API for large datasets.

Option D is incorrect because Google Cloud SQL is a relational database service and may not offer low-latency access for certain use cases.
Google Cloud Bigtable with the HBase API is designed for low-latency access to large datasets and is a suitable choice for optimizing access performance.

QUESTION 40

Answer - C) Assign IAM roles at the project level, giving each team access only to their respective projects.

Option A is incorrect because granting the Organization Administrator role to all developers does not provide resource isolation and can lead to excessive permissions. Option B is incorrect because using a single Google Cloud project for all development teams does not allow for proper isolation and resource management. Option D is incorrect because sharing a single service account across all projects can lead to security and access control issues. Option C is correct because assigning IAM roles at the project level allows each team to have access only to their respective projects, ensuring resource isolation and minimizing the risk of accidental deletion.

QUESTION 41

Answer - C) Assign IAM roles at the project level, giving each team access only to their respective projects.

Option A is incorrect because granting the Organization Administrator role to all developers does not provide resource isolation and can lead to excessive permissions. Option B is incorrect because using a single Google Cloud project for all development teams does not allow for proper isolation and resource management. Option D is incorrect because sharing a single service account across all projects can lead to security and access control issues. Option C is correct because assigning IAM roles at the project level allows each team to have access only to their respective projects, ensuring resource isolation and minimizing the risk of accidental deletion.

QUESTION 42

Answer - C) Create a new service account and select it while creating the new instance. Grant the service account permissions on Cloud Storage.

Option A is incorrect because granting permissions to an external IP address does not provide secure access control and isolation.
Option B is incorrect because using the same service account for all instances can lead to unintended access by other instances sharing the same account.
Option D is incorrect because relying on the default service account may not provide the necessary isolation and access control.
Option E is incorrect because granting permissions to all instances in the project does not meet the requirement of restricting access to the installation files.

QUESTION 43

Answer - A) Use App Engine to run your app. For each update, create a new version of the same service and send a small percentage of traffic to the new version using traffic splitting.

Option A is correct because it aligns with your goal of A/B testing. Using App Engine, you can create new versions of the same service and use traffic splitting to test updates on a small portion of live users while keeping the rest on the live version.
Option B is incorrect because creating a new service for each update would result in multiple instances of the app running simultaneously, which is not suitable for A/B testing.
Option C is incorrect because updating the deployment in Kubernetes Engine would direct all traffic to the new version, which does not allow for controlled A/B testing.
Option D is incorrect because creating a new deployment and updating the service would also direct all traffic to the new deployment, making it unsuitable for A/B testing.

QUESTION 44

Answer - A) Google Cloud Billing reports and Cost Explorer

Option A is correct because Google Cloud Billing provides reports and Cost Explorer, allowing you to analyze costs, identify underutilized resources, and rightsize virtual machines for cost savings.
Option B (Google Cloud Pub/Sub) is a messaging service and not related to cost optimization.
Option C (Google Cloud IAM) is for access control and does not provide cost optimization features.
Option D (Google Cloud Composer) is a workflow orchestration service and not focused on cost analysis.

QUESTION 45

Answer - A) Google Cloud Firestore

Option A is correct because Google Cloud Firestore is a globally distributed, fully managed NoSQL database service that offers automatic scaling, high availability, and a flexible schema-less data model, making it suitable for web applications.
Option B (Google Cloud Bigtable) is a NoSQL database but may not provide the same schema-less data model and flexibility.
Option C (Google Cloud SQL for PostgreSQL) is a relational database and may not offer the same NoSQL capabilities.
Option D (Google Cloud Spanner) is a globally distributed, strongly consistent database but may be overkill for a web application's needs.

QUESTION 46

Answer - A) Google Cloud Security Command Center

Option A is correct because Google Cloud Security Command Center provides tools for automated compliance checks, policy enforcement, and vulnerability detection, helping organizations ensure their resources comply with industry-specific regulations and standards.
Option B (Google Cloud IAM) is for access control and does not provide compliance checks.
Option C (Google Cloud KMS) is a key management service and does not address compliance checks.
Option D (Google Cloud Monitoring) is primarily for monitoring and observability, not for compliance checks and policy enforcement.

QUESTION 47

Answer - B) Implement Google Cloud Database Migration Service (DMS) for real-time database replication

Option B is correct because Google Cloud Database Migration Service (DMS) is specifically designed for real-time database replication and minimal downtime during migration. It keeps the on-premises and Google Cloud databases in sync, ensuring data consistency.
Option A is not the best choice because using Google Cloud Storage for backup and restore would require downtime during the migration, which is not ideal for minimal downtime scenarios.
Option C is not efficient because manually copying database files to Compute Engine instances would not provide real-time replication and could result in data inconsistency.
Option D is not designed for database migration but rather for data preparation and cleansing, making it unsuitable for this specific use case.

QUESTION 48

Answer - A) Configure GCP's Regional Managed Instance Groups (MIGs) for distributing VMs across multiple zones within a region

Option A is correct because Google Cloud's Regional Managed Instance Groups (MIGs) allow you to distribute VM instances across multiple zones within a region, providing high availability and redundancy. In case of VM failures in one zone, the application can continue to run in other zones within the same region.
Option B, C, and D are not directly related to achieving high availability and redundancy for VMs and applications in case of failures.

QUESTION 49

Answer – C) Container Registry, Kubernetes Deployment

A) Incorrect, containers can't be deployed directly; they need to be in a registry.
B) Incorrect, Cloud Storage is not the correct place for container images.
C) Correct, uploading to Container Registry and then creating a Deployment in GKE is the standard procedure.
D) Incorrect, Cloud Build is for building images, not directly deploying them.
E) Incorrect, Cloud Endpoints are for API management, not container deployment.

QUESTION 50

Answer – C) High-performance node pool

A) Incorrect, increasing resources equally is not cost-effective.
B) Incorrect, a custom scheduler is complex and may not be necessary.
C) Correct, different node pools allow for tailored resource allocation based on specific needs.
D) Incorrect, preemptible VMs offer cost savings but can be terminated unexpectedly, not suitable for all services.
E) Incorrect, anti-affinity rules help with distribution but don't address specific resource needs.

SET 9 - QUESTIONS ONLY

QUESTION 1

Your organization wants to migrate a legacy monolithic application to GCP for better scalability and maintenance. What approach would you recommend?

A) Refactor the application into microservices and deploy on GKE with Cloud Endpoints for API management.
B) Migrate the application as-is to Compute Engine and use Cloud Load Balancing for scalability.
C) Lift and shift the application to App Engine standard environment for automatic scaling.
D) Break down the application into functions and deploy on Cloud Functions for a serverless architecture.
E) Use Cloud Run to containerize the monolithic application, ensuring scalability and ease of deployment.
F) Migrate the application to a Kubernetes cluster on Anthos for hybrid cloud capabilities and scalability.

QUESTION 2

A global e-commerce company is using GCP to host its web application. The application uses Cloud Storage for product images, Cloud SQL for transactional data, and BigQuery for analytics. With Black Friday approaching, you need to ensure that the application scales efficiently to handle the surge in traffic. What combination of strategies and services should you employ for this scenario?

A) Implement horizontal pod autoscaling in GKE for the web front-end, use Cloud CDN for image delivery, and enable BigQuery slots for increased query capacity.
B) Scale up the Compute Engine VMs hosting the application, increase the Cloud SQL instance size, and use Dataflow for real-time analytics processing.
C) Use a Managed Instance Group for Compute Engine VMs with autoscaling, implement Cloud Spanner for transactional data, and optimize BigQuery queries for efficiency.
D) Configure a network load balancer for Compute Engine VMs, use Cloud Memorystore for caching, and set up a Dataflow job to stream analytics data to BigQuery.
E) Leverage preemptible VMs for the web front-end, increase the size of the Persistent Disks in Cloud SQL, and use BigQuery ML for on-demand analytics.

QUESTION 3

As part of your company's cloud security enhancement project, you are required to set up a system that can detect and alert on potential security breaches in real-time. Your GCP infrastructure includes Compute Engine, Cloud Storage, and BigQuery. Which combination of GCP services should you use to monitor and alert on security threats?

A) Configure Security Command Center to monitor all resources, and use Cloud Monitoring with alert policies for real-time alerts.
B) Implement custom audit logs for all services, stream them to Pub/Sub, and analyze using Dataflow for potential threats.
C) Set up VPC Flow Logs for network traffic analysis, and use Cloud Functions to trigger alerts based on log patterns.
D) Enable Access Transparency logs for all services, and use Cloud Logging with custom metrics for

alerting.
E) Utilize Cloud Armor for threat detection on Compute Engine and integrate with Cloud Pub/Sub for alert notifications.

QUESTION 4

In your company's GCP environment, you are tasked with setting up a secure and efficient way to manage SSH access to Compute Engine instances for multiple developers. You need to ensure that access is controlled and audited without managing individual SSH keys. What solution would you implement?

A) Configure the Compute Engine instances to use OS Login and manage access through IAM roles and permissions.
B) Set up individual SSH keys for each developer and store them in Secret Manager for secure access.
C) Use Identity-Aware Proxy (IAP) to control SSH access to Compute Engine instances based on developers' IAM roles.
D) Implement a third-party SSH key management tool to handle SSH access centrally and integrate it with GCP.
E) Create a VPN connection to the VPC and manage SSH access through network-level controls and firewall rules.

QUESTION 5

In your company, you need to implement a solution to manage GCP access for users who are managed in an on-premises Active Directory. The solution must ensure that users have the same level of access in GCP as they do in your internal systems. Which approach would best achieve this goal?

A) Use Cloud Identity and Google Cloud Directory Sync (GCDS) to synchronize user roles and permissions from Active Directory.
B) Manually assign GCP IAM roles to users that match their roles in Active Directory.
C) Develop a custom script that uses the Cloud Identity API to replicate Active Directory roles into GCP.
D) Configure a Security Assertion Markup Language (SAML) 2.0 identity provider for single sign-on (SSO) between Active Directory and GCP.
E) Implement a third-party identity and access management solution that integrates with both GCP and Active Directory.

QUESTION 6

In your development workflow on Ubuntu, you frequently interact with Cloud Bigtable. To streamline your development process, you need to test your application's Cloud Bigtable integration locally. What's the best approach to achieve this?

A) Set up a local HBase instance to mimic Cloud Bigtable's behavior for testing.
B) Use the Cloud Bigtable emulator available in the Google Cloud SDK for local testing.
C) Create a test Cloud Bigtable instance in GCP and use it exclusively for development.
D) Install a third-party Bigtable simulator that replicates the Cloud Bigtable environment.
E) Connect to a live Cloud Bigtable instance in GCP for all development and testing activities.

QUESTION 7

Your organization uses Active Directory for user management and needs to grant project-specific GCP access to users based on their Active Directory group memberships. What is the most effective way to implement this?

A) Directly assign GCP IAM roles to individual users based on their Active Directory group memberships.
B) Synchronize Active Directory groups with GCP IAM using Cloud Identity.
C) Create corresponding GCP IAM groups for every Active Directory group and manually manage memberships.
D) Use Cloud Directory Sync to map Active Directory groups to GCP resources and roles.
E) Implement a custom access management interface using Cloud Functions and Firebase.

QUESTION 8

To effectively manage GCP resources, you need a team member to monitor and manage Cloud Billing for all your projects. What minimum role should be assigned to this team member?

A) roles/billing.viewer
B) roles/billing.admin
C) roles/billing.user
D) roles/resourcemanager.projectViewer
E) roles/iam.billingViewer

QUESTION 9

In developing a new IoT application that collects data from various sensors and devices, you need to ensure efficient data ingestion, processing, and analysis in GCP. The application should be able to handle large-scale data streams and provide insights in near real-time. Which GCP services should you combine to achieve these objectives while maintaining cost-effectiveness and scalability?

A) Utilize IoT Core for device management, Dataflow for stream processing, and BigQuery for analysis. Leverage Preemptible VMs for cost-effective processing.
B) Implement Pub/Sub for data ingestion, Kubernetes Engine for data processing, and Looker for data analysis. Optimize costs using Custom Machine Types.
C) Choose Cloud IoT Edge for data ingestion, DataProc for processing, and Cloud SQL for analysis. Implement Autoscaling for balancing performance and cost.
D) Deploy Cloud Pub/Sub for data ingestion, Cloud Data Fusion for processing, and Data Studio for visualization and analysis. Use Persistent Disks for storage optimization.
E) Use Cloud Functions for lightweight data ingestion, Firestore for real-time processing, and AI Platform for advanced analytics. Implement Cloud Monitoring for performance optimization.

QUESTION 10

A company stores transactional data in Cloud Storage. The data is accessed frequently for the first 15 days, occasionally for the next 45 days, and then it should be archived. What is the most cost-effective lifecycle policy to set up?

A) Standard for 15 days, then Nearline for 45 days, and move to Archive thereafter.
B) Standard for 60 days, then move directly to Archive.

C) Nearline for 15 days, Coldline for the next 45 days, then Archive.
D) Standard for 15 days, Coldline for 45 days, then Archive.

QUESTION 11

As a GCP Cloud Engineer, you are optimizing resource utilization for a project. The project includes numerous Compute Engine instances, some of which are underutilized. What combination of GCP tools and features should you use to analyze and optimize these instances for cost and performance?

A) Implement Stackdriver Monitoring for real-time metrics and use custom Stackdriver dashboards to identify underutilized instances. Combine this with recommendations from the Compute Engine's Rightsizing Recommendations feature.
B) Use Cloud Functions to periodically check the utilization of each instance and manually adjust their sizes.
C) Rely on the GCP Pricing Calculator to estimate costs and manually inspect each Compute Engine instance for utilization metrics.
D) Configure a series of Cloud Pub/Sub events triggered by high CPU usage to resize instances dynamically using Cloud Functions.

QUESTION 12

As a cloud engineer, you are tasked with designing a robust and scalable application for processing streaming data from social media platforms. The application should efficiently process and analyze sentiment data in real time and store results for future analysis. What combination of GCP services would best suit these needs?

A) Utilize Cloud Pub/Sub for streaming data, implement Cloud Dataflow for real-time sentiment analysis, store results in Cloud Bigtable, and use BigQuery for deep historical analysis.
B) Set up Cloud Functions to process incoming streams, use Firestore for real-time data storage, and integrate with BigQuery for extended analysis.
C) Deploy Cloud Pub/Sub for data ingestion, Cloud Run for processing streams, store processed data in Cloud SQL, and analyze using Data Studio.
D) Use Cloud Endpoints for data intake, Cloud Spanner for storage and processing, and utilize Looker for both real-time and historical analysis.

QUESTION 13

In preparation for a financial audit, your team must configure IAM access for auditors to review transaction records in BigQuery and corresponding audit logs. What is the best practice to set up their access in GCP?

A) Create a group for the auditors and assign them 'bigquery.dataViewer' and 'logging.viewer' IAM roles.
B) Assign 'bigquery.admin' role to individual auditors for comprehensive access.
C) Grant the auditors group the 'project.editor' role for necessary permissions.
D) Provide individual auditors with 'bigquery.dataViewer' and 'logging.viewer' IAM roles.

QUESTION 14

In your organization, Cloud Storage is used to store customer interaction logs. For quality assurance purposes, you need to audit the activities of specific team members who edit or annotate these logs. What is the most straightforward way to track these user activities?

A) Review user activities related to editing or annotating logs in the Cloud Storage Audit logs.
B) Configure Stackdriver logging to monitor and alert on log file modifications.
C) Regularly inspect the version history of log files in the Cloud Storage console.
D) Develop a custom application to track and report any edits or annotations made to the log files.

QUESTION 15

As part of a security enhancement for your corporate web portal, you need a load balancer that can handle HTTPS traffic, perform SSL termination, and direct traffic based on URL paths to different backend services in GCP. Which load balancing service should you utilize?

A) Opt for an HTTP(S) Load Balancer with URL-based routing and SSL termination for optimal traffic distribution.
B) Choose a Global SSL Proxy Load Balancer to handle SSL traffic with URL path routing to backend services.
C) Use a TCP Proxy Load Balancer with added SSL certificates and custom scripts for URL path routing.
D) Implement an Internal Load Balancer with SSL termination and URL path-based routing for internal traffic management.

QUESTION 16

Your organization is focused on building a serverless application on Google Cloud to process real-time data from IoT devices. Which GCP service should you consider to ingest, process, and store the data efficiently while scaling automatically with demand?

A) Google Cloud Dataprep
B) Google Cloud Dataflow
C) Google Cloud Dataproc
D) Google Cloud Pub/Sub
E) Google Cloud Datastore

QUESTION 17

Your team is building a data analytics platform that requires processing large datasets in real-time. Which Google Cloud service should you consider for ingesting, processing, and analyzing streaming data at scale?

A) Google Cloud Dataprep for data preparation.
B) Google Cloud Bigtable for NoSQL storage.
C) Google Cloud Dataflow for stream and batch processing.
D) Google Cloud Spanner for globally distributed databases.

QUESTION 18

Your project involves deploying microservices-based applications on Google Kubernetes Engine (GKE). You want to ensure automated scaling of containers based on resource utilization. Which GCP service should you use for container orchestration and auto-scaling of microservices?

A) Google Cloud Functions.
B) Google Cloud App Engine.
C) Google Cloud Run.
D) Google Kubernetes Engine (GKE).

QUESTION 19

You need to analyze and visualize the logs generated by your Google Cloud resources in real-time. Which GCP service should you use for this purpose?

A) Cloud Monitoring
B) Cloud Logging
C) Cloud Pub/Sub
D) Cloud Dataflow
E) Cloud Storage
F) Cloud Bigtable

QUESTION 20

For an upcoming internal audit, auditors require temporary access to query data within a Cloud Spanner instance in your GCP project. They do not need to modify any data. What is the appropriate method to grant this access?

A) Grant each auditor the 'spanner.databaseUser' role.
B) Create a temporary Google Group for the auditors and assign the 'spanner.viewer' role.
C) Provide individual auditors with 'spanner.admin' role for complete access.
D) Manually share query results from Cloud Spanner with the auditors without granting direct access.

QUESTION 21

Your company needs to periodically upload large backup files, around 30 GB each, to Google Cloud Storage. Given the availability of a high-speed 500 Mbps internet connection, what technique would you recommend for efficient uploads?

A) Use the GCP console for its straightforward upload interface.
B) Opt for gsutil with parallel composite uploads to expedite the process.
C) Compress the files to smaller sizes before uploading.
D) Schedule uploads during off-peak hours to maximize bandwidth usage.

QUESTION 22

You need to allow a service account from a project 'network-admin' to manage network resources in another project 'global-network'. How can you securely provide the required access?

A) Transfer the service account from 'network-admin' to 'global-network' and assign it Network Admin role.
B) In 'global-network', assign the Network Admin role to the service account from 'network-admin'.
C) Generate and share the key of the service account from 'network-admin' with administrators in

'global-network'.
D) Create a shared VPC between 'network-admin' and 'global-network' and use the same service account.

QUESTION 23

For a financial analytics application in a GCP managed instance group, instances often scale up prematurely during data processing. The app takes about 90 seconds to start. What adjustment in autoscaling settings could optimize performance?

A) Lower the CPU utilization threshold for scaling down.
B) Set the health check initial delay to 90 seconds.
C) Increase the maximum instances.
D) Change the metric to network utilization.
E) Use predictive scaling based on historical data.

QUESTION 24

You have multiple GCP projects and need to confirm the project used for your recent App Engine deployment. What is the most efficient way to identify the project where the application is currently deployed?

A) Use gcloud services list to see all services in the current project.
B) Check the cloudbuild.yaml file for specified project details.
C) Run gcloud config list to verify the active project in your configuration.
D) Examine the app.yaml file for any project-specific configurations.
E) Look through Cloud Logging for deployment logs specifying the project.
F) Access the GCP Console and review the App Engine section in each project.

QUESTION 25

To handle an unexpected increase in traffic, you need to upgrade the memory of your existing Compute Engine instance from 4 GB to 8 GB. What is the correct procedure to follow on GCP?

A) Directly increase the memory allocation in the VM settings while it is running.
B) Temporarily stop the VM, change its machine type to one with 8 GB RAM, then restart.
C) Create a new VM instance with 8 GB RAM and migrate your applications to it.
D) Use the gcloud command-line tool to add more RAM to the instance without downtime.
E) Set up a load balancer to distribute traffic and reduce memory load on the instance.
F) Implement autoscaling to automatically adjust the memory based on traffic.

QUESTION 26

In light of a recent event where a Compute Engine instance was mistakenly deleted, what step can you take to ensure such critical instances are protected against accidental deletion in the future?

A) Switch to using Managed Instance Groups for better control over instance deletions.
B) Turn on the 'Deletion Protection' option on all key Compute Engine instances.
C) Modify the boot disk settings to make them independent of instance deletion.

D) Restrict access to instance management only to senior cloud engineers.
E) Create a detailed SOP for instance deletion and ensure all team members follow it.
F) Utilize the Resource Manager to apply a label that marks the instance as non-deletable.

QUESTION 27

For your accounting application on GCP, you need to ensure that each invoice uploaded by users is only accessible for 30 minutes and is deleted after 45 days. Which two GCP functionalities should you implement to meet these requirements?

A) Configure a Cloud Scheduler job to delete invoices older than 45 days.
B) Use Cloud IAM for granting temporary access to invoice data.
C) Implement signed URLs for secure and time-limited access to uploads.
D) Set up a lifecycle management policy in Cloud Storage for auto-deletion.
E) Enable versioning in Cloud Storage to manage file retention.
F) Create a custom Cloud Function to manage file access and deletion times.

QUESTION 28

You need to monitor and analyze the performance of your Google Cloud resources and set up alerting based on predefined conditions. Which GCP service should you use for this purpose?

A) Cloud Logging
B) Cloud Pub/Sub
C) Cloud Dataflow
D) Cloud Monitoring
E) Cloud Storage
F) Cloud Bigtable

QUESTION 29

You are tasked with ensuring that a Compute Engine-based application for a financial service only permits necessary egress traffic in its VPC. What firewall setup should you employ for optimal security?

A) Use a default high-priority rule to block all egress, with exceptions for required ports.
B) Create a low-priority egress rule to deny all traffic, supplemented by higher-priority rules for allowed ports.
C) Deploy a dedicated egress proxy to filter and control all outbound traffic.
D) Configure each Compute Engine instance with specific egress rules based on its role.
E) Establish a Cloud IDS to dynamically control and monitor egress traffic.
F) Set up a Cloud NAT gateway to manage and restrict all egress connections.

QUESTION 30

For an internal tool with usage limited to work hours and a requirement for zero costs outside these hours, which GCP service offers the most cost-effective solution?

A) Deploy on Compute Engine with scripts to start and stop instances based on a schedule.
B) Use Cloud Run (fully managed) with a configuration that allows scaling to zero instances.

C) Implement the application on App Engine Standard Environment with automatic scaling.
D) Set up the tool on a Google Kubernetes Engine cluster with a scheduled downscaling to zero nodes.
E) Configure the application on Cloud Functions to run only when invoked.
F) Utilize App Engine Flexible Environment with a custom scaling configuration.

QUESTION 31

In a scenario where a DevOps team needs access to production services in multiple GCP projects, what is the recommended approach to manage their permissions effectively?

A) Allocate the Project Owner role to the DevOps team for each project they need access to.
B) Use a service account with extensive permissions and share it with the DevOps team.
C) Assign the Project Viewer role to the DevOps team and add specific permissions as needed.
D) Create a custom role with necessary permissions and apply it to the DevOps team across projects.
E) Implement a central IAM policy that grants broad permissions to the DevOps team.
F) Set up a cross-project access group for the DevOps team with wide-ranging roles.

QUESTION 32

To manage files in Cloud Storage for a file-sharing app that requires frequent access for 30 days and a total retention period of 3 years, how should you structure the storage?

A) Utilize Standard storage for 30 days, then transition files to Coldline storage, and finally to Archive after a year.
B) Store files in Nearline storage for the first 30 days, followed by moving them to Coldline, and eventually to Archive.
C) Keep files in Standard storage for the initial 30 days, then transfer them to Archive storage for the 3-year duration.
D) Start with Coldline storage for frequent access, then shift to Archive storage for long-term retention.
E) Use a combination of Standard and Nearline storage for 30 days, then move files to Archive storage.
F) Implement a lifecycle policy that moves files from Standard to Nearline after 30 days, then to Coldline, and finally to Archive.

QUESTION 33

To ensure horizontal scalability and single IP exposure for a multiplayer game backend on Google Cloud that uses UDP packets, what should you implement?

A) Deploy an External HTTP(S) Load Balancer in front of the servers.
B) Set up an SSL Proxy Load Balancer for UDP traffic handling.
C) Use a Global UDP Proxy Load Balancer for traffic management.
D) Configure an External Network Load Balancer for UDP traffic distribution.
E) Implement an Internal UDP Load Balancer with a NAT gateway.
F) Create a series of forwarding rules with a single static IP for UDP traffic.

QUESTION 34

A retail company wants to optimize its supply chain management with real-time data analytics on GCP. They have multiple data sources, including online transactions and in-store sales. Which architecture would provide the best real-time analytics solution?

A) Stream data using Pub/Sub to Dataflow for processing, store in BigQuery for analysis, and visualize insights with Data Studio.
B) Use Cloud IoT Core for in-store data collection, transfer to Cloud SQL for storage, and analyze using Cloud Dataprep.
C) Collect data with Firebase, process using Cloud Functions, store in Firestore, and integrate with Looker for analytics.
D) Sync data to Bigtable for real-time processing, use Cloud Composer for orchestration, and analyze with BigQuery.
E) Deploy a custom data processing solution on Kubernetes Engine, store data in Cloud Spanner, and use AI Platform for predictive analytics.

QUESTION 35

Your team needs to provide controlled SSH access to Compute Engine VMs for a group of contractors working off-site. The contractors should have time-limited access and not have any other GCP permissions. What's the best approach to meet these requirements?

A) Use IAM conditional roles to grant temporary SSH access to the contractors.
B) Generate temporary SSH keys with an expiration date and add them to the VMs.
C) Create a temporary VPC with specific firewall rules and connect it to the contractors' network.
D) Set up Cloud Identity-Aware Proxy (IAP) with time-based access policies.
E) Implement a bastion host that contractors can SSH into, with access rules controlled by a script.

QUESTION 36

You want to monitor access to a Cloud Storage bucket in your GCP project and receive alerts if there are any access attempts from unauthorized IP addresses. How can you achieve this?

A) Use Cloud Storage Access Logs, export them to Cloud Logging, and set an alert for unauthorized IP access.
B) Implement a Cloud Function that triggers on Cloud Storage events and checks the IP addresses.
C) Configure a VPC Service Control perimeter around the Cloud Storage bucket for access control.
D) Set up a log sink to BigQuery for all bucket access logs and analyze them for unauthorized access.
E) Create a custom metric in Cloud Monitoring for access from unauthorized IP addresses.

QUESTION 37

You are tasked with setting up a disaster recovery (DR) plan for your company's critical applications on Google Cloud Platform. Which GCP service can help you achieve automated cross-region failover and recovery for your applications?

A) Google Cloud Spanner
B) Google Cloud VPN
C) Google Cloud Storage
D) Google Cloud Pub/Sub
E) Google Cloud Deployment Manager

QUESTION 38

Your organization operates a critical application that requires high availability and minimal downtime. You want to set up a disaster recovery (DR) solution in Google Cloud that can automatically fail over to another region in case of a regional outage. Which Google Cloud service or feature should you choose to achieve this cross-region failover and high availability?

A) Implement Google Cloud Memorystore for caching and load balancing for regional failover.
B) Configure Google Cloud VPN for secure cross-region communication and failover.
C) Use Google Cloud Deployment Manager to define and automate resource deployment for cross-region failover.
D) Deploy Google Cloud Functions for event-driven disaster recovery.
E) Utilize Google Cloud IAM (Identity and Access Management) for access control during DR scenarios.

QUESTION 39

Your team is responsible for ensuring data security in a Google Cloud project that uses multiple GCP services. To enhance security, you want to implement centralized access control and fine-grained permissions management. Which GCP service or feature should you use for this purpose?

A) Utilize Google Cloud Identity-Aware Proxy (IAP) for centralized access control.
B) Implement Google Cloud Armor for fine-grained permissions management.
C) Set up Google Cloud IAM (Identity and Access Management) for centralized access control and fine-grained permissions management.
D) Deploy Google Cloud Pub/Sub for access control and permissions management.

QUESTION 40

Your company is using Google Cloud Storage to store and manage large datasets. You want to implement a cost-effective solution to analyze and process this data using Google Cloud services. Which GCP service should you choose for cost-effective data processing with features like serverless data analysis and automatic scaling?

A) Use Google Cloud Dataprep to manually clean and preprocess data before analysis.
B) Deploy a self-managed Apache Hadoop cluster on Google Compute Engine for full control over data processing.
C) Utilize Google Cloud Dataflow to process data with serverless, automatic scaling capabilities.
D) Use Google Cloud Pub/Sub for data ingestion and processing.

QUESTION 41

Your company is using Google Cloud Storage to store and manage large datasets. You want to implement a cost-effective solution to analyze and process this data using Google Cloud services. Which GCP service should you choose for cost-effective data processing with features like serverless data analysis and automatic scaling?

A) Google Cloud Dataprep
B) Google Cloud Dataproc

C) Google Cloud Dataflow
D) Google Cloud Datastore

QUESTION 42

You have a Compute Engine instance running a third-party OTP application that needs to access installation files stored in a Cloud Storage bucket. You want to ensure that the access to these files is limited to only this instance. Which approach should you follow?

A) Use the default Compute Engine service account for the instance and restrict access in the Cloud Storage bucket ACL.
B) Grant permissions directly to the instance's external IP address for the Cloud Storage bucket.
C) Use a shared access key for the Compute Engine instance to access the Cloud Storage bucket.
D) Create a new service account and select it while creating the new instance. Grant the service account permissions on Cloud Storage.
E) Grant permissions to all Compute Engine instances in the project for the Cloud Storage bucket.

QUESTION 43

You are tasked with deploying a web application on GCP, and you need to implement a deployment strategy that allows for A/B testing by testing updates on a small portion of live users before full rollout. What is the recommended GCP deployment approach for achieving this goal?

A) Use App Engine to run your app. For each update, create a new version of the same service and send a small percentage of traffic to the new version using traffic splitting.
B) Use App Engine to run your app. For each update, create a new service and send a small percentage of traffic to the new version using traffic splitting.
C) Use Kubernetes Engine to run your app. For a new release, update the deployment to use the new version.
D) Use Kubernetes Engine to run your app. For a new release, create a new deployment for the new version and update the service to use the new deployment.

QUESTION 44

Your organization wants to ensure data security and compliance for sensitive data stored in Google Cloud Storage. You need to encrypt the data at rest and manage the encryption keys. Which encryption option should you choose to meet these requirements?

A) Google-managed keys for Google Cloud Storage
B) Customer-supplied keys for Google Cloud Storage
C) Firebase-managed keys for Google Cloud Storage
D) Google Identity Platform keys for Google Cloud Storage

QUESTION 45

Your organization is looking to set up a highly available and scalable Kubernetes cluster on Google Cloud. You want to choose a managed Kubernetes service that offers automated upgrades, monitoring, and scaling. Which Google Cloud Kubernetes service should you select for this purpose?

A) Google Kubernetes Engine (GKE)
B) Google Cloud Dataprep
C) Google Cloud Composer
D) Google Cloud Dataflow

QUESTION 46

Your organization is developing a real-time data streaming application that requires low-latency data ingestion and processing. You want to choose a Google Cloud service that can handle high-throughput data streams and provide real-time analytics capabilities. Which Google Cloud service should you select for this use case?

A) Google Cloud Dataflow
B) Google Cloud Dataprep
C) Google Cloud Pub/Sub
D) Google Cloud Datastore

QUESTION 47

Your organization is running a high-availability web application on Google Cloud Platform (GCP). You want to ensure that the application remains available even if a single zone or region experiences an outage. What GCP service can help you achieve multi-region redundancy and high availability?

A) Utilize Google Cloud Global Load Balancer for traffic distribution.
B) Implement Google Cloud Resource Manager for automated zone failover.
C) Leverage Google Cloud CDN (Content Delivery Network) for regional redundancy.
D) Use Google Cloud Spanner for globally distributed databases .

QUESTION 48

Your organization is building a real-time analytics platform on Google Cloud. You need to ingest, process, and analyze large volumes of streaming data from various sources. Which GCP service can help you efficiently handle real-time data processing and analytics?

A) Use Google Cloud Dataprep for data preprocessing and batch analytics.
B) Implement Google Cloud Dataflow for stream processing and real-time analytics.
C) Deploy Google BigQuery for batch data processing and analysis.
D) Leverage Google Cloud Dataproc for long-running Hadoop and Spark jobs.

QUESTION 49

You have been given the task of deploying a newly developed API, packaged as a Docker image, onto Google Kubernetes Engine. Which of the following steps should you take to successfully deploy this API?

A) Build the Docker image using Cloud Build, upload it to Cloud Storage, and then deploy it on GKE.
B) Upload the Docker image to Artifact Registry, then use a Kubernetes Service in GKE to run the image.
C) Use Cloud Build to automatically deploy the Docker image to GKE upon successful image build.
D) Upload the Docker image to Container Registry, then create a Kubernetes Deployment in GKE.
E) Store the Docker image in a private Git repository and deploy it directly from there to GKE.

QUESTION 50

You are managing a GKE cluster with multiple microservices, where a few require high network throughput. What is the most efficient way to accommodate these varying network demands?

A) Configure all microservices with enhanced network capabilities to match the highest demand.
B) Use Network Policies to prioritize network traffic for high-demand microservices.
C) Allocate dedicated network resources to each microservice based on its individual needs.
D) Create a node pool with high network throughput capabilities for the demanding microservices.
E) Implement a service mesh to manage and optimize network traffic across all microservices.

SET 9 - ANSWERS ONLY

QUESTION 1

Answer - A) Refactor into microservices

A) Correct, refactoring into microservices and deploying on GKE with Cloud Endpoints offers scalability and improved maintenance.
B) Incorrect, simply migrating to Compute Engine may not fully leverage the benefits of cloud scalability and maintenance.
C) Incorrect, App Engine standard environment is more suited for lightweight applications and may not handle a legacy monolithic application effectively.
D) Incorrect, breaking into functions may not be feasible for all monolithic applications and could lead to complexities.
E) Incorrect, while Cloud Run offers scalability, it may not be the best for complex monolithic applications.
F) Incorrect, Anthos is a robust solution but may be more than required for this scenario and involves more complexity.

QUESTION 2

Answer - A) Horizontal pod autoscaling, Cloud CDN, BigQuery slots

A) Correct, horizontal pod autoscaling for the web front-end, Cloud CDN for efficient image delivery, and BigQuery slots for analytics ensure scalability during traffic surges.
B) Incorrect, simply scaling up VMs and SQL instance size may not provide the most efficient scaling strategy, and Dataflow for real-time analytics might be overkill.
C) Incorrect, while Managed Instance Groups provide scalability, Cloud Spanner may introduce unnecessary complexity for transactional data handling.
D) Incorrect, network load balancing is less effective for HTTP traffic, and Memorystore is not mentioned as part of the existing architecture.
E) Incorrect, preemptible VMs are not reliable for peak traffic times, and changing the database structure and analytics approach may not be feasible in the short term.

QUESTION 3

Answer - A) Security Command Center and Cloud Monitoring

A) Correct, Security Command Center provides comprehensive monitoring, while Cloud Monitoring can be configured for real-time alerts.
B) Incorrect, while custom audit logs are useful, setting up a complete streaming and analysis pipeline is complex and may not provide immediate alerts.
C) Incorrect, VPC Flow Logs are useful for network analysis but do not cover all aspects of security monitoring.
D) Incorrect, Access Transparency logs are more about governance and compliance, not real-time threat detection.
E) Incorrect, Cloud Armor is specific to web security and does not provide complete infrastructure

monitoring.

QUESTION 4

Answer - A) OS Login and IAM roles

A) Correct, OS Login integrates with IAM roles to manage SSH access efficiently and securely without handling individual SSH keys.
B) Incorrect, managing individual SSH keys, even with Secret Manager, adds complexity and doesn't offer centralized control.
C) Incorrect, Identity-Aware Proxy is primarily used for web applications, not for managing SSH access to Compute Engine instances.
D) Incorrect, a third-party tool adds complexity and may not be necessary when GCP offers integrated solutions like OS Login.
E) Incorrect, a VPN adds network complexity and doesn't provide an efficient way to manage SSH access at the user level.

QUESTION 5

Answer - A) Cloud Identity and GCDS

A) Correct, using Cloud Identity and GCDS to synchronize user roles and permissions from Active Directory ensures consistency in access levels.
B) Incorrect, manually assigning roles is time-consuming and error-prone.
C) Incorrect, developing a custom script is unnecessary when GCDS provides a ready-made solution.
D) Incorrect, while SAML 2.0 provides SSO, it does not by itself ensure role and permission synchronization.
E) Incorrect, a third-party solution might add unnecessary complexity and cost compared to using Cloud Identity and GCDS.

QUESTION 6

Answer - B) Cloud Bigtable emulator in Google Cloud SDK

A) Incorrect, while HBase is similar, it doesn't perfectly replicate Cloud Bigtable's behavior.
B) Correct, the Cloud Bigtable emulator allows for accurate local testing and development without connecting to GCP.
C) Incorrect, this approach does not constitute local testing.
D) Incorrect, a third-party simulator may not replicate all features of Cloud Bigtable accurately.
E) Incorrect, connecting to a live instance is not a local testing approach.

QUESTION 7

Answer - B) Synchronize Active Directory groups with GCP IAM

A) Incorrect, direct assignment of IAM roles to individual users is inefficient and does not leverage Active Directory group memberships.
B) Correct, synchronizing Active Directory groups with GCP IAM using Cloud Identity provides an effective and automated way to manage access based on group memberships.

C) Incorrect, manually creating and managing corresponding IAM groups is time-consuming and error-prone.
D) Incorrect, Cloud Directory Sync synchronizes users but does not directly map groups to specific GCP resources and roles.
E) Incorrect, developing a custom interface is unnecessary and complex when existing solutions can meet the requirement.

QUESTION 8

Answer - B) roles/billing.admin

A) Incorrect, roles/billing.viewer allows viewing billing information but not managing it.
B) Correct, roles/billing.admin provides the necessary permissions to manage and monitor Cloud Billing.
C) Incorrect, roles/billing.user allows managing billing for a project but may not include monitoring across all projects.
D) Incorrect, roles/resourcemanager.projectViewer allows viewing project resources but not specific to billing management.
E) Incorrect, roles/iam.billingViewer does not exist in GCP IAM roles.

QUESTION 9

Answer – A) Utilize IoT Core for device management, Dataflow for stream processing, and BigQuery for analysis. Leverage Preemptible VMs for cost-effective processing.

Option A is a comprehensive solution for the IoT application requirements. IoT Core effectively manages device connectivity and data collection. Dataflow provides powerful stream processing capabilities, suitable for handling large-scale data streams. BigQuery allows for efficient analysis of the processed data, providing near real-time insights. The use of Preemptible VMs in Dataflow jobs can help manage costs without compromising on scalability. Option B, while viable, may not offer the same level of streamlined integration and real-time processing capability. Option C's choice of Cloud SQL for analysis may not be optimal for large-scale IoT data. Option D, using Data Studio for analysis, is more suited for visualization rather than in-depth, large-scale data analysis. Option E's use of Firestore for real-time processing is an interesting choice, but it may not provide the same level of efficiency and scalability for large IoT datasets as Dataflow, and AI Platform, while powerful, might introduce unnecessary complexity and cost for the stated requirements.

QUESTION 10

Answer - A) Standard for 15 days, then Nearline for 45 days, and move to Archive thereafter.

A) Correct. This setup optimizes cost while aligning with the data access pattern: Standard for initial frequent access, Nearline for occasional access, then archiving.
B) Incorrect as it does not reflect the reduced access after 15 days.
C) Incorrect, as Nearline is not used for the initial frequent access phase.
D) Incorrect, as Coldline is more expensive than Nearline for the occasional access phase.

QUESTION 11

Answer - A) Implement Stackdriver Monitoring for real-time metrics and use custom Stackdriver dashboards to identify underutilized instances. Combine this with recommendations from the Compute Engine's Rightsizing Recommendations feature.

A) Correct. Provides a comprehensive approach using Stackdriver for monitoring and Compute Engine's Rightsizing Recommendations for optimization.
B) Not efficient and requires manual intervention.
C) Helps estimate costs but doesn't provide active monitoring or optimization.
D) Focuses only on high CPU usage and may not address all aspects of instance optimization.

QUESTION 12

Answer - A) Utilize Cloud Pub/Sub for streaming data, implement Cloud Dataflow for real-time sentiment analysis, store results in Cloud Bigtable, and use BigQuery for deep historical analysis.

A) Correct. Offers a complete solution for real-time processing, scalable storage, and deep analysis, ideal for streaming data scenarios.
B) Cloud Functions and Firestore are more suited to event-driven applications than high-volume streaming data.
C) Cloud Run and Cloud SQL are not optimized for high-throughput stream processing and sentiment analysis.
D) Cloud Endpoints and Looker do not specifically cater to the real-time processing of streaming data.

QUESTION 13

Answer - A) Create a group for the auditors and assign them 'bigquery.dataViewer' and 'logging.viewer' IAM roles.

A) Ideal for providing auditors with the necessary access to BigQuery data and logs, while maintaining security and ease of management.
B) Too broad, giving unnecessary administrative access.
C) 'project.editor' grants more permissions than needed for auditing.
D) Managing access through groups is more efficient than individual accounts.

QUESTION 14

Answer - A) Review user activities related to editing or annotating logs in the Cloud Storage Audit logs.

A) Audit logs in Cloud Storage provide a detailed and direct way to monitor specific user activities such as editing or annotating log files.
B) Stackdriver can be configured for this, but it is more complex than using audit logs.
C) Version history doesn't specifically audit user activities.
D) A custom application is less efficient and might not capture all relevant data as effectively as audit logs.

QUESTION 15

Answer - A) Opt for an HTTP(S) Load Balancer with URL-based routing and SSL termination for optimal traffic distribution.

A) HTTP(S) Load Balancer is the best fit as it supports SSL termination and URL path-based routing,

essential for directing traffic to appropriate backend services.
B) SSL Proxy Load Balancer cannot route based on URL paths.
C) TCP Proxy Load Balancer does not support URL path routing and operates at the TCP level.
D) Internal Load Balancer is designed for internal traffic and does not meet the requirements for a public-facing web portal.

QUESTION 16

Answer - D) Google Cloud Pub/Sub

Option D: This is the correct choice as Google Cloud Pub/Sub is a messaging service designed for ingesting and distributing real-time data, making it suitable for IoT data ingestion and processing.
Option A: Google Cloud Dataprep is for data preparation and cleaning, not real-time data ingestion.
Option B: Google Cloud Dataflow is a data processing service and may not be the most efficient choice for data ingestion.
Option C: Google Cloud Dataproc is for running Hadoop and Spark clusters and may not be suitable for serverless data processing.
Option E: Google Cloud Datastore is a NoSQL database and not designed for real-time data ingestion and processing.

QUESTION 17

Answer - C) Google Cloud Dataflow for stream and batch processing.

Option C: This is the correct choice as Google Cloud Dataflow is designed for ingesting, processing, and analyzing streaming data at scale, making it suitable for real-time data analytics.
Option A: Google Cloud Dataprep focuses on data preparation, not real-time data processing.
Option B: Google Cloud Bigtable is a NoSQL database and may not be the ideal choice for real-time data analytics.
Option D: Google Cloud Spanner is a globally distributed database and may not be optimized for real-time data processing.

QUESTION 18

Answer - D) Google Kubernetes Engine (GKE).

Option D is the correct choice as Google Kubernetes Engine (GKE) is a managed Kubernetes service that provides container orchestration and automated scaling capabilities for microservices-based applications.
Option A is for serverless functions, Option B is for platform-as-a-service, and Option C is for containerized serverless applications.

QUESTION 19

Answer - B) Cloud Logging

Option B, "Cloud Logging," is the correct choice. It allows you to collect, view, and analyze logs generated by various GCP resources in real-time. Cloud Monitoring (Option A) is focused on monitoring metrics, not logs. Cloud Pub/Sub (Option C) deals with event streaming, and Cloud Dataflow (Option D) is for data processing. Cloud Storage (Option E) and Cloud Bigtable (Option F) are storage and database services, respectively, not log analysis tools.

QUESTION 20

Answer - B) Create a temporary Google Group for the auditors and assign the 'spanner.viewer' role.

B) This approach allows for efficient management of auditor access, granting them the ability to query data without the risk of modification. Grouping enhances security and simplifies access revocation post-audit.
A) The 'spanner.databaseUser' role permits data modification, which is unnecessary.
C) The 'spanner.admin' role provides excessive access for an audit.
D) Manually sharing results is inefficient and could lead to delays or data omission.

QUESTION 21

Answer - B) Opt for gsutil with parallel composite uploads to expedite the process.

B) Parallel composite uploads via gsutil enable the large files to be broken into smaller parts and uploaded simultaneously, taking full advantage of the high-speed connection and reducing the overall upload time.
A) The GCP console isn't optimized for handling large files.
C) Compression can reduce file size but doesn't utilize bandwidth as effectively as parallel uploading.
D) While off-peak scheduling can help, it doesn't inherently speed up the upload process like parallel uploads do.

QUESTION 22

Answer - B) In 'global-network', assign the Network Admin role to the service account from 'network-admin'.

B) This method correctly grants the service account from 'network-admin' the necessary permissions to manage network resources in 'global-network'. It's a secure and straightforward approach to cross-project resource management.
A) Service accounts cannot be transferred between projects.
C) Sharing service account keys is insecure and not recommended.
D) Creating a shared VPC is an option but may not be necessary solely for service account access.

QUESTION 23

Answer - B) Set the health check initial delay to 90 seconds.

A) Lowering the CPU threshold for scaling down affects when instances are removed, not added.
B) Correct. Aligns health checks with app start-up time, preventing premature scaling.
C) Increasing maximum instances doesn't address the timing issue with health checks.
D) Changing the scaling metric doesn't impact the health check timing.
E) Predictive scaling is useful, but doesn't specifically address the health check timing issue.

QUESTION 24

Answer - C) Run gcloud config list to verify the active project in your configuration.

C) This is the quickest and most reliable way to identify the active project in your gcloud configuration, indicating where the App Engine app was deployed.
A) Listing services only works if you already know the project.
B) The cloudbuild.yaml file is not always used in App Engine deployments.
D) The app.yaml file typically doesn't specify the project for deployment.
E) Sifting through logs can be time-consuming and may not clearly indicate the project.
F) Checking each project in the Console is less efficient than using the gcloud command.

QUESTION 25

Answer - B) Temporarily stop the VM, change its machine type to one with 8 GB RAM, then restart.

B) This is the standard procedure for resizing a Compute Engine instance in GCP. Stopping the VM allows for safe reconfiguration of its resources, and then it can be restarted with the new specifications.
A) It's not possible to change memory allocation of a running VM directly in the VM settings.
C) Creating a new VM is an option but is more complex than simply resizing the existing VM.
D) The gcloud tool does not offer an option to add RAM to a running instance.
E) While load balancing can distribute traffic, it doesn't solve the issue of inadequate memory.
F) Autoscaling adjusts the number of instances, not the memory of individual instances.

QUESTION 26

Answer - B) Turn on the 'Deletion Protection' option on all key Compute Engine instances.

B) Enabling 'Deletion Protection' directly prevents the accidental deletion of Compute Engine instances, adding an additional layer of security to your critical cloud infrastructure.
A) Managed Instance Groups offer scaling and management benefits but don't prevent individual instance deletions.
C) Changing boot disk settings helps with data persistence but not with preventing instance deletion.
D) Limiting access is a good security practice but may not be feasible for all operations.
E) SOPs are important but rely on human compliance, which is not foolproof.
F) Labels in Resource Manager are for organization and do not enforce operational restrictions like deletion.

QUESTION 27

Answer - C) and D)

C) Signed URLs in Cloud Storage provide a secure method for users to upload invoices, with the ability to set an expiration time (30 minutes in this case) for access control.
D) Lifecycle management policies in Cloud Storage allow for the automatic deletion of objects after a set period, addressing the requirement for deleting invoices after 45 days.
A) Cloud Scheduler is for scheduling tasks, less efficient for managing file deletion in Cloud Storage.
B) Cloud IAM controls access but does not provide temporary or time-based access features.
E) Versioning in Cloud Storage is for maintaining file versions, not for setting access times or auto-deletion.

F) Writing custom Cloud Functions for this purpose is more complex than using existing Cloud Storage features.

QUESTION 28

Answer - D) Cloud Monitoring

Option D - Cloud Monitoring allows you to monitor the performance of various GCP resources, set up alerting based on predefined conditions, and gain insights into your system's health and performance.
Option A - Cloud Logging deals with collecting and analyzing logs, not performance monitoring.
Option B - Cloud Pub/Sub is for event streaming.
Option C - Cloud Dataflow is for data processing.
Option E - Cloud Storage is an object storage service, and
Option F - Cloud Bigtable is a NoSQL database.

QUESTION 29

Answer - B) Create a low-priority egress rule to deny all traffic, supplemented by higher-priority rules for allowed ports.

B) This approach ensures that by default, all egress traffic is blocked, creating a secure baseline. Then, allowing specific necessary traffic through higher-priority rules provides the needed flexibility without compromising security. It's ideal for a financial service application where data security is paramount.
A) High-priority deny rules might prevent necessary traffic from being allowed.
C) An egress proxy adds complexity and may not be as effective as direct firewall rules.
D) Configuring individual instances is less scalable than VPC-wide rules.
E) Cloud IDS is more focused on intrusion detection than specific egress control.
F) Cloud NAT manages IP addresses but doesn't offer granular port control.

QUESTION 30

Answer - B) Use Cloud Run (fully managed) with a configuration that allows scaling to zero instances.

B) Cloud Run (fully managed) is the ideal choice because it can automatically scale down to zero instances when the application is not in use, thus not incurring any costs outside of work hours. This perfectly aligns with the need for cost-saving during idle times.
A) Compute Engine scripts require manual intervention and do not guarantee zero costs when idle.
C) App Engine Standard Environment scales down but not to zero.
D) GKE cannot scale down to zero nodes by default.
E) Cloud Functions are event-driven and not ideal for a continuous use application.
F) App Engine Flexible Environment does not scale down to zero instances.

QUESTION 31

Answer - D) Create a custom role with necessary permissions and apply it to the DevOps team across projects.

D) Creating a custom role that includes only the necessary permissions needed for the DevOps team's tasks across multiple projects is the most efficient and secure way to manage their access. This method ensures they have the required access without the risk of excessive privileges, adhering to the principle of least privilege.

A) Project Owner role is too broad and may pose security risks.
B) Sharing a service account with extensive permissions is not a recommended practice.
C) Project Viewer is too restrictive as a starting point for DevOps responsibilities.
E) A central IAM policy with broad permissions can lead to security vulnerabilities.
F) Cross-project access groups with wide-ranging roles might grant more access than necessary.

QUESTION 32

Answer - C) Keep files in Standard storage for the initial 30 days, then transfer them to Archive storage for the 3-year duration.

C) This strategy is efficient for both access and cost. Standard storage is suitable for the first 30 days when files are frequently accessed. Afterwards, moving to Archive storage for the 3-year retention period optimizes costs, as Archive storage is designed for infrequent access and offers lower rates, ideal for long-term retention.

A) Transitioning through Coldline before Archive adds unnecessary complexity and costs.
B) Nearline followed by Coldline is not as cost-effective as directly moving to Archive.
D) Coldline is not designed for the frequent access required in the initial 30 days.
E) A combination of Standard and Nearline is not necessary and may increase costs.
F) Multiple transitions through storage classes can incur higher costs and complexity.

QUESTION 33

Answer - D) Configure an External Network Load Balancer for UDP traffic distribution.

D) An External Network Load Balancer is the ideal solution for this scenario. It is capable of handling UDP traffic, which is crucial for the game's communication protocol, and allows for the use of a single external IP address. This facilitates the horizontal scaling of servers while maintaining a consistent point of access for the game's multiplayer functionality.

A) External HTTP(S) Load Balancers do not support UDP traffic.
B) SSL Proxy Load Balancers are for TCP-based SSL traffic, not UDP.
C) Global UDP Proxy Load Balancer is not a commonly available service in Google Cloud.
E) Internal UDP Load Balancers are meant for private networks and don't provide a public IP.
F) Forwarding rules with a static IP are less efficient and scalable compared to a load balancer.

QUESTION 34

Answer – A) Pub/Sub, Dataflow, BigQuery, Data Studio

A) Correct, offers a scalable and efficient real-time analytics pipeline with visualization capabilities.
B) Incorrect, Cloud IoT Core and Cloud SQL are not the best fit for this scenario.
C) Incorrect, Firebase and Firestore are more suited for app development than complex supply chain analytics.
D) Incorrect, Bigtable and Cloud Composer are more complex than necessary.
E) Incorrect, overly complex and may not offer real-time processing efficiency.

QUESTION 35

Answer – B) Temporary SSH keys

A) Incorrect, IAM conditional roles do not provide SSH access management.
B) Correct, temporary SSH keys with expiration dates offer a secure and time-limited access method.
C) Incorrect, creating a temporary VPC is overly complex for this requirement.
D) Incorrect, Cloud IAP doesn't specifically manage time-limited SSH access.
E) Incorrect, a bastion host adds complexity and does not inherently limit access time.

QUESTION 36

Answer – A) Cloud Storage Access Logs, Cloud Logging alert

A) Correct, exporting access logs to Cloud Logging and setting up alerts is an efficient way to monitor and get notified about unauthorized access.
B) Incorrect, Cloud Functions are more for event-driven operations, not continuous monitoring.
C) Incorrect, VPC Service Controls provide access control but not specific alerting on unauthorized access.
D) Incorrect, this approach lacks real-time alerting.
E) Incorrect, custom metrics in Cloud Monitoring are not typically used for IP address monitoring.

QUESTION 37

Answer - E) Google Cloud Deployment Manager (Correct)

Option A is incorrect because while Google Cloud Spanner provides high availability, it does not directly offer automated cross-region failover and recovery for applications.
Option B is incorrect because Google Cloud VPN is a network connectivity service and not a DR tool.
Option C is incorrect because Google Cloud Storage is an object storage service and does not provide automated cross-region failover.
Option D is incorrect because Google Cloud Pub/Sub is a messaging service, not a DR solution.
Option E is correct because Google Cloud Deployment Manager can be used to define and automate the deployment and management of resources across regions, allowing for automated cross-region failover and recovery in the event of application failures.

QUESTION 38

Answer - C) Use Google Cloud Deployment Manager to define and automate resource deployment for cross-region failover. (Correct)

Option A is incorrect because while Memorystore can be used for caching, it does not provide automated cross-region failover capabilities.
Option B is incorrect because Google Cloud VPN is for network connectivity and secure communication but does not offer automated resource deployment and cross-region failover.
Option D is incorrect because Google Cloud Functions are designed for event-driven functions and may not be the best choice for automated disaster recovery.
Option E is incorrect because Google Cloud IAM is related to access control and not automated disaster

recovery planning.

Option C is correct because Google Cloud Deployment Manager allows you to define and automate the deployment and management of resources across regions, enabling automated cross-region failover and high availability in case of application failures or regional outages.

QUESTION 39

Answer - C) Set up Google Cloud IAM (Identity and Access Management) for centralized access control and fine-grained permissions management. (Correct)

Option A is incorrect because Google Cloud Identity-Aware Proxy (IAP) primarily focuses on identity verification and access control for web applications and does not provide fine-grained permissions management.

Option B is incorrect because Google Cloud Armor is a DDoS protection service and does not offer fine-grained permissions management.

Option D is incorrect because Google Cloud Pub/Sub is a messaging service and not designed for access control and permissions management at the project level.

Option C is correct because Google Cloud IAM (Identity and Access Management) allows for centralized access control and fine-grained permissions management at the project level, enhancing data security across multiple GCP services.

QUESTION 40

Answer - C) Utilize Google Cloud Dataflow to process data with serverless, automatic scaling capabilities.

Option A is incorrect because Google Cloud Dataprep is a data preparation tool, not a serverless data processing solution. Option B is incorrect because deploying a self-managed Apache Hadoop cluster requires manual management and does not offer serverless capabilities. Option D is incorrect because Google Cloud Pub/Sub is a messaging service, not a data processing service. Option C is correct because Google Cloud Dataflow provides serverless data analysis and automatic scaling, making it a cost-effective solution for data processing and analysis with ease of use.

QUESTION 41

Answer - C) Google Cloud Dataflow

Option A, Google Cloud Dataprep, is focused on data preparation and cleaning, not serverless data analysis. Option B, Google Cloud Dataproc, is a managed Spark and Hadoop service but requires cluster management and may not be as cost-effective as serverless options. Option D, Google Cloud Datastore, is a NoSQL database and not intended for data processing. Option C, Google Cloud Dataflow, offers serverless data processing with automatic scaling and is suitable for cost-effective data analysis and processing.

QUESTION 42

Answer - D) Create a new service account and select it while creating the new instance. Grant the service account permissions on Cloud Storage.

Option A is incorrect because relying on the default service account may not provide the necessary isolation and access control.
Option B is incorrect because granting permissions to an external IP address does not provide secure access control.
Option C is incorrect because using a shared access key may not offer the required security and granularity of access control.
Option E is incorrect because granting permissions to all instances in the project does not restrict access to the specific instance that requires it.

QUESTION 43

Answer - A) Use App Engine to run your app. For each update, create a new version of the same service and send a small percentage of traffic to the new version using traffic splitting.

Option A is correct because it aligns with your goal of A/B testing. Using App Engine, you can create new versions of the same service and use traffic splitting to test updates on a small portion of live users while keeping the rest on the live version.
Option B is incorrect because creating a new service for each update would result in multiple instances of the app running simultaneously, which is not suitable for A/B testing.
Option C is incorrect because updating the deployment in Kubernetes Engine would direct all traffic to the new version, which does not allow for controlled A/B testing.
Option D is incorrect because creating a new deployment and updating the service would also direct all traffic to the new deployment, making it unsuitable for A/B testing.

QUESTION 44

Answer - B) Customer-supplied keys for Google Cloud Storage

Option B is correct because using customer-supplied keys for Google Cloud Storage allows you to maintain control over the encryption keys used to encrypt data at rest, ensuring data security and compliance.
Option A (Google-managed keys) means Google manages the keys, not the customer.
Option C (Firebase-managed keys) is related to Firebase, not Google Cloud Storage encryption.
Option D (Google Identity Platform keys) is not used for encrypting data at rest in Google Cloud Storage.

QUESTION 45

Answer - A) Google Kubernetes Engine (GKE)

Option A is correct because Google Kubernetes Engine (GKE) is a managed Kubernetes service that offers automated upgrades, monitoring, and scaling, making it suitable for highly available and scalable Kubernetes clusters.
Option B (Google Cloud Dataprep) is a data preparation tool and not related to Kubernetes.
Option C (Google Cloud Composer) is for workflow orchestration and not specific to Kubernetes.
Option D (Google Cloud Dataflow) is for data processing and not related to Kubernetes cluster management.

QUESTION 46

Answer - C) Google Cloud Pub/Sub

Option C is correct because Google Cloud Pub/Sub is a real-time messaging service that can handle high-throughput data streams and is designed for low-latency data ingestion and processing, making it suitable for real-time data streaming applications.
Option A (Google Cloud Dataflow) is a data processing service and may not provide real-time ingestion.
Option B (Google Cloud Dataprep) is a data preparation tool, not a real-time data streaming service.
Option D (Google Cloud Datastore) is a NoSQL database and does not provide real-time data streaming capabilities.

QUESTION 47

Answer - D) Use Google Cloud Spanner for globally distributed databases

Option D is correct because Google Cloud Spanner is a globally distributed, horizontally scalable, and strongly consistent relational database service. It can provide multi-region redundancy and high availability by distributing data across multiple regions, ensuring that the application remains available even if a single zone or region experiences an outage.
Option A is not designed for multi-region redundancy but rather for global traffic distribution.
Option B is related to resource management and does not directly address multi-region redundancy.
Option C focuses on content delivery and caching but does not provide multi-region redundancy for the application itself.

QUESTION 48

Answer - B) Implement Google Cloud Dataflow for stream processing and real-time analytics

Option B is correct because Google Cloud Dataflow is a fully managed stream and batch data processing service that allows you to efficiently handle real-time data processing and analytics. It is well-suited for ingesting, processing, and analyzing large volumes of streaming data from various sources in real-time.
Option A focuses more on data preparation and batch analytics, not real-time processing.
Option C emphasizes batch data processing and analysis with BigQuery, which is not designed for real-time stream processing.
Option D is more suitable for long-running batch jobs using Hadoop and Spark but does not address real-time analytics needs.

QUESTION 49

Answer – D) Container Registry, Kubernetes Deployment

A) Incorrect, Cloud Storage is not for container images.
B) Incorrect, Artifact Registry can be used but Kubernetes Deployment is the right choice, not Service.
C) Incorrect, Cloud Build automates the build process but doesn't deploy directly to GKE.
D) Correct, uploading to Container Registry and then creating a Deployment in GKE is the standard deployment process.
E) Incorrect, a private Git repository is not a container registry and doesn't integrate directly with GKE for deployments.

QUESTION 50

Answer – D) Node pool with high network throughput

A) Incorrect, enhancing network capabilities for all services is inefficient.
B) Incorrect, Network Policies control traffic flow, not network resource allocation.
C) Incorrect, dedicated network resources per service can be complex and may not be supported directly in GKE.
D) Correct, a node pool with high network throughput for specific services ensures efficient network resource use.
E) Incorrect, service meshes manage traffic but don't inherently increase network throughput.

SET 10 - QUESTIONS ONLY

QUESTION 1

You need to design a secure network architecture on GCP for a multi-tier web application. What should your design include?

A) Implement VPC with private subnets for each tier, use Cloud VPN for secure access, and Cloud Armor for DDoS protection.
B) Set up a public subnet for the web tier, private subnets for application and database tiers, and use Cloud IDS for intrusion detection.
C) Create a single VPC with shared subnets for all tiers, implement Identity-Aware Proxy for access control, and use Cloud NAT for outbound traffic.
D) Use Shared VPC to host all tiers, implement Cloud Firewall rules for inter-tier communication, and use Cloud Load Balancing for traffic distribution.
E) Configure separate VPCs for each tier with VPC peering, use Cloud Interconnect for dedicated network access, and Cloud IAM for access management.
F) Establish a VPC with public and private subnets, use Cloud Endpoints for API management, and implement Cloud DNS for domain name resolution.

QUESTION 2

You are tasked with improving the security posture of your company's cloud infrastructure. The current setup includes various GCP services such as Compute Engine, Cloud Functions, and Cloud Storage. There is a need to implement a more robust identity and access management (IAM) policy. Which of the following steps should you prioritize to enhance security effectively?

A) Enforce the principle of least privilege by reviewing and minimizing IAM roles assigned to users and service accounts.
B) Migrate all services to a Virtual Private Cloud (VPC) with private access only, and use VPC Service Controls for all projects.
C) Implement a third-party identity provider for all GCP services and enforce two-factor authentication for all user accounts.
D) Create custom IAM roles tailored to specific job functions within your organization and assign them to users and service accounts.
E) Use Cloud Identity-Aware Proxy to control access to applications and services based on user identity and context.

QUESTION 3

In your GCP environment, you need to ensure that all Compute Engine VM instances are compliant with the company's security standards, including OS hardening and software updates. You also need to be able to report on compliance status regularly. What approach would you recommend to automate this process and maintain compliance?

A) Use OS Config Patch Management to manage and apply OS patches, and generate compliance reports using Cloud Logging.

B) Implement a set of custom scripts to check each VM for compliance, and use Cloud Functions to automate the process and log results.
C) Deploy a third-party configuration management tool on each VM to ensure compliance, and integrate with GCP for reporting.
D) Set up a regular snapshot schedule for VMs, and use Cloud Monitoring to check snapshots for compliance standards.
E) Utilize Compute Engine's instance metadata to store compliance configuration, and check each VM against these metadata values.

QUESTION 4

Your organization runs a mission-critical application on GCP, which heavily relies on real-time data processing and analysis. You need to choose a database service that offers high throughput, low latency, and horizontal scalability. Which GCP database service would you recommend?

A) Cloud SQL for its managed relational database capabilities.
B) Cloud Spanner for its global scalability and strong consistency.
C) Bigtable for high throughput and scalability for large amounts of unstructured data.
D) Firestore for its real-time data synchronization and NoSQL document database features.
E) Memorystore for its in-memory data store capabilities for low latency access.

QUESTION 5

You are configuring access control for a GCP project that will be used by various departments in your company. The employees' access to GCP resources needs to be controlled based on their department, which is defined in your on-premises Active Directory. What is the most effective way to manage this access control?

A) Assign GCP IAM roles to users based on departmental membership defined in Active Directory.
B) Create separate GCP projects for each department and manage access at the project level.
C) Utilize Cloud Identity and synchronize departmental groups from Active Directory to manage access.
D) Implement a role-based access control (RBAC) system in GCP that mirrors the departmental structure in Active Directory.
E) Set up individual service accounts for each department and grant IAM roles to these service accounts.

QUESTION 6

Your team uses Ubuntu for application development and requires frequent interaction with Cloud SQL. For local development and testing, what method would you recommend to emulate Cloud SQL behavior without connecting to the actual service in GCP?

A) Use the Cloud SQL Proxy for local testing of Cloud SQL interactions.
B) Install a local MySQL or PostgreSQL database that matches the Cloud SQL configuration.
C) Connect to a development instance of Cloud SQL in GCP with limited data.
D) Set up a Docker container running a Cloud SQL mock for local testing.
E) Implement a custom database emulator that mimics Cloud SQL features.

QUESTION 7

To ensure secure access to GCP services, your organization wants to implement Multi-Factor Authentication (MFA) for users accessing GCP, using the existing Active Directory setup. How can you achieve this?

A) Configure MFA on Active Directory and integrate it with GCP IAM using SAML SSO.
B) Enable MFA on each GCP IAM user account individually.
C) Implement an MFA solution within GCP and require users to register their devices.
D) Use a third-party MFA tool and integrate it with both Active Directory and GCP.
E) Set up a Cloud VPN that requires MFA for users accessing GCP resources.

QUESTION 8

As the startup owner, you need to ensure that your cloud infrastructure is compliant with financial regulations. You want to assign a role to an external auditor that allows them to review IAM policies, Cloud Storage bucket policies, and BigQuery dataset permissions. Which role should you assign?

A) roles/iam.securityReviewer
B) roles/complianceAuditor
C) roles/iam.policyViewer
D) roles/iam.roleViewer
E) roles/securitycenter.auditViewer

QUESTION 9

Your company is migrating a legacy application to Google Cloud. The application requires a highly available relational database. It also needs to support a legacy interface that relies on specific SQL extensions. What is the most appropriate database solution on GCP for this scenario, considering performance, scalability, and compatibility with legacy SQL extensions?

A) Cloud Spanner
B) Cloud SQL
C) Bigtable
D) Firestore
E) Cloud Memorystore
F) BigQuery

QUESTION 10

Your application generates log files that are stored in Cloud Storage. These logs are analyzed daily for the first week, weekly for the next month, and then need to be kept for compliance for 5 years without access. What lifecycle policy should be applied?

A) Use Standard for 7 days, then Nearline for 30 days, and finally move to Archive, retaining for 5 years.
B) Use Standard for 37 days and then Archive for 5 years.
C) Store everything in Archive as logs are infrequently accessed.
D) Use Nearline for 7 days, Coldline for 30 days, and Archive for 5 years.

QUESTION 11

Your company is deploying a new application on GCP that requires secure, low-latency connections between GCP services and on-premises data centers. The application will heavily rely on BigQuery for data analytics. Which of the following approaches ensures optimal performance and security for this hybrid architecture?

A) Configure a Dedicated Interconnect to establish a direct physical connection between the on-premises network and GCP, and use Cloud VPN as a backup. Ensure that BigQuery data is stored in a region geographically close to the on-premises data center.
B) Rely solely on Cloud VPN for connectivity and use Cloud Storage for intermediate data storage before loading into BigQuery.
C) Use Cloud Endpoints for secure API management and Cloud Pub/Sub for data transfer between on-premises and GCP services.
D) Implement a serverless architecture using Cloud Functions to interact with BigQuery and manage data processing, relying on public internet for connectivity.

QUESTION 12

You're developing a disaster recovery plan for a GCP-hosted application that is critical to your business operations. The application is deployed across multiple Compute Engine instances and uses Cloud SQL for data storage. To ensure minimal downtime and data loss in case of a regional outage, which strategy should you implement?

A) Set up a secondary set of Compute Engine instances in another region, use Cloud SQL cross-region replication, and regularly test failover procedures.
B) Rely on GCP's live migration feature to automatically handle any regional outages, and use persistent disks for data redundancy.
C) Implement a load balancer with a global configuration, use regional persistent disks for Compute Engine instances, and rely on Cloud SQL's automatic backups.
D) Configure Compute Engine instances for preemptible VMs to reduce costs and use Cloud SQL with read replicas in the same region for high availability.

QUESTION 13

As part of enhancing transparency, your company wants to provide external consultants with limited access to review Cloud Pub/Sub configurations and related audit logs. How should you set up their IAM access in accordance with Google Cloud's best practices?

A) Add the consultants to a group and assign them 'pubsub.viewer' and 'logging.viewer' IAM roles.
B) Grant the 'pubsub.admin' role to individual consultant accounts for in-depth access.
C) Allocate the 'project.viewer' role to the consultant group for broad access.
D) Assign 'pubsub.viewer' and 'logging.viewer' roles to each consultant's user account.

QUESTION 14

Your team uses Cloud Storage to maintain a repository of software artifacts. As a part of an internal audit, you need to track which team members uploaded or replaced artifacts in the past six months. Which method should you employ to gather this information accurately?

A) Investigate the upload and replacement activities using the Cloud Storage Audit logs.
B) Filter the Stackdriver logging for upload and replacement events in Cloud Storage.
C) Analyze the Cloud Storage usage reports in the GCP console for user activities.
D) Use Cloud Monitoring to set up alerts and view past activities related to artifact uploads and replacements.

QUESTION 15

Your company's internal reporting tool, hosted on GCP, needs to be accessible over HTTPS with SSL termination at the load balancer level. It also requires session affinity to maintain user sessions with specific backend instances. What load balancing setup should you implement?

A) Deploy an HTTP(S) Load Balancer with SSL termination and session affinity based on client IP addresses.
B) Use a Global SSL Proxy Load Balancer with SSL offloading and configure session affinity in backend configurations.
C) Configure a TCP Proxy Load Balancer with SSL termination and enable session affinity using custom configurations.
D) Set up a Network Load Balancer with SSL offloading and session affinity based on client cookies.

QUESTION 16

You need to implement access control policies for a Google Cloud project, ensuring that only specific users and groups have access to certain resources. Which Google Cloud service provides centralized identity and access management for this purpose?

A) Google Cloud IAM
B) Google Cloud KMS
C) Google Cloud Identity-Aware Proxy (IAP)
D) Google Cloud Identity Platform
E) Google Cloud Security Command Center

QUESTION 17

You are responsible for securing access to your Google Cloud resources. You want to enforce identity and access management policies consistently across all services. Which Google Cloud feature or service should you use for centralized access control and policy enforcement?

A) Google Cloud IAM (Identity and Access Management).
B) Google Cloud Identity for user identity management.
C) Google Cloud Security Command Center for threat detection.
D) Google Cloud Key Management Service for encryption key management.

QUESTION 18

Your organization is planning to set up a disaster recovery strategy for its critical applications running on Google Cloud. You need a solution that ensures minimal data loss and rapid recovery in case of failures. Which GCP service should you consider for disaster recovery and data replication across multiple regions?

A) Google Cloud Filestore.
B) Google Cloud Memorystore.
C) Google Cloud Datastore.
D) Google Cloud Storage.

QUESTION 19

You want to grant specific users SSH access to instances in a Google Compute Engine (GCE) project, but you want to limit access based on tags assigned to instances. What IAM role should you assign to the users at the project level, and what should you configure in the firewall rule?

A) Project Editor and target as 'Tag'
B) Compute Instance Admin and target as 'Label'
C) Network Admin and target as 'Network'
D) Compute OS Login and target as 'Instance'
E) Security Admin and target as 'Resource'
F) Compute OS Login and target as 'VM Instance'

QUESTION 20

A development team in your organization is working on a new feature that requires them to intermittently access and update a Cloud Spanner database. What is the most effective way to manage their access to ensure security and ease of administration?

A) Individually assign the 'spanner.databaseUser' role to each developer.
B) Establish a Google Group for the development team and allocate the 'spanner.databaseUser' role to the group.
C) Grant the 'spanner.admin' role to the development team for unrestricted access.
D) Allow the development team 'spanner.viewer' role and elevate permissions as needed.

QUESTION 21

You are moving a 45 GB database backup to a Google Cloud Storage Coldline Bucket for long-term storage. To maximize the use of your organization's 800 Mbps internet connection, what is the most effective upload method?

A) Directly upload the backup through the GCP console.
B) Leverage gsutil for parallel composite uploads of the backup file.
C) First split the backup into smaller files, then upload them sequentially.
D) Change the storage class to Standard for the duration of the upload for increased speed.

QUESTION 22

Your team is responsible for monitoring and managing compute resources in a project named 'resource-management'. A specific service account from another project 'monitoring-tools' needs to access these resources. What steps should you follow to enable this?

A) In 'resource-management', grant the Compute Viewer role to the service account from 'monitoring-tools'.

B) Transfer the 'monitoring-tools' service account to the 'resource-management' project and assign appropriate roles.
C) Create an identical service account in 'resource-management' and duplicate the roles from 'monitoring-tools'.
D) Configure the service account from 'monitoring-tools' to generate OAuth tokens for accessing resources in 'resource-management'.

QUESTION 23

In a GCP managed instance group hosting a media streaming service, you notice unnecessary scaling when traffic spikes. The service's initialization time is around 2 minutes. Which configuration change would most effectively address this?

A) Increase the minimum number of instances.
B) Decrease the health check initial delay to 60 seconds.
C) Increase the health check initial delay to 120 seconds.
D) Adjust the CPU utilization threshold for scaling.
E) Change from HTTP to TCP health checks.

QUESTION 24

As a freelancer juggling multiple GCP projects, you need to confirm the deployment target of an App Engine application. Which method provides a quick and accurate way to identify the project used for the latest deployment?

A) Look at the app.yaml file for any project identifier.
B) Run gcloud app services list to view services in the current project.
C) Check the cloudbuild.yaml file for deployment project details.
D) Execute gcloud config list to see the active project configuration.
E) Review the build history in Cloud Build for the deployment project.
F) Inspect the source code repository for project-specific deployment scripts.

QUESTION 25

Your Compute Engine VM, vital for real-time data processing, needs a memory upgrade from 4 GB to 8 GB to improve performance. How can you effectively perform this upgrade?

A) Adjust the VM's settings to increase RAM allocation and apply the changes immediately.
B) Stop the VM, modify its machine type to increase RAM to 8 GB, and then restart the instance.
C) Allocate additional memory through the instance's operating system configuration.
D) Utilize vertical autoscaling to automatically increase the VM's memory.
E) Deploy a new instance with 8 GB RAM and redirect traffic to it.
F) Use a custom script via the gcloud tool to enhance the VM's memory.

QUESTION 26

Following an accidental deletion of a production Compute Engine instance by a junior team member, which feature should you enable to protect against such mistakes in the future?

A) Activate 'Automatic Restart' on all critical instances.
B) Implement a policy that only allows instance deletion during maintenance windows.
C) Enable 'Deletion Protection' on all production and critical instances.
D) Use custom service accounts with restricted permissions for instance management.
E) Configure a Cloud Monitoring alert for any instance deletion attempts.
F) Establish a required approval process for deleting any Compute Engine instances.

QUESTION 27

In your multi-tenant accounting software, it's essential to restrict user access to their uploaded invoices for 30 minutes and ensure the files are deleted after 45 days. What two GCP features should you use to implement these functionalities?

A) Apply a Cloud Identity-Aware Proxy (IAP) to control and log access to the invoices.
B) Configure signed URLs for temporary access to the invoices in Cloud Storage.
C) Use Cloud Storage lifecycle policies to delete invoices automatically after 45 days.
D) Implement a Cloud SQL database with expiration policies for invoice data.
E) Create a custom service account to manage invoice access and deletion.
F) Set up Stackdriver Logging to monitor and enforce the access and deletion rules.

QUESTION 28

Your company is building a microservices-based application on Google Kubernetes Engine (GKE). You want to ensure that the pods automatically scale based on CPU and memory utilization. What should you add to the GKE deployments to achieve this?

A) Horizontal Pod Autoscaler (HPA)
B) Vertical Pod Autoscaler (VPA)
C) Cluster Autoscaler
D) Pod Disruption Budgets
E) GKE Node Pool Scaling

QUESTION 29

In configuring a secure environment for a sensitive financial transaction system on Compute Engine, how can you ensure that egress traffic is strictly controlled to only essential ports?

A) Implement application-level egress controls within each Compute Engine instance.
B) Set up a VPC firewall with a default low-priority rule to block all egress, and specific allow rules for necessary ports.
C) Configure a Cloud VPN to route and control all egress traffic from the VPC.
D) Use network tags on Compute Engine instances to define egress rules.
E) Create a high-priority rule in the VPC firewall to block all non-essential egress traffic.
F) Employ a third-party network security solution to manage egress traffic.

QUESTION 30

To ensure minimal costs for a containerized internal tool used exclusively during business hours, what is the best GCP deployment option that incurs no charges when idle?

A) Set up the application on Google Kubernetes Engine with pod autoscaling and node preemption.
B) Deploy the application on Cloud Run (fully managed) with the ability to scale to zero instances.
C) Use App Engine Flexible Environment with aggressive autoscaling settings.
D) Configure a Compute Engine virtual machine with scheduled start and stop times.
E) Implement the tool on Cloud Functions, activating only upon requests.
F) Create a managed instance group in Compute Engine with auto-scaling based on CPU utilization.

QUESTION 31

For granting a DevOps team access to multiple production services in GCP projects, while minimizing the risk of excessive permissions, what is the best practice?

A) Assign the DevOps team predefined roles like Compute Engine Admin in each project.
B) Create individual IAM roles for each member of the DevOps team tailored to their specific tasks.
C) Implement a custom role with the exact required permissions for the DevOps team across all projects.
D) Grant the DevOps team the Security Admin role to ensure broad access to necessary services.
E) Set up a centralized administration project and grant the DevOps team access from there.
F) Use Resource Manager to assign the DevOps team project-level access as needed.

QUESTION 32

For a file-sharing application that stores files on Cloud Storage with high access for the first 30 days and a legal requirement to retain files for 3 years, what is the most cost-effective storage plan?

A) Use Standard storage for 30 days, transition to Nearline for 1 year, then to Coldline, and finally to Archive.
B) Keep files in Coldline storage for the initial 30 days, then move them to Archive storage for 3 years.
C) Start with Nearline storage for 30 days, then shift files to Archive storage for the remaining period.
D) Utilize Standard storage for the first 30 days, followed by transferring files to Archive storage for 3 years.
E) Implement a policy to store files in Archive storage throughout the entire 3-year period.
F) Store files in Standard storage for 30 days, then use a combination of Coldline and Archive for the rest of the period.

QUESTION 33

For a multiplayer online game that updates server actions via UDP packets and requires horizontal scaling on Google Cloud, which load balancing solution should you use?

A) Set up an External HTTP(S) Load Balancer for the game's backend servers.
B) Implement an SSL Proxy Load Balancer to manage the UDP traffic.
C) Configure a Global UDP Proxy Load Balancer for distributing traffic.
D) Use an External Network Load Balancer for handling UDP packet distribution.
E) Create an Internal UDP Load Balancer with external exposure capabilities.
F) Employ Cloud DNS with weighted load balancing for UDP traffic management.

QUESTION 34

Your company is developing a new mobile application that requires a backend service to store user data securely and scale automatically based on user load. The data includes user profiles, preferences, and app settings. Which GCP solution would best fit these requirements?

A) Deploy a backend using App Engine with Firestore for data storage, and integrate with Cloud Identity for secure authentication.
B) Utilize Compute Engine with auto-scaling groups, store data in Cloud SQL, and secure user data using Cloud IAM roles and permissions.
C) Implement a containerized backend on Kubernetes Engine, use Cloud Spanner for scalable data storage, and manage security with Cloud Endpoints.
D) Set up a serverless architecture with Cloud Functions, store user data in Bigtable, and ensure data security with VPC Service Controls.
E) Create a Firebase backend for the app, use Firebase Realtime Database for data storage, and secure access with Firebase Authentication.

QUESTION 35

Your company has a strict policy of logging and reviewing all administrative actions taken on its cloud resources. You need to ensure that all actions performed via SSH on Compute Engine instances are logged and reviewable. Which solution will fulfill this requirement?

A) Implement Stackdriver Logging for Compute Engine and configure it to capture SSH session logs.
B) Configure OS Login on Compute Engine VMs and integrate it with Cloud Audit Logs.
C) Set up a third-party SSH gateway that logs all SSH activities and forwards them to Cloud Logging.
D) Use IAM roles with logging permissions and enable detailed activity logging on each VM.
E) Enable Cloud IAP for SSH and configure it to send logs to Cloud Logging for review.

QUESTION 36

You are responsible for monitoring a set of Compute Engine instances. You need to set up an alerting mechanism to notify you when any instance has a system load above 80% for more than 5 minutes. Which approach should you take?

A) Use the Compute Engine API to regularly check the system load and send notifications if the threshold is exceeded.
B) Create a custom metric in Cloud Monitoring for system load and set an alert for when the threshold is exceeded.
C) Implement a Stackdriver Logging filter to capture high system load events and configure an alert policy.
D) Set up a log sink to export Compute Engine logs to BigQuery and analyze them for high load events.
E) Rely on the built-in Compute Engine monitoring tools to automatically send alerts for high system load.

QUESTION 37

Your team is working on a project that requires the real-time processing of streaming data from various sources. Which Google Cloud service is best suited for ingesting, processing, and analyzing streaming data with low latency?

A) Google Cloud Dataflow
B) Google Bigtable
C) Google Cloud Pub/Sub
D) Google Cloud Dataprep
E) Google Cloud BigQuery

QUESTION 38

Your team is working on a global-scale web application that requires low-latency content delivery to users worldwide. Which Google Cloud service should you choose to ensure fast and efficient content delivery with minimal latency?

A) Configure Google Cloud Load Balancing for regional content distribution.
B) Utilize Google Cloud CDN (Content Delivery Network) with Google Cloud Storage for static content hosting.
C) Set up Google Cloud Identity-Aware Proxy (IAP) for access control and security.
D) Deploy Google Cloud Functions for serverless web application serving.
E) Implement Google Cloud Pub/Sub for content distribution to global users.

QUESTION 39

Your company is running a fleet of virtual machines (VMs) on Google Cloud Compute Engine. You want to ensure that each VM can access specific Google Cloud APIs based on their roles. What should you do to achieve this access control?

A) Assign the same service account to all VMs for uniform access.
B) Use instance metadata to define API access for each VM.
C) Create a custom IAM role for each VM instance.
D) Use service accounts to grant permissions to each VM instance.

QUESTION 40

Your team is responsible for optimizing cost management in a Google Cloud project that uses multiple GCP services. You want to identify opportunities for cost reduction and analyze resource usage. Which GCP service or feature can you use for cost optimization and resource usage analysis?

A) Implement Google Cloud Billing Reports for cost reduction and resource usage analysis.
B) Configure Google Cloud Monitoring for real-time cost tracking and analysis.
C) Utilize Google Cloud Cost Explorer for cost optimization and resource usage analysis.
D) Set up Google Cloud Security Command Center for cost management and resource usage analysis.

QUESTION 41

Your team is building a web application that requires a reliable and scalable database solution. You want to use a managed database service on Google Cloud that provides automatic failover, automated backups, and high availability. Which GCP database service should you choose for this scenario?

A) Google Cloud SQL
B) Google Cloud Firestore
C) Google Cloud Bigtable
D) Google Cloud Spanner

QUESTION 42

You have multiple Compute Engine instances in a project, and you need to grant access to a specific Cloud Storage bucket for one instance only to install a third-party OTP application. What is the most secure way to achieve this while ensuring that other instances are not affected?

A) Grant permissions to all Compute Engine instances in the project for the Cloud Storage bucket.
B) Grant permissions directly to the instance's external IP address for the Cloud Storage bucket.
C) Create a new service account and select it while creating the new instance. Grant the service account permissions on Cloud Storage.
D) Use the default Compute Engine service account for the instance and restrict access in the Cloud Storage bucket ACL.
E) Use a shared access key for the Compute Engine instance to access the Cloud Storage bucket.

QUESTION 43

You are building a web application on GCP and require a deployment strategy that enables A/B testing by testing updates on a small portion of live users. What is the recommended GCP deployment approach to achieve this objective effectively?

A) Use App Engine to run your app. For each update, create a new version of the same service and send a small percentage of traffic to the new version using traffic splitting.
B) Use App Engine to run your app. For each update, create a new service and send a small percentage of traffic to the new version using traffic splitting.
C) Use Kubernetes Engine to run your app. For a new release, update the deployment to use the new version.
D) Use Kubernetes Engine to run your app. For a new release, create a new deployment for the new version and update the service to use the new deployment.

QUESTION 44

Your organization is planning to deploy a highly available web application on Google Cloud. The application must be resilient to regional outages and provide low-latency access to users worldwide. Which Google Cloud service or feature should you leverage for this purpose?

A) Google Cloud CDN
B) Google Cloud VPN
C) Google Cloud Load Balancing with multiple regions
D) Google Cloud AutoML

QUESTION 45

Your organization needs to ensure data durability and availability for its critical cloud-native applications. You want to choose a Google Cloud storage service that replicates data across multiple geographic locations automatically and provides 99.999999999% durability. Which Google Cloud storage option should you select for this data storage requirement?

A) Google Cloud Standard Storage
B) Google Cloud Nearline Storage
C) Google Cloud Coldline Storage
D) Google Cloud Multi-Regional Storage

QUESTION 46

Your organization is planning to deploy a highly available web application on Google Cloud. The application needs to be globally distributed to minimize latency and provide redundancy. Which Google Cloud service should you use for global load balancing and content delivery?

A) Google Cloud Network Load Balancer
B) Google Cloud HTTP(S) Load Balancer
C) Google Cloud Internal TCP/UDP Load Balancer
D) Google Cloud Armor

QUESTION 47

Your organization is deploying a containerized application on Google Kubernetes Engine (GKE). You want to ensure that the application can recover quickly in case of a failure and automatically scale based on resource utilization. Which GKE feature can help you achieve this goal?

A) Use GKE's Horizontal Pod Autoscaling (HPA) to automatically adjust the number of pods based on CPU or memory usage.
B) Configure GKE's Static IP addresses for persistent network identities.
C) Enable GKE's Role-Based Access Control (RBAC) for fine-grained access management.
D) Deploy GKE's Ingress Controllers for managing external access to services.

QUESTION 48

Your organization is migrating a legacy on-premises application to Google Cloud. The application relies on an Oracle database. Which Google Cloud service can you use to host the Oracle database while minimizing operational overhead and ensuring compatibility?

A) Deploy the Oracle database on Google Compute Engine instances.
B) Use Google Cloud SQL for Oracle to manage the Oracle database.
C) Set up Oracle database on Google Kubernetes Engine (GKE) for containerized management.
D) Utilize Google Cloud Bigtable for hosting relational databases.

QUESTION 49

As part of a new project, you need to deploy a series of microservices, all containerized using Docker, onto Google Kubernetes Engine. What are the key steps you should follow for this deployment?

A) Deploy the Docker containers directly to GKE from your local machine.
B) Use Cloud Build to create Docker images, upload them to Container Registry, and then deploy on GKE.
C) Upload the Docker images to Container Registry and then use Helm charts to deploy on GKE.
D) Store the Docker images in Cloud Source Repositories and deploy them to GKE.
E) Upload the Docker images to Container Registry, then create Kubernetes Deployments for each microservice in GKE.

QUESTION 50

In your GKE deployment, you have a mix of CPU-intensive and I/O-intensive microservices. How should you optimize the cluster for such a diverse workload?

A) Deploy all microservices on the same type of nodes for simplicity and management ease.
B) Use GKE's default settings for all microservices, relying on its built-in optimization.
C) Segment the microservices into different node pools, each optimized for CPU or I/O-intensive workloads.
D) Implement custom resource quotas at the namespace level to manage the resource usage of each microservice.
E) Rely on Kubernetes' inherent scheduling and resource allocation to optimize resource usage automatically.

SET 10 - ANSWERS ONLY

QUESTION 1

Answer - A) Implement VPC with private subnets

A) Correct, a VPC with private subnets for each tier, along with Cloud VPN and Cloud Armor, offers a secure and scalable network architecture.
B) Incorrect, while this setup provides some security, it lacks comprehensive protection like DDoS and does not fully isolate each tier.
C) Incorrect, a single VPC with shared subnets may not provide the necessary isolation and security for a multi-tier application.
D) Incorrect, Shared VPC is more suited for larger organizations with multiple projects, not specifically for a multi-tier web application.
E) Incorrect, separate VPCs for each tier could lead to unnecessary complexity and may not be the most efficient architecture.
F) Incorrect, while Cloud Endpoints and Cloud DNS are useful, they do not constitute a complete network architecture for a multi-tier application.

QUESTION 2

Answer - A) Principle of least privilege

A) Correct, implementing the principle of least privilege by minimizing IAM roles enhances security without overhauling the entire infrastructure.
B) Incorrect, while VPCs add security, migrating all services might not be necessary and could be disruptive.
C) Incorrect, introducing a third-party identity provider is complex and may not be the most immediate step for enhancing IAM policies.
D) Incorrect, creating custom roles is beneficial but should come after ensuring that the principle of least privilege is applied.
E) Incorrect, Cloud Identity-Aware Proxy is useful, but prioritizing IAM role review is a more fundamental and immediate step for enhancing security.

QUESTION 3

Answer - A) OS Config Patch Management

A) Correct, OS Config Patch Management automates OS patching and integration with Cloud Logging helps in reporting compliance.
B) Incorrect, custom scripts are less efficient and more error-prone compared to using built-in GCP tools.
C) Incorrect, deploying third-party tools adds complexity and may not integrate seamlessly with GCP for reporting.
D) Incorrect, using snapshots for compliance checks is not practical or efficient for ongoing compliance monitoring.
E) Incorrect, instance metadata is useful for configuration but does not provide an automated solution for compliance monitoring and reporting.

QUESTION 4

Answer - C) Bigtable

A) Incorrect, Cloud SQL is a managed relational database but may not meet the high throughput and scalability requirements for real-time data.
B) Incorrect, Cloud Spanner offers scalability and consistency but might be overkill in terms of cost and complexity for certain real-time applications.
C) Correct, Bigtable provides high throughput and scalability, making it well-suited for applications with large amounts of unstructured data and real-time processing needs.
D) Incorrect, Firestore offers real-time data sync but may not provide the same level of throughput and scalability as Bigtable.
E) Incorrect, Memorystore is primarily for caching and may not serve as a primary database for real-time data processing and analysis.

QUESTION 5

Answer - C) Cloud Identity synchronization

A) Incorrect, assigning IAM roles directly does not leverage the existing structure in Active Directory.
B) Incorrect, creating separate projects can lead to management complexity and is not necessary for access control.
C) Correct, using Cloud Identity to synchronize departmental groups from Active Directory is an effective way to manage access based on department.
D) Incorrect, implementing a separate RBAC system in GCP is more complex than synchronizing with Active Directory.
E) Incorrect, using service accounts for departments is not a standard practice for user access management and complicates IAM role assignments.

QUESTION 6

Answer - B) Local MySQL/PostgreSQL database

A) Incorrect, Cloud SQL Proxy connects to an actual Cloud SQL instance, not a local emulator.
B) Correct, installing a local MySQL or PostgreSQL database provides a close approximation for Cloud SQL during local development.
C) Incorrect, this is not a local testing method but rather a connection to a real Cloud SQL instance in GCP.
D) Incorrect, there is no official Docker container that accurately mocks Cloud SQL.
E) Incorrect, creating a custom emulator is unnecessary and complex when a local database can suffice.

QUESTION 7

Answer - A) MFA on Active Directory integrated with GCP IAM

A) Correct, configuring MFA on Active Directory and integrating it with GCP IAM using SAML SSO allows for secure access with existing setups.
B) Incorrect, enabling MFA individually on GCP IAM accounts does not leverage the existing Active Directory setup.
C) Incorrect, implementing a separate MFA solution within GCP is redundant and does not utilize the

existing Active Directory.
D) Incorrect, a third-party tool is not necessary if Active Directory can be integrated directly with GCP.
E) Incorrect, Cloud VPN provides network access control but is not directly related to MFA for GCP service access.

QUESTION 8

Answer - A) roles/iam.securityReviewer

A) Correct, roles/iam.securityReviewer allows viewing IAM policies and resource policies, which is necessary for compliance auditing.
B) Incorrect, roles/complianceAuditor is not a standard role in GCP.
C) Incorrect, roles/iam.policyViewer does not exist in GCP IAM roles.
D) Incorrect, roles/iam.roleViewer is focused on viewing custom IAM roles, not resource policies.
E) Incorrect, roles/securitycenter.auditViewer is specific to the Security Command Center and does not cover IAM policies and resource policies in general.

QUESTION 9

Answer – B) Cloud SQL

A) Cloud Spanner is designed for horizontal scaling and global consistency, but it may not support specific legacy SQL extensions.
B) Cloud SQL supports standard SQL and offers options for MySQL, PostgreSQL, and SQL Server, making it suitable for legacy applications needing specific SQL extensions. It provides high availability and can be scaled vertically.
C) Bigtable is a NoSQL database suitable for large analytical and operational workloads but does not support SQL.
D) Firestore is a NoSQL document database, not ideal for legacy SQL-based applications.
E) Cloud Memorystore offers managed Redis and Memcached but is not a relational database.
F) BigQuery is designed for large-scale analytics and does not support transactional workloads typical of relational databases.

QUESTION 10

Answer - A) Use Standard for 7 days, then Nearline for 30 days, and finally move to Archive, retaining for 5 years.

A) Correct. This policy aligns with the access pattern and compliance requirements: Standard for initial frequent analysis, Nearline for less frequent access, and then Archive for long-term retention.
B) Incorrect as it does not optimize costs during the weekly access period.
C) Incorrect, as Archive class is not suitable for the initial analysis periods.
D) Incorrect, as Nearline and Coldline do not match the specified access patterns.

QUESTION 11

Answer - A) Configure a Dedicated Interconnect to establish a direct physical connection between the on-premises network and GCP, and use Cloud VPN as a backup. Ensure that BigQuery data is stored in a region geographically close to the on-premises data center.

A) Correct. Provides a secure, high-performance connection suitable for heavy data transfer and low latency requirements.
B) May not meet performance needs for heavy data analytics workloads.
C) Focuses on API management and messaging but does not address the core requirement of low-latency connectivity.
D) Serverless architecture simplifies management but does not adequately address network performance and security for hybrid connections.

QUESTION 12

Answer - A) Set up a secondary set of Compute Engine instances in another region, use Cloud SQL cross-region replication, and regularly test failover procedures.

A) Correct. Ensures business continuity with cross-region redundancy and regular testing of failover processes.
B) Live migration is helpful but not sufficient for full disaster recovery.
C) Global load balancing is beneficial but does not address region-specific outages for back-end components.
D) Preemptible VMs are cost-effective but not suitable for critical applications where continuous availability is required.

QUESTION 13

Answer - A) Add the consultants to a group and assign them 'pubsub.viewer' and 'logging.viewer' IAM roles.

A) This method provides the consultants with the necessary access to review Pub/Sub configurations and logs, while grouping users for easier access management.
B) The 'pubsub.admin' role is overly permissive for this purpose.
C) 'project.viewer' might give broader access than required for this specific task.
D) Using groups is more efficient and manageable than individual user accounts.

QUESTION 14

Answer - A) Investigate the upload and replacement activities using the Cloud Storage Audit logs.

A) Audit logs are the most suitable tool for this requirement, offering detailed insights into specific actions like uploads or replacements by users.
B) While possible, Stackdriver logging requires more setup and is less direct than audit logs.
C) Usage reports provide general usage statistics but not specific user activity details.
D) Cloud Monitoring is geared towards real-time monitoring and alerting, not historical audit reviews.

QUESTION 15

Answer - A) Deploy an HTTP(S) Load Balancer with SSL termination and session affinity based on client IP addresses.

A) HTTP(S) Load Balancer supports both SSL termination and session affinity, making it suitable for maintaining user sessions with backend services while providing secure HTTPS access.

B) SSL Proxy Load Balancer does not support session affinity.
C) TCP Proxy Load Balancer does not inherently support session affinity or SSL termination at the load balancer level.
D) Network Load Balancer does not offer SSL offloading and is more suited for TCP/UDP traffic without HTTP(S) features.

QUESTION 16

Answer - A) Google Cloud IAM

Option A: This is the correct choice as Google Cloud IAM (Identity and Access Management) provides centralized identity and access management, allowing you to define and enforce access control policies for resources.
Option B: Google Cloud KMS is a key management service and not primarily focused on identity and access management.
Option C: Google Cloud Identity-Aware Proxy (IAP) is used for secure user access to applications but is not for resource-level access control.
Option D: Google Cloud Identity Platform is focused on identity management but not access control.
Option E: Google Cloud Security Command Center is a security management tool but does not provide centralized access control.

QUESTION 17

Answer - A) Google Cloud IAM (Identity and Access Management).

Option A: This is the correct choice as Google Cloud IAM is designed for centralized access control and policy enforcement across all Google Cloud services, ensuring consistent security policies.
Option B: Google Cloud Identity focuses on user identity management, not access control for resources.
Option C: Google Cloud Security Command Center is for threat detection and not access control.
Option D: Google Cloud Key Management Service is for encryption key management, not access control policies.

QUESTION 18

Answer - D) Google Cloud Storage.

Option D is the correct choice as Google Cloud Storage provides robust data replication and disaster recovery capabilities, allowing you to store data across multiple regions to minimize data loss and enable rapid recovery in case of failures.
Option A is for managed file storage, Option B is for in-memory data caching, and Option C is for NoSQL data storage.

QUESTION 19

Answer - D) Compute OS Login and target as 'Instance'

Option D, "Compute OS Login" (IAM role), should be assigned to users at the project level. In the firewall rule, the target should be set as 'Instance,' and tags can be used to limit access based on instance tags. Option B is incorrect as it suggests using 'Label' instead of 'Tag' for access control, and the other options do not align with the requirement to limit access based on instance tags.

QUESTION 20

Answer - B) Establish a Google Group for the development team and allocate the 'spanner.databaseUser' role to the group.

B) Utilizing a Google Group to manage team access is efficient and secure. The 'spanner.databaseUser' role provides the necessary read and write permissions while maintaining control and simplifying access management.
A) Assigning roles to individuals is less manageable and secure.
C) The 'spanner.admin' role is overly permissive and may pose security risks.
D) The 'spanner.viewer' role does not allow the necessary update capabilities.

QUESTION 21

Answer - B) Leverage gsutil for parallel composite uploads of the backup file.

B) Utilizing gsutil's parallel composite upload feature is the most effective way to upload large files. It splits the backup into smaller segments that are uploaded in parallel, utilizing the full capacity of the 800 Mbps connection efficiently.
A) The GCP console is not the most efficient tool for large file uploads.
C) Sequential uploads do not fully utilize the available bandwidth.
D) Changing the storage class doesn't impact the upload speed, only storage pricing and availability.

QUESTION 22

Answer - A) In 'resource-management', grant the Compute Viewer role to the service account from 'monitoring-tools'.

A) Granting the necessary IAM role to the service account from 'monitoring-tools' in the 'resource-management' project is the most straightforward and secure way to provide access. It allows the service account to perform its monitoring duties without transferring accounts or duplicating roles.
B) Service accounts cannot be transferred between projects.
C) Creating a duplicate service account is unnecessary and complicates access management.
D) Using OAuth tokens for this purpose adds unnecessary complexity.

QUESTION 23

Answer - C) Increase the health check initial delay to 120 seconds.

A) Increasing the minimum number might reduce scaling but doesn't solve the health check timing issue.
B) Decreasing the delay would lead to more instances being prematurely marked unhealthy.
C) Correct. This ensures the instances are fully operational before the health check starts.
D) Adjusting the CPU threshold could help but doesn't align with the service's initialization time.
E) Changing the health check type doesn't address the specific issue of timing with service readiness.

QUESTION 24

Answer - D) Execute gcloud config list to see the active project configuration.

D) The gcloud config list command provides immediate information about the current gcloud configuration, including the active project, making it the most efficient way to identify the project of the latest deployment.
A) The app.yaml file usually doesn't contain the project identifier.
B) Listing services is helpful but requires knowing the project beforehand.
C) The cloudbuild.yaml may not be used for all App Engine deployments.
E) Cloud Build history is useful but may require combing through multiple builds.
F) Source code repositories might not have clear project-specific deployment scripts.

QUESTION 25

Answer - B) Stop the VM, modify its machine type to increase RAM to 8 GB, and then restart the instance.

B) This is the recommended method for resizing a VM in GCP. Stopping the instance allows you to safely change its machine type to one with more memory, and then you can restart it with the upgraded configuration.
A) GCP doesn't support on-the-fly RAM allocation adjustments for running VMs.
C) Memory allocation for a VM is managed through GCP, not the operating system.
D) Vertical autoscaling is not a feature currently offered in GCP for automatic memory adjustments.
E) While deploying a new instance is possible, it's more complex than resizing the existing one.
F) Custom scripts cannot be used to change the hardware configuration of a running VM in GCP.

QUESTION 26

Answer - C) Enable 'Deletion Protection' on all production and critical instances.

C) 'Deletion Protection' is a specific feature in GCP that prevents Compute Engine instances from being deleted, which is an effective measure to avoid accidental deletions and ensure the stability of critical systems.
A) 'Automatic Restart' is for VM recovery from failures, not for preventing deletion.
B) Having a policy for deletion windows is a procedural measure but can still allow for accidental deletions.
D) Restricting permissions is good practice but may not be effective against all types of mistakes.
E) Alerts notify after an action is attempted or completed, which may be too late.
F) An approval process adds a layer of security but also depends on manual oversight.

QUESTION 27

Answer - B) and C)

B) Signed URLs in Cloud Storage effectively limit the access time for users to upload and access their invoices, providing control over the 30-minute access window.
C) Cloud Storage lifecycle policies automate the deletion of invoices after a predetermined time (45 days), ensuring data retention compliance without manual intervention.
A) Cloud IAP is for securing applications and doesn't directly manage file access or deletion.
D) Cloud SQL expiration policies are not designed for managing files in Cloud Storage.
E) Custom service accounts manage access but don't automate deletion or temporary access limits.
F) Stackdriver Logging is for monitoring, not for enforcing access or deletion policies.

QUESTION 28

Answer - A) Horizontal Pod Autoscaler (HPA)

Option A - Horizontal Pod Autoscaler (HPA) automatically adjusts the number of pod replicas based on CPU and memory utilization, allowing pods to scale in response to demand.
Option B - Vertical Pod Autoscaler (VPA) adjusts resource requests and limits within pods.
Option C - Cluster Autoscaler manages node scaling, not pod scaling.
Option D - Pod Disruption Budgets define constraints on pod disruptions, and
Option E - GKE Node Pool Scaling deals with node pool size.

QUESTION 29

Answer - B) Set up a VPC firewall with a default low-priority rule to block all egress, and specific allow rules for necessary ports.

B) Setting a low-priority rule in the VPC firewall to block all egress traffic establishes a secure default posture. Then, crafting specific high-priority rules to allow only the necessary ports ensures that the financial transaction system only communicates through essential channels.
A) Application-level controls are good but not as comprehensive as VPC firewall rules.
C) Cloud VPN is for secure connections, not specific egress control.
D) Network tags help organize instances but don't control egress traffic.
E) High-priority block rules might override necessary allow rules.
F) Third-party solutions might not be necessary given GCP's built-in firewall capabilities.

QUESTION 30

Answer - B) Deploy the application on Cloud Run (fully managed) with the ability to scale to zero instances.

B) Cloud Run (fully managed) stands out as the most suitable option because it offers the capability to scale down to zero instances, ensuring no costs are incurred when the application is not being used. This is in line with the requirement for a cost-effective solution during non-business hours.
A) Kubernetes Engine does not naturally scale down to zero nodes.
C) App Engine Flexible Environment does not scale to zero, resulting in ongoing costs.
D) Compute Engine VMs with scheduled times require manual management and do not scale to zero.
E) Cloud Functions are for event-driven applications, not suited for this use case.
F) Managed instance groups in Compute Engine do not scale down to zero.

QUESTION 31

Answer - C) Implement a custom role with the exact required permissions for the DevOps team across all projects.

C) Implementing a custom role that precisely defines the required permissions for the DevOps team across all projects is the most effective way to manage their access. This approach ensures that they have the specific access they need without the risk of over-privileging, which aligns with the principle of least privilege and enhances security.
A) Predefined roles like Compute Engine Admin may provide more access than necessary.
B) Individual roles for each team member can be cumbersome to manage and maintain.

D) The Security Admin role might be overly broad for DevOps tasks.
E) A centralized administration project does not necessarily restrict access to only what is needed.
F) Resource Manager provides broad access, which may not be ideal for controlled permissions.

QUESTION 32

Answer - D) Utilize Standard storage for the first 30 days, followed by transferring files to Archive storage for 3 years.

D) This approach effectively balances the need for accessibility and cost efficiency. Standard storage supports the initial high-access demand, and Archive storage is the most economical option for the subsequent long-term retention. Moving files to Archive after the first 30 days minimizes costs while ensuring compliance with the 3-year retention requirement.
A) Multiple transitions between storage classes are less efficient and may increase costs.
B) Coldline storage is not ideal for high access in the first 30 days.
C) Nearline storage is less cost-effective for the initial high-access period compared to Standard storage.
E) Archive storage throughout the 3-year period is not cost-effective for the initial high-access demand.
F) Using Coldline after Standard storage adds unnecessary cost for the period before moving to Archive.

QUESTION 33

Answer - D) Use an External Network Load Balancer for handling UDP packet distribution.

D) The External Network Load Balancer is the most suitable choice for managing UDP traffic for a multiplayer online game on Google Cloud. It supports UDP packets, crucial for the game's communication, and provides a single IP address for horizontal scaling. This ensures efficient and balanced distribution of player traffic across multiple VMs, maintaining game performance and scalability.
A) External HTTP(S) Load Balancers are not suitable for UDP packet handling.
B) SSL Proxy Load Balancers are intended for SSL/TLS traffic, not UDP.
C) Global UDP Proxy Load Balancer is not a standard load balancing option in Google Cloud.
E) Internal UDP Load Balancers are designed for internal network traffic, not external access.
F) Cloud DNS does not offer direct load balancing for specific protocols like UDP.

QUESTION 34

Answer – A) App Engine, Firestore, Cloud Identity

A) Correct, provides a scalable, secure, and managed environment suitable for app backends.
B) Incorrect, might be overkill and less efficient for a mobile app backend.
C) Incorrect, Kubernetes Engine is more complex than needed for this use case.
D) Incorrect, Bigtable is not ideal for user profile data.
E) Incorrect, Firebase is suitable but doesn't offer the same level of scalability and security integration as the App Engine and Firestore combination.

QUESTION 35

Answer – B) OS Login, Cloud Audit Logs

A) Incorrect, Stackdriver Logging does not capture SSH session logs by default.
B) Correct, OS Login with Cloud Audit Logs provides a centralized way to log and review SSH actions.
C) Incorrect, a third-party SSH gateway introduces complexity and potential security risks.
D) Incorrect, IAM roles with logging permissions do not specifically capture SSH actions.
E) Incorrect, Cloud IAP is not primarily for logging SSH sessions.

QUESTION 36

Answer – B) Custom metric in Cloud Monitoring, Alert

A) Incorrect, using the Compute Engine API for regular checks is inefficient.
B) Correct, a custom metric in Cloud Monitoring with an alert for the specific threshold provides real-time monitoring and alerting.
C) Incorrect, Stackdriver Logging is not the best tool for system load monitoring.
D) Incorrect, this method lacks real-time monitoring and alerting.
E) Incorrect, built-in tools may not provide alerts for specific thresholds without additional configuration.

QUESTION 37

Answer - E) Google Cloud BigQuery (Correct)

Option A is incorrect because Google Cloud Dataflow is a data processing service, but it may not provide the real-time analysis capabilities of streaming data compared to Google Cloud BigQuery.
Option B is incorrect because Google Bigtable is a NoSQL database and not designed for real-time data processing.
Option C is incorrect because Google Cloud Pub/Sub is a messaging service and not a data processing service.
Option D is incorrect because Google Cloud Dataprep is a data preparation tool, not a streaming data processing service.
Option E is correct because Google Cloud BigQuery provides real-time streaming data ingestion and analysis capabilities with low latency, making it suitable for real-time processing of streaming data from various sources.

QUESTION 38

Answer - B) Utilize Google Cloud CDN (Content Delivery Network) with Google Cloud Storage for static content hosting. (Correct)

Option A is incorrect because Google Cloud Load Balancing primarily focuses on load distribution and may not provide the same content caching and distribution capabilities as Google Cloud CDN.
Option C is incorrect because Google Cloud Identity-Aware Proxy (IAP) is focused on access control and security, not content delivery and latency optimization.
Option D is incorrect because Google Cloud Functions are designed for serverless functions and may not be the most efficient way to serve static web content with minimal latency.
Option E is incorrect because Google Cloud Pub/Sub is a messaging service and not specifically designed for content distribution to global users.

Option B is correct because Google Cloud CDN, when used in conjunction with Google Cloud Storage for hosting static content, provides a secure and efficient content delivery network with low-latency content delivery worldwide, meeting the requirements for a global-scale web application.

QUESTION 39

Answer - D) Use service accounts to grant permissions to each VM instance. (Correct)

Option A is incorrect because assigning the same service account to all VMs may not allow for granular access control to specific Google Cloud APIs.
Option B is incorrect because using instance metadata to define API access is not a recommended method for access control and does not provide granularity.
Option C is incorrect because creating a custom IAM role for each VM instance can become cumbersome to manage and may not provide the necessary flexibility.
Using service accounts allows you to assign specific roles and permissions to each VM instance, ensuring fine-grained access control to Google Cloud APIs.

QUESTION 40

Answer - C) Utilize Google Cloud Cost Explorer for cost optimization and resource usage analysis.

Option A is incorrect because Google Cloud Billing Reports are primarily for billing and invoice management, not for in-depth cost optimization and resource usage analysis. Option B is incorrect because Google Cloud Monitoring provides real-time monitoring and alerting capabilities but does not specialize in cost optimization analysis. Option D is incorrect because Google Cloud Security Command Center focuses on security-related aspects and does not directly address cost management and resource usage analysis. Option C is correct because Google Cloud Cost Explorer is a tool that allows you to analyze your Google Cloud spending, identify cost-saving opportunities, and gain insights into resource usage, making it a suitable choice for cost optimization and resource analysis in a GCP project.

QUESTION 41

Answer - D) Google Cloud Spanner

Option A, Google Cloud SQL, offers managed relational databases but may not provide the same level of scalability and high availability as Google Cloud Spanner. Option B, Google Cloud Firestore, is a NoSQL document database and may not meet the requirement for a scalable relational database. Option C, Google Cloud Bigtable, is a NoSQL database optimized for large analytical and operational workloads, not a relational database. Option D, Google Cloud Spanner, is a fully managed, scalable, and highly available relational database service that offers automatic failover, automated backups, and high availability, making it suitable for the described scenario.

QUESTION 42

Answer - C) Create a new service account and select it while creating the new instance. Grant the service account permissions on Cloud Storage.

Option A is incorrect because granting permissions to all instances in the project does not provide

isolation and access control for the specific instance that needs access.
Option B is incorrect because granting permissions to an external IP address does not offer sufficient access control.
Option D is incorrect because relying on the default service account may not provide the necessary isolation and control.
Option E is incorrect because using a shared access key may not provide the required security and granularity of access control.

QUESTION 43

Answer - A) Use App Engine to run your app. For each update, create a new version of the same service and send a small percentage of traffic to the new version using traffic splitting.

Option A is correct because it aligns with your goal of A/B testing. Using App Engine, you can create new versions of the same service and use traffic splitting to test updates on a small portion of live users while keeping the rest on the live version.
Option B is incorrect because creating a new service for each update would result in multiple instances of the app running simultaneously, which is not suitable for A/B testing.
Option C is incorrect because updating the deployment in Kubernetes Engine would direct all traffic to the new version, which does not allow for controlled A/B testing.
Option D is incorrect because creating a new deployment and updating the service would also direct all traffic to the new deployment, making it unsuitable for A/B testing.

QUESTION 44

Answer - C) Google Cloud Load Balancing with multiple regions

Option C is correct because Google Cloud Load Balancing with multiple regions allows you to distribute traffic across multiple regions, ensuring high availability and low-latency access for users worldwide, even during regional outages.
Option A (Google Cloud CDN) is for content delivery and may not provide regional failover.
Option B (Google Cloud VPN) is for secure connectivity and does not address regional resiliency.
Option D (Google Cloud AutoML) is for machine learning and not related to web application resilience.

QUESTION 45

Answer - D) Google Cloud Multi-Regional Storage

Option D is correct because Google Cloud Multi-Regional Storage automatically replicates data across multiple geographic locations, providing high data durability and availability with 99.999999999% durability.
Option A (Google Cloud Standard Storage) is for standard storage and does not provide the same level of geographic replication.
Option B (Google Cloud Nearline Storage) is for infrequently accessed data and does not offer multi-regional replication.
Option C (Google Cloud Coldline Storage) is for archival data and does not provide multi-regional replication.

QUESTION 46

Answer - B) Google Cloud HTTP(S) Load Balancer

Option B is correct because Google Cloud HTTP(S) Load Balancer is a global, fully-distributed load balancer that provides global load balancing and content delivery, making it suitable for highly available web applications with low latency and redundancy.
Option A (Google Cloud Network Load Balancer) is regional and may not provide global distribution.
Option C (Google Cloud Internal TCP/UDP Load Balancer) is for internal load balancing within a single VPC.
Option D (Google Cloud Armor) is a security service and does not provide load balancing or content delivery capabilities.

QUESTION 47

Answer - A) Use GKE's Horizontal Pod Autoscaling (HPA) to automatically adjust the number of pods based on CPU or memory usage

Option A is correct because GKE's Horizontal Pod Autoscaling (HPA) allows you to automatically adjust the number of pods in your application based on CPU or memory utilization. It ensures quick recovery in case of failures and efficient resource utilization.
Option B is related to IP address management and does not address recovery or scaling.
Option C is focused on access control and security but does not directly address recovery or scaling.
Option D is related to managing external access to services but does not handle application scaling or recovery.

QUESTION 48

Answer - B) Use Google Cloud SQL for Oracle to manage the Oracle database

Option B is correct because Google Cloud SQL for Oracle is a fully managed database service that provides compatibility with Oracle databases while minimizing operational overhead. It allows you to host and manage Oracle databases in Google Cloud, ensuring a smooth migration of your legacy application.
Option A would require manual management of Oracle on Compute Engine instances, increasing operational overhead and complexity.
Option C is not the best choice for hosting Oracle databases, as it is more suitable for containerized workloads and may not provide the required compatibility.
Option D is not designed for relational databases like Oracle and is not a suitable choice for this use case.

QUESTION 49

Answer – E) Container Registry, Kubernetes Deployments

A) Incorrect, containers must be in a registry before deployment to GKE.
B) Incorrect, Cloud Build is for building images, not for deployment.
C) Correct, but more advanced; uploading to Container Registry and deploying with Helm is a viable approach, especially for complex deployments.
D) Incorrect, Cloud Source Repositories is not for Docker images.
E) Correct, this is the straightforward and standard process for deploying containerized microservices on

GKE.

QUESTION 50

Answer – C) Different node pools

A) Incorrect, using the same node type for all services can lead to inefficiencies.
B) Incorrect, default settings may not be optimized for such diverse requirements.
C) Correct, segmenting services into different node pools allows for tailored resource optimization.
D) Incorrect, resource quotas manage usage but don't optimize the underlying resource allocation.
E) Incorrect, Kubernetes scheduling is effective but works best when supplemented with tailored node pools for diverse workloads.

ABOUT THE AUTHOR

Step into the world of Anand, and you're in for a journey beyond just tech and algorithms. While his accolades in the tech realm are numerous, including penning various tech-centric and personal improvement ebooks, there's so much more to this multi-faceted author.

At the heart of Anand lies an AI enthusiast and investor, always on the hunt for the next big thing in artificial intelligence. But turn the page, and you might find him engrossed in a gripping cricket match or passionately cheering for his favorite football team. His weekends? They might be spent experimenting with a new recipe in the kitchen, penning down his latest musings, or crafting a unique design that blends creativity with functionality.

While his professional journey as a Solution Architect and AI Consultant, boasting over a decade of AI/ML expertise, is impressive, it's the fusion of this expertise with his diverse hobbies that makes Anand's writings truly distinctive.

So, as you navigate through his works, expect more than just information. Prepare for stories interwoven with passion, experiences peppered with life's many spices, and wisdom that transcends beyond the tech realm. Dive in and discover Anand, the author, the enthusiast, the chef, the sports lover, and above all, the storyteller.

Made in the USA
Coppell, TX
08 July 2024